LANDSCAPE AND LEGACY

The Splendor of Nature, History, and Montana's Rocky Mountain Front

WRITTEN & COMPILED BY
DR. JOHN A. VOLLERTSEN

ISBN 10: 1-59152-124-6
ISBN 13: 978-1-59152-124-2

Published by John A. Vollertsen

©2013 by John A. Vollertsen

Cover photo: Ear Mountain by John Vollertsen

Back cover photo: Rocky Mountain Front by John Vollertsen

All rights reserved. This book may not be reproduced in whole or in part by any means (with the exception of short quotes for the purpose of review) without the permission of the publisher.

You may order extra copies of this book by calling Farcountry Press toll-free at (800) 821-3874.

sweetgrassbooks
a division of Farcountry Press

Produced by Sweetgrass Books.
PO Box 5630, Helena, MT 59604; (800) 821-3874;
www.sweetgrassbooks.com

The views expressed by the author/publisher in this book do not necessarily represent the views of, nor should be attributed to, Sweetgrass Books. Sweetgrass Books is not responsible for the content of the author/publisher's work.

Printed in the United States of America.

17 16 15 14 13 1 2 3 4 5

Dedicated to our future visionaries,
especially my grandchildren
Rachel, Addyson, Alyssa, Chase, Brooke, and Mason.

ACKNOWLEDGMENTS

The authors would like to thank the many cooperators for allowing interviews and sharing documents. We thank Christopher Preston for his assistance in assembling part of the bibliography. Special thanks to Shana Harrington for copy-editing and bringing the manuscript to a higher level of professionalism. Thanks to Beverly Magley for skillful proofreading and fine-tuning. We also thank Barbara Fifer for her meticulous attention to indexing. Particular thanks and heartfelt gratitude to Kathy Springmeyer and staff at Sweetgrass Books for their attention to a multitude of details, recommendations, and guidance throughout the process of producing this book.

TABLE OF CONTENTS

TABLE OF CONTENTS *continued*

INTRODUCTION

Ever wonder why Montana's Rocky Mountain Front has become one of this nation's brightest natural resource focal points? Ever wonder why, after one visit to the "Front," visitors are immediately stricken with the compulsion to keep coming back? Why is this piece of landscape so important to so many Americans?

Learn from the experts why this landscape is so appealing to hundreds of animal and plant species, and to tens of thousands of human beings. Let expert authors of the chapters in this amazing book explain in plain and simple language the diverse amenities that Montana's Rocky Mountain Front has to offer. Tap into the knowledge offered by wildlife biologists, historians, land managers, and experienced local residents who represent over five hundred years of combined experience on the Front.

This book represents a small contribution from a much larger tapestry of knowledge, education, and experience. The principal reason for writing this book can be summed up in one word - advocacy. The Front has so much to offer. Somewhere between loving it to death and exploiting it to unsustainable proportions, the Front requires advocacy to maintain its monolithic appeal. It is the goal of this book to enlighten reasonable people to enact reasonable decisions about the Front, for the next one hundred or more generations.

Whether a recreational reader or a college researcher, consumers of this well-written book will emerge better informed, better qualified, and broadly respected for their knowledge of one of the country's last remaining and truly wild places.

Inside each chapter you will learn from each author's expert experiences. Some of the authors integrate years of their own on-the-ground professional and academic research results in very practical and heartfelt words that reflect deep attachment to the people, natural resources, and clean, crisp landscapes of the Front. Additionally, some of the authors bring wisdom, experience, and love for the land through their living, working, or recreating on the Front. Read expert conclusions, opinions, and personal experiences, never before openly revealed.

People connect to the Front in a thousand different ways. It is the intent of this book to challenge people of all walks of life—old timers and new comers—to indulge in decades of condensed research, experience, and stories of flat-out neighborly love for the land. Learn from ordinary people who truly talk from the heart.

The chapter titles and subtitles will help readers to quickly concentrate on areas of particular interest, whether it is wildlife, natural history, Native Americans, great regional writers, environmental advocacy, or what the legislative future of the Front may look like. Examine and evaluate factual documentation and quotations from experts.

What is the geologic make-up of the Front? What are the prominent animal species? When did Native Americans first visit? Why wilderness? Why energy extraction? Who left their mark? These and many other questions are answered in the illuminating chapters ahead. Read for pleasure, read for research, read for spokesmanship. Regardless of the reason, be part of the future of this beautiful, peaceful, and sacred landscape . . . and continue a premier legacy.

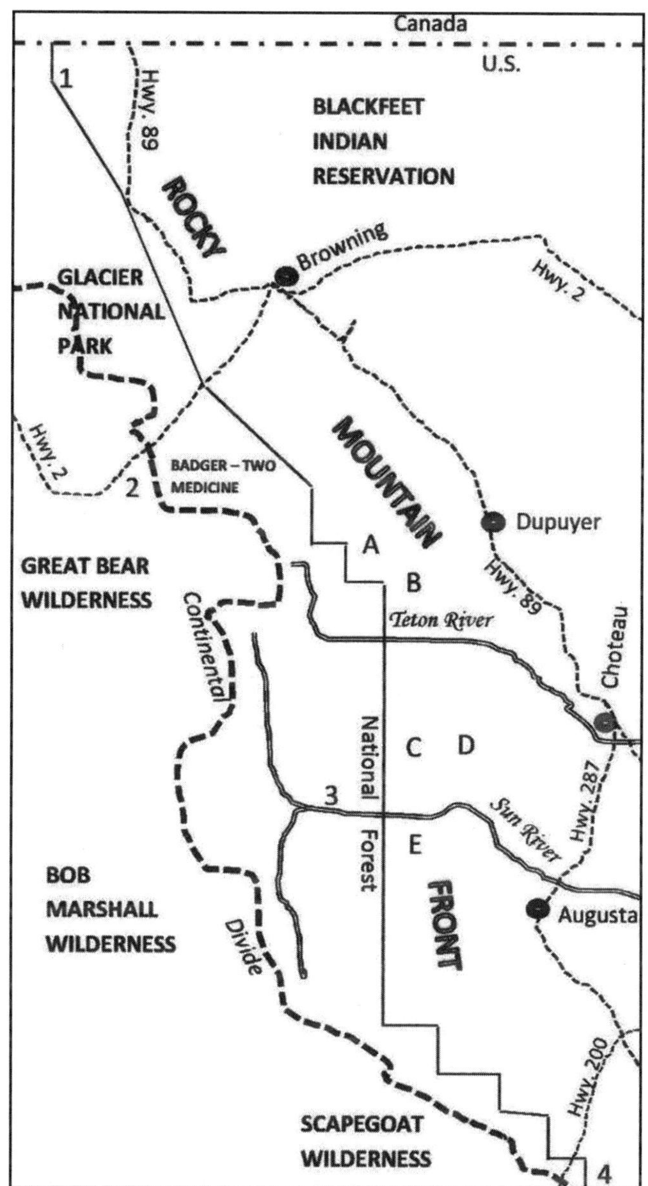

Map Legend for Montana's Rocky Mountain Front:
1. Chief Mountain; **2.** Marias Pass; **3.** Gibson Reservoir; **4.** Rogers Pass; **A.** Theodore Roosevelt Memorial Ranch; **B**. Blackleaf Wildlife Management Area (WMA); **C.** Ear Mountain WMA; **D.** Pine Butte Swamp Preserve; **E.** Sun River WMA.

Chapter 1

EAST FRONT GEOLOGY

Karen W. Porter

The Montana Rocky Mountain Front, as the term is generally used, is a region of primarily public lands, contained by various existing land-use boundaries, and stretching in a broad arc from Glacier National Park to Montana Highway 200. In spite of its somewhat arbitrary delineation, the Front does have a specific and recognizable topography and geology over much of its area.

Where and What Is the Montana Rocky Mountain Front?

From a vantage point on the High Plains at Augusta or Choteau, the Montana Rocky Mountain Front stretches from about Bowman's Corner on the south (junction of MT Highway 200 and US Highway 287) to East Glacier on the north. Within the Front, this unique landscape lies between Rogers Pass and Marias Pass, south to north, with the north end tucked against the southeastern edge of Glacier National Park. The western boundary of the Front generally coincides with the eastern boundary of the Bob Marshall Wilderness Complex, based substantially on drainage-divide topography; elevations within the Front are often as high as those within the wilderness. The eastern boundary generally corresponds with a topographic shift from the Front's linear ridge-and-valley topography to flatter landscape out over the High Plains. The southern end of the Front is not easily recognized topographically and is somewhat arbitrarily placed at Rogers Pass.

Some of the same rock units and geologic structures that occur in the Front also occur in Glacier National Park and southern Canada. However, the northern boundary of the Front against the Park is established by the abrupt eastern swing of a major thrust fault, the Lewis Thrust, which completely cuts out the rock types that dominate the Front. Similarly, geologic structures typical of the Front also underlie the High Plains, beyond the Front's eastern edge.

The Front's characteristic ridge-and-valley topography of closely spaced thrust sheets of Paleozoic and Mesozoic rocks continues for several miles west of the Front into the Bob Marshall Wilderness Complex. But thereafter, the faults become more widely spaced and steeper. All of the Mesozoic and most of the Paleozoic rocks have been eroded away, and the ancient Precambrian rocks form the landscape.

Most of the Rocky Mountain Front lies well east of the Continental Divide, which wanders northwesterly through the Bob Marshall Wilderness country. But the Divide swings east briefly to form the western edge of the Front at Teton Pass before swinging back northwesterly and bisecting the Badger–Two Medicine country of the Front all the way to Marias Pass.

To both the trained and the untrained eye, much of the Front looks like a series of high ridges separated by lower valleys or gulches, forming linear, subparallel landforms with a north to northwesterly orientation. Where rock exposures are good, an observer also notices that nearly all of the rock layers seem to be tilted generally west rather than lying flat. In some places, the tilt, or dip, is quite steep, even near vertical; elsewhere, it is nearly flat. The observer also makes a puzzling observation while hiking or riding horseback progressively deeper (westward) into the landscape; he sees the same few rock types over and over. These observations have to do with the mountain-building processes that produced this landscape.

Major drainages, such as Birch Creek, the Teton River, Deep Creek, and the Dearborn River, originate within this landscape. The Sun River originates farther west. Although all of these waters ultimately flow eastward onto the High Plains, long stream segments run south through valleys within the Front until reaching an east-flowing stream that has breached the dominant north-south–oriented topography.

Much of the Front is forested, but open valleys, isolated peaks, and sheer cliffs, sometimes called *reefs*, provide visual breaks in the monochromatic green of the forests. Many of these unforested landmarks are well known in the landscape, such as Scarface and Choteau Mountains, the Fairview Plateau, and Castle and Walling Reefs. Other open vistas in both the Front and the Bob Marshall to the west result from forest fires that denuded the forest and provide new views of the landscape.

This Montana Rocky Mountain Front landscape is also known to geologists as the Disturbed Belt, suggesting that the geology here is distinctive, and different from most other Montana mountain country. Though the Front is mountainous country, the story of these mountains begins before they were mountains.

Stories the Rocks Tell

Nearly all of the rocks exposed in the Rocky Mountain Front are sedimentary in origin. What we notice most about them are their color and texture, the many small details within them (including fossils), and the relative degree to which they erode. Together, these features indicate a wide range of depositional settings of the original sediments, from terrestrial (land) environments, such as streambeds, swamps, and lakes, to marine environments, such as tidal flats or an ocean basin.

Additionally, these sedimentary rocks represent a very long period of geologic time (see following figure)—from late Precambrian time (Proterozoic era), about 1,400 million years ago, to deposits of glacial origin, perhaps 10,000 to 12,000 years ago, and modern-day deposits in streams and terraces.

Nonetheless, some parts of the geologic time frame are not represented here, either because sediments were not deposited in this area during those times or because such deposits were eroded away before younger ones were deposited.

Geologic Time Scale

(modified from Hendrix, 2011)[1]

EON	ERA	PERIOD		EPOCH	TIME*
					Present
Phanerozoic	Cenozoic	Quaternary		Holocene	12,000 years ago
				Pleistocene	2.6 million years ago
		Tertiary	Neogene	Pliocene	5
				Miocene	23
			Paleogene	Oligocene	34
				Eocene	56
				Paleocene	65 million years ago
	Mesozoic	Cretaceous			145
		Jurassic			201
		Triassic			251 million years ago
	Paleozoic	Permian			299
		Pennsylvanian			318
		Mississippian			359
		Devonian			416
		Silurian			444
		Ordovician			488
		Cambrian			542 million years ago
Precambrian	Proterozoic				2,500 million years ago
	Archean				4.6 billion years ago

(Shaded box) Indicates rocks present in the Montana Rocky Mountain Front.

By thinking of these sedimentary rocks in their time sequence, with their particular physical and biological features that tell where and how the sediment was laid down, geologists are able to read the record of a changing landscape through geologic time. However, because the Rocky Mountains, including the Montana Rocky Mountain Front, were formed by compressive mountain-building stresses, all of the rocks have been pushed into their present places from somewhere to the west; thus, reconstructing ancient landscapes is complicated at best.

Proterozoic Rocks: The Oldest Sedimentary Record

Western Montana and adjacent Idaho and Canada have one of the most fascinating sedimentary rock sequences on the continent. In Montana, it is named the Belt Supergroup. Though named for limited exposures near Belt, Montana, this group of rocks is visible along most of western Montana's highways, valley walls, and backcountry. It has *supergroup* status because of its tremendous thickness—over eighteen kilometers (54,000 feet; ten miles!) in some places. Additionally, portions of the vertical sequence have been repeated by faulting. Not surprisingly, establishing divisions of this extraordinarily thick sequence has been difficult and contentious for over a century. Today, students of Belt rocks have, with reasonable confidence, defined and named the sequence of rock formations that make up the Belt Supergroup.

What is so remarkable about the Belt sedimentary rocks is that while nearly everywhere else in the world, rocks this old (Middle Proterozoic: deposited 1,470 million to 1,400 million years ago) have been extensively "cooked" and deformed by various mountain-building events through time, Belt rocks have been only very slightly affected by deformational events, even with uplift during formation of the Rocky Mountains. They have been heated enough to make them very hard and resistant to erosion but not enough to destroy any of their physical features. We can easily tell the sandstones (now quartzites) from the mudstones (now argillites) from the carbonates.

Belt rocks are a particular challenge to students of earth history not only because of their great thickness but also because they were deposited, as sediments, in a variety of land and water environments before the appearance of animal life-forms with hard parts (such as shells) that could be fossilized. Thus, an important geologic tool, the fossil record, cannot be applied to these rocks. Nonetheless, an amazing array of physical features can be observed in these ancient sandstones, mudstones, and carbonates, such as imprints of raindrops, casts from long-gone salt crystals, cross-bedding of sedimentary layers, and a variety of wave and current ripples. Additionally, certain carbonates show distinct features of primitive algal-like colonies.

Within the Front, Proterozoic Belt Supergroup rocks are exposed mostly in the southernmost part, in the Rogers Pass–Alice Creek–Silver King Mountain area. Farther north, rocks of this age lie west of the Front within the Bob Marshall Wilderness Complex. They are the predominant rocks of Glacier National Park's spectacular landscapes.

Paleozoic Rocks

In the northern Rocky Mountains, Paleozoic sedimentary rocks are predominantly carbonates (limestone and dolomite). The original sediment was calcareous mud, laid down in shallow seas that commonly covered much of the North American continent prior to Mesozoic crustal unrest that culminated in uplift of the Rocky Mountains. The calcareous content comes from abundant shells and other skeletal parts of invertebrate animals and calcareous algae, and from the direct precipitation of carbonate from warm seas. In the dry climate of the West, carbonates are resistant rock units, so they form most of the ridges and escarpments of the Front. The Paleozoic carbonates of the Rocky Mountain Front, and, indeed, of all of the Northern Rockies, are of Cambrian, Devonian, and Mississippian age, oldest to youngest. Sandstones and mudstones (shales) are less abundant in the Paleozoic rock record but form some of the valley topography within the Front because they are also less resistant to erosion.

Familiar to many backcountry travelers are names like the Madison Group, whose lower formation is the Allan Mountain Limestone and whose upper formation is the Castle

Mountain Dolomite, both named for prominent landforms of the Front. The Mississippian-age Madison composes most of the high escarpments of the Front. It is 1,200 to 1,500 feet thick, which contributes to high escarpments, as does the multiple stacking of thrust plates.

Cambrian-age rocks everywhere record the earliest forms of life, already quite diverse but now preserved because of protective shells and other hard parts that become fossilized. Trilobites, a long-extinct group of arthropods, were undergoing rapid evolution in Cambrian time and have left an abundant fossil record that is well recorded in the Cambrian rocks of the Trilobite Range west of the Front in the Bob Marshall Wilderness. Within the Front, Cambrian rocks occur along the upper North Fork of Whitetail Creek on the southwestern flank of Feather Woman Mountain near Heart Butte. These outcrops extend southeastward across the North Fork of Birch Creek, west of Swift Reservoir. Another narrow band of Cambrian rocks is mapped across Gibson Reservoir on the Sun River, northward across the eastern flank of Arsenic Mountain and southward along the eastern flank of Allan Mountain.

Mesozoic Rocks

Both Jurassic and Cretaceous rocks were originally widely deposited in the northern Rocky Mountain region. However, these rocks were long ago eroded from the high elevations west of the Front. Further, they are poorly preserved within the Front because their relative weakness caused them to be squeezed out by the much more rigid and resistant Paleozoic carbonates as east-pushing compressive mountain building intensified. Thus, within the Rocky Mountain Front, Jurassic and Cretaceous sandstones and shales are not common. Where preserved, they are usually narrow bands in swales on the back (western) sides of resistant ridges.

The most easily recognized rock unit is the Kootenai Formation, composed of red, green, and purple sandstones and mudstones. Kootenai deposits were laid down in early Cretaceous streams, lakes, and floodplains east of the newly rising Rocky Mountains. Later Cretaceous deposits are thick marine shales of the Blackleaf, Marias River, and Virgelle-Telegraph

Creek Formations that record the presence of a vast seaway in the region at this time. Only the Blackleaf has been recognized within the Front. Still younger Cretaceous deposits of the Two Medicine, Horsethief, and St. Mary's River Formations record a return to dominantly land environments. None of these rocks are preserved within the Front.

A wide, northwest-oriented swath of Cretaceous rocks, primarily marine shales, lies west of Gateway Pass in the Bob Marshall Wilderness Complex, along Strawberry Creek and the North Fork of the Sun River. East of the Front, Cretaceous sandstones and shales extend in rolling folds and thrust faults for many miles, at the surface and beneath the High Plains. Their deformation reflects the same east-pushing stresses observed within the Front and the adjacent Bob Marshall.

Made into Mountains

About 250 million years ago, the Farallon plate (oceanic crust) slowly began shoving its way beneath the western edge of the North American plate (continental crust). This subduction began to raise the western part of North America. By about 145 million years ago, at the start of the Cretaceous period, the subduction was applying enormous eastward-pushing compressive stresses to western North America, from Mexico into Canada. This compression folded and faulted great masses of rock, carrying some eastward for many miles. Different parts of the mountainous region responded at slightly different times and with different deformation styles as the Rocky Mountains formed.

In western Montana, the east-pushing compression uplifted large blocks of deeply buried Precambrian "basement" rocks along steep faults, and rumpled younger, more plastic Paleozoic and Mesozoic rocks into large folds (anticlines and synclines). These folds frequently broke (faulted) and thrust over one another, forming tilted, repeated slabs of rock stacked like shingles. By both uplift and overthrusting, the long-buried sedimentary layers were raised to form mountains.

By early Cretaceous time, the weight of the continued piling of rock was causing a downwarp of the crust in front of the rising Rocky Mountains. This downwarp allowed the continent's interior to be flooded by ocean waters, forming the great Cretaceous Interior Seaway, which stretched from the Arctic to the Gulf of Mexico. Everywhere, the continuously uplifted rocks became the source of new sediments carried by streams to the Cretaceous basin, a process that continued for millions of years, finally filling the basin.

By about 65 million years ago, in early Paleocene time, the compressive forces and resulting uplift were largely over. The interior of North America was a broad plain east of the new Rocky Mountains; basin filling and regional upwarp of the crust had drained the seaway from the continent.

Since the main mountain-building period of the late Cretaceous—and through many other events, including volcanism, climate variations, and glaciation—the Rocky Mountains have been under erosion. Across the Montana Rockies, Mesozoic and Paleozoic rocks have largely been removed from the mountain ranges behind the Front, exposing the ancient Precambrian "basement" rocks. The Front itself is dominated by multiple, thin, repeated, thrust-stacked wedges of Paleozoic and Mesozoic rocks. It is this repetition of the same rock units and their variable resistance to erosion that, together, form the ridge-and-valley topography that characterizes much of the Front. One prominent long ridge of Madison Limestone, sometimes fault-paired and continuous for nearly thirty miles, has been named the Sawtooth Range.

Cenozoic History of the Front: Igneous Intrusions and Glaciation

Intrusive igneous sills, dikes, and plugs of varying composition record several episodes of magmatic intrusion in the region during late Cretaceous and Cenozoic time. These rocks are now being exposed by erosion and are minimally recognized east of the Rocky Mountain Front. None have been recognized within the Front. Haystack Butte is a crystalline dacite plug. An inconspicuous monzonite plug with associated dikes occurs south of Bean Lake and is cut by the Dearborn River. The Adel Mountains east of Highway 287 at the south end of the Front are volcanic in origin.

The Rocky Mountain Front, as well as all of the Northern Rockies, was covered by the Cordilleran Ice Sheet, a continental glacier that advanced and retreated several times across the region during the Pleistocene epoch. This last great ice sheet on the North American continent, which produced the spectacular landscape of Glacier National Park, began its final retreat about 12,000 years ago. Based on preserved glacial deposits, the eastern edge of the ice sheet appears to have closely coincided with the edge of the Rocky Mountain Front. Moving ice carried tons of scoured rock debris eastward to the edge of the mountains, where it was dumped in outwash deposits of boulders, gravel, sand, and mud. These glacial deposits are preserved at the edge of the Front in several high benches west of Augusta and in the Heart Butte area at the northern end of the Front. Since then, and continuing today, these gravels have been picked up by modern streams, reworked along with freshly eroded debris from the mountain front, and redeposited far out onto the Plains.

The Present-Day Landscape

The Front continues to be modified daily, though usually with little notice by us. Each year, snowmelt and rains percolate into slopes, gather in small creeks, and run through the major valleys of the Teton, Sun, and other rivers. Stream banks cave in, boulders tumble, freeze-thaw action splits away slabs from a rock face, ground saturates and begins to slide down slope, and stream energy carries away millions of tons of the landscape to be deposited (temporarily) eastward on the High Plains. Fire significantly alters the type and rate of erosion of this landscape. Slopewash and scour can occur across denuded slopes, replacing the slower sink-off and percolation of water into streams where vegetation is preserved.

To appreciate the geology and geologic history of the Front, just walk out into it and keep your eyes open. Look for the general themes of this history: (1) the rocks in the Front are repetitive, meaning the same few units are repeated as you go west, and each repetition is a separate thrust sheet; (2) the rock layers tilt, or dip, to the west, the direction from which they were pushed (rarely, a complete fold is observed where it did not break and the east limb of the fold is preserved); (3) the resistant ridges are Paleozoic carbonate rocks, either Mississippian or Devonian in age; (4) these ridges of Paleozoic rocks were shoved eastward and repeatedly stacked on themselves and onto younger rocks, so they have a thrust fault at their base; and (5) the back sides of the carbonate ridges may have rock units younger than the ridges (look for shale or sandstone—Jurassic or Cretaceous in age), and these are in the right order (younger rocks on top of older rocks). Remember that you have clues to what is around you from the loose slabs and boulders you can study close-up on slopes and talus piles; streambed debris can be helpful but may have been transported some distance.

KAREN PORTER is retired from the Montana Bureau of Mines and Geology (MBMG), in Butte, Montana, where she directed the geologic mapping program and conducted field research. Her research focused primarily on Montana's geologic history, particularly of the Cretaceous-age rocks of central Montana, on which she has numerous publications. Prior to being at MBMG, Porter was an independent consultant in the petroleum industry, working in Colorado, Wyoming, and Montana. Porter holds a B.A. in geology-zoology from Mount Holyoke College, an M.S. in geology from the University of Michigan, and a Ph.D. in geology from the Colorado School of Mines. She lives in Butte.

[1] Marc S. Hendrix, *Geology Underfoot in Yellowstone Country* (Missoula, MT: Mountain Press Publishing Co., 2011), 11.

Chapter 2

WILD HEART AND SOUL OF MONTANA

Bill Cunningham

Two centuries ago when Lewis and Clark explored the vast land we now call Montana, they encountered a wilderness of some 93 million acres. Today, less than a tenth of this land remains wild and undisturbed, and much of this surviving wild country clings to the most isolated reaches of the Continental Divide between Marias and Rogers Passes. As such, wilderness and, arguably, its most dominant topographical feature—the Continental Divide—interconnect so as to form the wild heart and soul of Montana.

If there is any widely accepted sacred ground in Montana, it is the revered Bob Marshall country—aptly dubbed the flagship of our nation's wilderness fleet. In shorthand, we affectionately call this vast, wild region "The Bob," to include not only the 1.5-million-acre designated wilderness core but the surrounding 1 million acres of contiguous—but unprotected—federally owned wildland that wraps around the core like a giant horseshoe. Ironically, the wildest part of this entire magnificent complex is de facto wilderness, lacking in any form of legislative recognition or protection. This is the eastern face of the Bob Marshall country—the Rocky Mountain Front—and it harbors the wildest and least-visited land in the entire complex.

What do we mean by the term Rocky Mountain Front? How might we geographically define this sweeping landscape? We could assemble a dozen locals who know and love this majestic land and come up with that many different definitions of the Front. So, for starters, I'll quote myself when I once wrote that the boundaries of the Front "stretch from Marias Pass 110 miles south to Rogers Pass and extend from the Continental Divide east to where the foothills interface with the Northern Great Plains. The country exemplifies a genuine 'east of the mountains' feeling marked by wind, eastward-leaning trees, sparse vegetation, great limestone reefs, narrow canyon mouths bound by sheer rock walls, along with a full complement of wild critters."[1]

The above might serve as a thumbnail snapshot, but let's take a closer look. Those of us who live for wild country naturally assume that the deeper a person penetrates the backcountry the wilder it is. Usually, that is the case, but the Front is a rare exception. You're likely to experience deeper solitude and truer naturalness along the outer eastern fringes of the Front than in the center of the sprawling Bob Marshall Wilderness far to the west.

The Front is the most startling wild geography in America's Northern Rockies south of the Canadian border, a boundary appropriately known by Native Americans as the "Medicine Line." Although I am fortunate to live near the Front and have visited it countless times over the past forty-plus years, I never cease to marvel at this abrupt transition between mountains and prairie. From the Blackfeet holy land of the Badger-Two Medicine, the country stretches south in a grand spectacle of jagged limestone peaks, sheer walls, parallel reefs, and deep canyons, most of which is managed by the Forest Service as part of the Lewis and Clark National Forest. These nearly

400,000 acres of roadless federal land on the Rocky Mountain Front are an integral part of Montana's largest expanse of unroaded terrain: the 2.5-million-acre Bob Marshall Wilderness Complex, which itself is part of an even larger, mostly intact ecosystem extending well into Canada.

However, as impressive as these mountains are, much of the country's mystique comes from the direction of the rising sun. Immediately east of the great gray ramparts, a virtually undeveloped expanse of foothills and prairie unfold in a mix of private, state, and Bureau of Land Management (BLM) ownership. This is classic *front of the Front* country, separated from the main upthrust of the Rocky Mountains. As a result, Montana's share of the Rocky Mountain Front is the last and largest unspoiled meeting of peaks and plains between Canada and Mexico.

This country east of the Continental Divide is drier, colder, and windier than its west-side counterpart approximately eighty miles to the west. Of course, dryness is relative. The Badger–Two Medicine is comparatively moist, with the Front becoming progressively drier to the south. The lushness of the Badger may be due to the descent of the Continental Divide barrier, which reaches its lowest point in Montana at 5,215-foot Marias Pass. Prevailing storms from the west funnel into the Badger, where they mix with arctic air to produce abundant moisture. All along the Front, vegetation is sparse, lending a spacious, open character to the land bordering on the austere. Only a few hardy trees survive on exposed ridges and slopes. Gnarled limber pine cling like living statues sculpted into grotesque shapes by an almost constant wind.

Wind is truly the signature climatic reality along the Front. When it eases, it is merely catching its breath so as to gather more strength. Here, we find a landscape where the trees lean east, away from the wind, and the people lean west, into the wind. The sometimes hurricane force of wind drove out most of the homesteaders during the 1910s and 1920s and deserves at least partial credit for limiting human population and development, a sort of cleansing agent helping to keep the country wild.

The Front is the kind of place that will raise your spirits while instilling humility to your soul.

A Glimpse at Wild Origins

The Rocky Mountain Front is a confused jumble of displaced rock formations that slid eastward, like a stack of buttered pancakes, when the Rocky Mountains were thrust upward, forcing the older formations on top of the younger formations in reverse of their normal order. As a result of this overthrust faulting, massive slabs of rock were displaced as much as fifty miles to the east onto the plains over a period of some 3 million years. Today's landscape on the Front—composed of remarkably straight, north-south ridges and canyons—is the product of these forces. The mountains are known as the Sawtooth Range and are distinguished by jagged ridges and escarpments of Madison limestone with an average thickness of 2,000 feet. If you poke along the bases of these cliffs, you'll likely find fossilized coral honeycombed into the rock.

A Century of Stewardship

The Front is the wildest part of Montana's wilderness heartland, placing it among the most pristine lands in the contiguous forty-eight states. One can argue that the wildness of the Front has survived to this day because of its self-protection, a fortuitous accident of geography and climate. Indeed, the land is geographically blessed by being both incredibly rugged and far removed from population centers. Further, it is bitterly cold for months on end and blasted by screaming winds. Perhaps the best indicator of the Front's wildness is that it remains home to almost all of its indigenous historical flora and fauna.

All that aside, the preservation of the wild essence of the Front has been anything but accidental. Instead, it has been only through endless pressure endlessly applied by highly determined and dedicated people over the past century that the land and its denizens are in the excellent condition they are today.

Open south-facing gulches in this *Serengeti of North America* provide winter forage for thousands of migrating elk. The largest concentration is the famed Sun River elk herd. During winter, more than 3,000 elk graze the mixed and rough fescue grasslands of the Sun River Wildlife Management

Area below the monumental massif of Sawtooth Ridge. This herd was the centerpiece of an inspiring heritage of wildlife restoration that began in 1913 when the Montana legislature established the 200,000-acre Sun River Game Preserve within what is now the Bob Marshall Wilderness. Today, there are three sportsmen-purchased state wildlife management areas (WMAs) along the Front, as well as The Nature Conservancy's Pine Butte Preserve and the Theodore Roosevelt Memorial Ranch owned by the Boone and Crockett Club. All of these special state and private places are dedicated to the enhancement of wildlife in wild country. Each is contiguous to unroaded public land along the Front, and each contains wildland within its borders. The Rocky Mountain Front lies between the Bob Marshall Wilderness and these wildlife preserves, so, as the Front goes, so goes the adjacent wildland and its wild inhabitants.

Thousands of white-tailed and mule deer roam these benches and coulees along the front of the Front. The higher ground is home to our nation's largest herd of native Rocky Mountain bighorn sheep. Rugged pinnacles provide vital cliff security for one of Montana's major mountain goat populations.

Fortunately, the country is wild and big enough to harbor an array of nonhuman predators to help balance this large and varied prey base. Secluded fens and foothills along the Front provide the last remaining front of the Front habitat between Canada and Mexico where the plains grizzly makes its last stand. All of the front of the Front is grizzly country. Knowing this makes the peaks beyond stand taller and the wildness all the more profound.

Wolves have recolonized the Front from the north, and today several packs are well established from the Sun River to the upper tributaries of Dupuyer Creek to the Medicine Line. As a recovered species recently removed from federal endangered status, the future of this top-end predator becomes all the more dependent on human tolerance combined with the already excellent wild habitat and plentiful natural food sources of the Front. There are few, if any, sounds in the wilderness that better stir our imaginations than the haunting howl of a wolf on a cold, moonlit night.

Grizzlies and wolves may be expanding on the Front, but the most abundant predators are the big cats. You almost certainly won't see this reclusive feline, but if you venture beyond the road near ridges, reefs, and rocks, you can be sure that a mountain lion is keeping a wary eye on you.

Most abundant and diverse along the Front are birds of prey and other avians. During any time of year, you're likely to see bald and golden eagles, saw-whet owls, prairie falcons, and maybe even a rare glimpse of a peregrine falcon. Over the years, I've caught at least fleeting blurs of every denizen of the Front, but one in particular is deeply embedded in my memory. I was hiking near the rugged canyon mouth of Badger Creek when suddenly there was a pair of harlequin ducks floating and diving in a rush of whitewater rapids. They were having such a good time I felt like joining them.

All of this diversity of wild critters reflects the varied *ecotone* nature of this transitional mixing bowl of foothills, coulees, and benches wedged between the distinctly different landforms of mountain and prairie. Vegetation, the foundation of this diversity, is shaped by the complex interactions of geology, soils, climate, and fire. In turn, because of so many different elevations, the ecotone of the Front is home to far more species than the mountains to the west or the northern mixed grass and rough fescue prairies to the east.

In Wildness is the Preservation of the Front

As with the definition of the Rocky Mountain Front, there are numerous definitions and perspectives of *wilderness.* But in 1964, Congress, in passing the landmark National Wilderness Preservation Act, defined the term to mean an area of undeveloped federal land set aside for *enduring* preservation in its natural state. It is a place where humans are visitors who do not remain. It is a place where the land and its community of life are *untrammeled,* not *untrampled,* as the term is often misconstrued. A trammel is Old English for a net. Thus, untrammeled wilderness is unnetted or uncontrolled by humans. Using lack of human domination and control as a yardstick, the Front far exceeds the minimum legal requirements for *wilderness* as defined in the Wilderness Act.

In so many ways, the permanent protection of wildland for its own sake is the ultimate expression of human respect and humility toward the earth and its inhabitants. I have seen grizzly bears, mountain goats, and trumpeter swans along the Front and I am reminded that these species cannot live close to people. Wilderness is for their benefit and survival as well as ours. As a wilderness guide, I have seen the stress and anxiety of urban-bound people evaporate from their faces and minds as they've wandered the serpentine crest of the Sawtooth Range gazing out across the northern Great Plains to infinity.

A Closer Look from North to South

Following is a description of the roadless components along the Rocky Mountain Front, each of which is separated by the few access roads that reach a little way into the Front between Marias Pass and Rogers Pass. Keep in mind that each is part of a contiguous whole within the greater Bob Marshall Wilderness ecosystem.

Badger–Two Medicine

The 120,000-acre Badger–Two Medicine roadless area is strategically positioned between Glacier Park, the Great Bear and Bob Marshall Wilderness Areas, and the high plains of the Blackfeet Nation. Most significantly, it functions as a connecting biological corridor between Glacier Park and the Bob Marshall Wilderness Complex, a genetic link for wildlife habitat and travel.

The Badger is a huge, complicated wildland, made even more so by its irreplaceable role as sacred land in the practice of traditional Blackfeet religion. This practice is completely dependent on the pristine nature of the Badger–Two Medicine. In the words of one nine-year-old tribal member, the Badger "is the last place we have to practice our religion in an undisturbed manner—if they build roads the animals would not have a place to live."

Unlike the rest of the Bob Marshall Country, the Badger retains traditional Indian place names. This is only because a group of Blackfeet chiefs journeyed to Washington, D.C., in 1915 to protest white man names for sacred lands along the east side of Glacier and the Badger. The spiritual importance of mountain peaks here is reflected by such names as Little Plume, Feather Woman, Morningstar, Scarface, Poia, Running Owl, Bull Shoe, Curly Bear, Running Crane, and Spotted Eagle.

There are two distinct, contrasting provinces of the Badger–Two Medicine. One is the incredibly rugged peaks in the southern end—from the North Fork of Birch Creek to Badger Creek, along with the northwest extension of the Continental Divide. The other is the broad, gentle valley of the South Fork Two Medicine River to the north. Absent are the ice walls, horn peaks, and alpine lakes characteristic of next-door Glacier Park. Instead, the Badger is a pleasing patchwork of primeval forest, rugged limestone peaks, rushing streams, and wide, glaciated valleys bordered by gentle slopes.

Steep limestone mountains dissected by narrow canyons and waterways punctuate the east-flowing Badger Creek drainage. The roughness and remoteness of the country lends needed seclusion to grizzlies and gray wolves, along with protective cliffs for mountain goats. The signs of wildlife increases markedly in the more subdued South Fork Two Medicine drainage with higher populations of elk, deer, moose, sheep, and black bear. With a rich mosaic of riparian forest and meadow habitat, it's possible to flush a nesting Canada goose and then meet a grizzly around the next bend, as I did one time. Beaver ponds dot the valley, hosting an array of ducks, coots, rails, grebes, and snipes.

Widespread fires between 1889 and 1910 created vast areas of alpine tundra. Unrelenting wind blows away the snow, exposing forage for wildlife. Due to topographic and climatic patterns, as noted earlier, vegetation is unusually lush and diverse for east-of-the-Divide country.

To better illustrate this amazing wildland, please allow me to recount some of the highlights of a monumental eight-day, seventy-mile backpack across the entire Badger–Two Medicine. The group consisted of college students in a wilderness field course, and our southeasterly route went from Marias Pass to the mouth of Blackleaf Canyon.

A dozen miles along the Continental Divide from Marias Pass to 8,006-foot Bullshoe Mountain provided a grand overview of one of Montana's wildest stretches of the Divide. Our backpack along the "Backbone of the World," the Blackfeet name for the Great Divide, presented a vivid portrait of the Badger as an ecological link among mountains, plains, Glacier Park, and the Bob. Dropping off the divide into the lush green meadows of Lee Creek, and then on down to the forks of the Badger, took us through the central forested valleys of the roadless complex. We took advantage of a layover day to climb Goat Mountain, dramatically isolated from its surrounding pinnacles.

The following day, we found ourselves on a long, rocky ridge that led southward to the summit of Morningstar Mountain—central sentinel of the more rugged southern portion of the Badger–Two Medicine. We could only rejoice in the wildness and vastness of a seemingly limitless mountainscape. With Feather Woman to the east, Scarface—with a family of nimble mountain goats—to the south, and Spotted Eagle rising to the west, the sight was more than our senses could absorb. At 8,376 feet, the sharp apex of Morningstar is the region's highest peak and is thus the place in this sacred land first touched by the light of the rising sun. I don't know if this lofty pinnacle has any special powers, but I do know that I felt an enhanced clarity about what this country is all about.

Afterward, we hiked to the lovely sloping greenery of Mowitch Basin by way of a rare old-growth lodgepole pine forest at the head of Lookout Creek, where some of us struggled to the rocky overhang of 6,863-foot Heart Butte. The top of this inspirational overlook lies precisely on the boundary between the reservation and the national forest where it changes from a diagonal to a longitudinal line. Nowhere else does one obtain a stronger impression of the Front, a sense of ecological mixing between peaks and prairie. To the south, a patchwork of aspen parklands dotted with small, glaciated lakes stretched to the horizon.

Continuing south behind the massive formation of Major Steele Backbone, we crossed the austere open head of Hungry Man Creek en route to the foaming waters of the North Fork of Birch Creek. This is where we left the *ceded strip* of the Badger, once part of the Blackfeet Reservation before a starving tribe was manipulated into selling the land to the U.S. government in 1896. We crossed into the only part of the Front currently protected as wilderness—the Birch Creek country of the Bob Marshall. As mentioned previously, prevailing storms from the west funnel into the Badger, where they mix with arctic air to produce abundant moisture. During our mid-August backpack, as we traveled from Mowitch Basin to Birch Creek, we were pounded with heavy rain and hail for three days—while the surrounding country basked in sunshine and high pressure.

Teton Peaks—Choteau Mountain

Soaring peaks, parallel reefs along limestone cliffs, hanging valleys, and looming, remote drainages characterize Teton Peaks-Choteau Mountain, a 77,572-acre roadless expanse in the northern reaches of the Front. This unprotected wildland borders thirty-two miles of the Bob Marshall Wilderness while encompassing some twenty miles of the eastern Front. It begins from 8,237-foot Old Man of the Hills, overlooking the Boone and Crockett Theodore Roosevelt Memorial Ranch, southward to the unmistakable sloping profile of 8,580-foot Ear Mountain, rising majestically above The Nature Conservancy's 17,000-acre Pine Butte Preserve. Included in this varied foothill-prairie complex are the Blackleaf and Ear Mountain Wildlife Management Areas and the Bureau of Land Management (BLM) Blind Horse Outstanding Natural Area (ONA). The Teton River portion of the Front consists of three major drainages, accessed by two road corridors.

The plains grizzly makes its last stand in these remote fens and foothills, particularly in the aspen thickets of the Pine Butte fen. To the west along the crest of the Sawtooth Range, the Teton Peaks are the highest pinnacles on the Front. Formed by thrust faults with steep east faces and gentle west slopes, these mountains are sliced by a maze of canyons, valleys, and rushing streams.

It is not uncommon to spot grizzlies and mountain goats the same day when climbing the apex of both the Front and the Bob Marshall—massive 9,392-foot Rocky Mountain Peak, which dominates the head of the Teton River's south fork. From this unparalleled vantage point, the senses are filled with impressions of gleaming limestone, gnarled limber pine, and wind, always the wind.

Once, on a rambling late-spring hike, I saw mountain sheep, goats, elk, mule and white-tailed deer, and a black bear within or adjacent to the Blind Horse ONA—all within one incredible day. There aren't many places left with that much diversity and abundance. This is just one reason the area is formally classified as an outstanding natural area.

I recall a similar trek when I was angling steeply across rock talus side slopes to the southwest summit ridge of Old Baldy. Suddenly, I spotted a large brown shape moving slowly on the grassy saddle between the twin summits of Old Baldy. Sure enough, it was a big, lone grizzly doing the same thing I was doing: ambling in the high country on a glorious summer morning. Wisely deciding that the mountain was his, I did a quick 180.

An impression of wildness that has stayed with me over the years was gained after a tricky late-spring scramble on loose scree that finally brought me to a high point directly below Choteau Mountain. The entire front of the Front Blind Horse ONA unfolded below in vibrant greens. Just beyond, I could pick out remnants of the Old North Trail, established by Eurasian people who crossed the land bridge between Siberia and Alaska 12,000 years ago and began migrating along the ice-free corridor adjacent to the Front. For a long time, I watched four elk graze peacefully on a grassy bench overlooking Chicken Coulee. The Front, from where I sat, to the Continental Divide is the "Backbone of the World" to the Blackfeet Indians and to the ancients who traversed the Old North Trail. "Something there is sacred," says Gene Sentz, that grizzled guardian of the Front from Choteau.

While most of this stretch of the Front is wild and remote, it might be best to avoid Our Lake in the upper South Fork of the Teton if you're looking for solitude. This sparkling gem, also known as Hidden Lake by locals, is by far the most popular day-hike destination on the Front, and for good reason, with its classic alpine beauty combined with an almost sure bet of seeing mountain goats. Nearby, from 7,743-foot Headquarters Pass, is the most spectacular gateway into the Bob and presents a magnificent view southwest to the distant Chinese Wall.

Deep Creek

In the heart of this great meeting ground between mountains and plains is a roadless expanse of 52,329 acres spanning thirteen miles of the Front. Known simply as Deep Creek, it extends from the Deep Creek–Teton Divide south to the Sun River. This roadless area averages six to nine miles in width, from the stark 8,400-foot crest of the Sawtooth Range eastward to mile-high prairies.

From the Deep Creek–Teton Divide, steep, narrow side drainages feed to the east-flowing North and South Forks of Deep Creek. These upper tributaries are characterized by incredibly rugged canyon mouths. The crest of the Front Range along the current Bob Marshall Wilderness boundary overlooks a series of high, parallel overthrust limestone reefs to the east, which separate deep, sparsely forested valleys. In the sheltered nooks of these drainages, a scattered forest of mostly lodgepole pine and aspen is slowly being replaced by climax spruce and fir, broken by large meadows, with small clearings higher up. Beaver ponds in Blacktail Gulch and along Arsenic Creek are lined with dense willow, alder, dogwood, and berry bushes. Rocky ridgetops are dotted with twisted limber pine, juniper, and mats of kinnikinnick.

The awesome slanted form of 8,330-foot Castle Reef guards the north side of the Sun River Canyon, where Indian pictographs mark the entrance to the bighorn sheep range of Wagner Basin. The sheer limestone turrets of the Castle's east face are visible from far out in the Plains, one of the Front's most distinctive landmarks, as is Ear Mountain eleven miles due north.

Open, south-facing gulches provide vital winter forage for thousands of migrating Sun River elk, mule deer, and white-tailed deer, and up to 1,000 bighorn sheep. Secluded benches, ridges, and steep side slopes make up the central winter range of the largest native bighorn sheep herd in the lower forty-eight. Mountain goats, far fewer in number, prefer the rugged backbone of the Front and the towering cliffs of Castle Reef. Little wonder that Deep Creek and the rest of the Front are known as *North America's Serengeti.*

The three major top-end predators (bears, wolves, and cougars) live here during different times of the year depending on where their food supply happens to be. Another exciting symbol of wildness, the rare peregrine falcon, has been spotted along the Deep Creek front during fall migration. Abundant unoccupied peregrine habitat, where extensive cliffs rise above stream bottoms, is ideally suited for expansion of the species.

One of the more enjoyable Front summits to climb is 8,488-foot Arsenic Peak. Heading north from Mortimer Gulch, the climb is a vigorous twelve mile round-trip. The trail climbs steadily through open, grassy parks before crossing a small pass into Big George. From here, a prominent south ridge leads to the lower east summit and onto the top. The reward is one of the best 360-degree vistas from any peak in the Bob. From this high point, all of the Deep Creek country unfolds like a giant relief map.

It is difficult to imagine Deep Creek being anything other than what it has always been—a wild stretch of that formidable barrier we call the Rocky Mountain Front. In 1987, the late Walkin' Jim Stoltz, noted Montana minstrel of the wilds, led the two-month long *Great Bob Trek*—a monumental hike through unprotected wildlands around the Bob to draw support for their preservation. While hiking through Deep Creek, Walkin' Jim was inspired to write, "The feel of the morning in the Deep Creek Wilderness, reborn and alive, will walk with me always. It gives us a feeling . . . a sense of being alive that no other place or experience can imitate."[2]

Sawtooth Ridge

The ragged roaring rampart of Sawtooth Ridge is arguably the most dramatic uplift of the entire 110-mile-long sweep of the Front between Marias and Rogers Passes. With deeply incised fangs, a severely serrated summit, sheer cliffs, and a complex lattice of avalanche chutes, it is surely the Front's most distinctive feature. It forms the monumental south gate of Sun River Canyon, complementing perfectly Castle Reef to the north.

Sadly, Sawtooth was *orphaned* when it was severed from the 2.5-million-acre Bob Marshall Wilderness Complex by the ill-conceived Beaver-Willow Road after the devastating 1964 flood. The road forms the western boundary of a 21,000-acre roadless area of mostly national forest along with the upper west end of the state Sun River WMA. A typical west-east cross section reveals land that rises and falls an average of 1,000 feet in a series of parallel reefs and canyons before climbing 2,500 feet to the highest "tooth" of Sawtooth Ridge, at 8,179 feet. Then comes a 1,000-foot plummet followed by a more gradual 2,500-foot descent to the Plains—all within a linear distance of less than five miles.

Depending on the severity of the winter, the WMA *game range* supports between 1,000 and 3,000 elk. By late spring, the elk move west, past Sawtooth, following the green-up of vegetation.

We humans need an occasional lesson in humility, as Sawtooth dished out some years back. I was perched on the windswept north lip of Sawtooth Ridge within 100 yards of the north *tooth* of Sawtooth. I was stopped by an exposed footwide ledge leading to a narrow gap that was easily jumpable—except for a sheet of ice on the far side. If I gauged it wrong, I'd fall 1,000 feet on one side or 200 feet on the other. Same difference. I looked cautiously over the east edge, straight down to a jumble of talus rock 1,000 feet below. For one mad moment, I envisioned taking flight, to follow the skyward path of the golden eagle gliding past me on rising thermals. Vertigo struck, as did nausea. Head spinning, I backed away from the precipice to regain balance.

After a deep breath, I reflected on what the mountain has taught me. Foremost is humility. Reaching the tippy top is far less important than showing respect for this special wild place. As I inched back down the knife ridge, the wind let up and the sun brightened. Surely this was a sign for me? Of course not. The land yields equally to elk, bear, lichen, and human. As I contemplated my insignificance amid such grandeur, I felt both empty and exhilarated.

Another stark memory stands out. We had set up an early-spring camp at the head of Home Gulch. That night, the wind shook our camp like a giant hand. We awoke to see the splintered remains of a huge fir tree that had been snapped in two by the windstorm. The complete skeleton of a bighorn ram lay frozen into the ice of the creek, perhaps the victim of winter kill. Harsh and unforgiving is this Sawtooth country.

Renshaw

The 57,611-acre Renshaw roadless subregion of the Front is bounded by the Sun River/Gibson Reservoir on the north and the popular Benchmark road to the south. These highlands rise from the plains about twenty-five miles west of Augusta. This diverse mountainscape is made up of three distinct landforms. Patrick's Basin drains north to the Sun River through a wide, densely forested valley used by migrating Sun River elk. Tucked within this secluded enclave is some of the best grizzly habitat on the Front. Next, the high, grassy, relatively gentle Fairview–Ford Creek plateau, with its alternating stringers of Douglas fir and lodgepole pine, is a blend of winter and spring range for elk and bighorn sheep. This midsection of the Front on north to the Teton River is home to the largest native population of bighorns on the continent. Renshaw encompasses more than 10,000 acres of elk winter range—the most winter range on national forest anywhere on the Front.

The third landform, the South Fork of the Sun River, includes the most popular east-side route into the Bob Marshall Wilderness, which heads out from Benchmark. The imposing east face of 8,246-foot Fairview Mountain is seen far out on the Plains. Nearly vertical limestone reefs above foothills and prairie grade to sharp peaks, forests, and high parks to the west that were converted to grasslands by fires during the 1920s.

If the Rocky Mountain Front is one man's religion, as it was for one Pulitzer Prize–winning author, the late A. B. Guthrie Jr., then Renshaw is surely a fitting cathedral within which to practice this religion. There is something thrilling about trekking a wild, windswept ridge, seeing a fresh grizzly track in the snow, or simply gazing west with the knowledge that the mountains endure—wild and free—to the distant horizon and beyond. I'll never forget the most dramatic of the very few mountain lion sightings I've ever had, which took place in the wide open swales of Fairview Plateau. The reclusive big cat was stalking a weak calf that was falling behind a herd of cow elk. The stalking cougar and we human intruders became aware of each other at precisely the same moment. Somehow, this six-foot-long, 150-pound animal literally vanished before our eyes, lending new meaning to how secretive these felines really are.

Falls Creek—Silver King

The southernmost buttress of the Rocky Mountain Front, south of Benchmark, is 75,417 roadless acres of high peaks and steep canyons adjacent to the Scapegoat Wilderness. It is called Falls Creek–Silver King after a major drainage on the east side and a major peak west of the Divide. This is the first part of the Front seen when heading east from Rogers Pass on Highway 200. About two thirds of this roadless subregion of the Front lies east of the Continental Divide, with the remaining 25,000 acres draining into the upper Blackfoot River.

The western backbone of the country is formed by Wood Creek Hogback, the crest of the Front Range, and the Continental Divide. It is high, dry, cold, and windy, with a sense of space magnified by bare rock, sparse vegetation, and charred forest from the 240,000-acre Canyon Creek Fire of 1988. Bizarre shapes of gale-battered limber and whitebark pine clinging tenaciously to exposed ridges heighten the drama.

Falls Creek is the largest unprotected pristine watershed on the Front south of the Badger–Two Medicine. Grizzlies den and elk calve at the head of the East Fork of Falls Creek. The head of Falls Creek is bound by the Continental Divide, which is distinctly marked by wind-carved sandstone pedestals twenty to fifty feet high. Born on Scapegoat Mountain, the wild Dearborn River cuts a steep-walled gorge through Devil's Glen. Rapids alternate with deep emerald pools before the river flattens out into a wide, rocky valley.

Varied habitat in and around this southern rampart of the Front provides room to roam for both grizzlies and wolves. During winter, I've observed hundreds of deer and elk foraging along the foothills both north and south of the Dearborn River. Since the 1988 fire, it seems that elk in particular are using the grass-rich burn much more.

Fire, Wilderness, and the Front

Fire is a hot-button issue on the Rocky Mountain Front, no pun intended. Some ill-informed locals oppose any and all additions to the Bob Marshall Wilderness on the grounds that the Forest Service cannot control wildfire within wilderness, which, in turn, places adjacent private property at risk. In fact, the Wilderness Act permits the managing agency to take any necessary measures in wilderness to control fire, insects, and diseases. This provision is reaffirmed by the Rocky Mountain Front Heritage Act, proposed by local citizens along the Front and first introduced by Senator Max Baucus (D-MT) in 2011.

Let's take a closer look at the hot issue of fire. In Montana's mountains, vegetation has evolved with the driving forces of fire and climate. Fire is part of a complex interaction of ecological forces that act on the ecosystem. If we are to preserve wild forests in the Front and elsewhere, we must also preserve the processes through which these forests evolve. Periodic large fires within wilderness and the Front are both necessary and inevitable.

A recent dramatic example includes the 240,600-acre Canyon Creek Fire of 1988, which roared across the Continental Divide and scorched much of the Dearborn and Falls Creek drainages on the Front all the way to Haystack Butte far out on the Plains. Three huge wildfires along the Front during the hot, dry summer of 2007 further fanned the flames of this heated topic. The Skyland Fire burned much of the South Fork Two Medicine drainage in the northern end of the Badger–Two Medicine. At the same time, the Fool Creek Fire escaped the Bob at Washboard Reef and burned much of the West and North Forks of the Teton. Then came the Ahorn Fire, the eastern perimeter of which extended into the proposed Renshaw Addition to the Bob on the Front. Each of these three large fires averaged around 60,000 acres. The latter two were prescribed natural fires ignited within the wilderness by lightning strikes.

A century of fire suppression has caused an unnaturally heavy buildup of forest fuel in portions of the Front. It's not surprising that giant wildfires, like Canyon Creek, Fool Creek, and Ahorn, burned more intensely than they otherwise would were it not for our interruption of natural fire frequencies. The life cycles of some trees, such as lodgepole and ponderosa pine, depend on fire. Many lodgepole cones will not release their seeds unless opened by the heat of a hot fire. The thick bark of mature ponderosa allows it to survive a natural fire regimen of low-intensity, high-frequency ground fires. As the surrounding vegetation burns off, young trees can better compete for water and nutrients.

It is widely recognized that wilderness designation means that the land is protected from roads, timber harvest, motorized vehicles and equipment, and commercial uses except livestock grazing and outfitting. Less understood is the equally vital but subtler goal of protecting the *natural processes* that shape the land. Fire is the dominant natural process influencing forests of the Front and elsewhere in the Northern Rockies. Thus, recognizing and respecting the natural role of fire is the foundation of long-term, sustainable wilderness stewardship.

Where Do We Go from Here?

Wilderness designation under the 1964 Wilderness Act is the *gold standard* of federal land protection. Except for a buffer of perhaps a quarter mile around the half dozen or so major public access roads leading into the Front, virtually all of the national forest and BLM roadless acreage found here far exceeds the minimum legal requirements for inclusion in our nation's wilderness system. Wilderness suitability of these unsurpassed wildlands is enhanced even further by their contiguity with the already protected 1.5-million-acre core of the Bob Marshall Wilderness Ecosystem, of which they are an integral part.

Real or perceived resource or user conflicts always dominate the question of whether Congress should designate a given tract of public land as wilderness. By any measure, such conflicts on the Front are among the lowest of any wilderness candidate since passage of the act nearly fifty years ago. With only a few exceptions, the recently adopted Forest Service Travel Plan for the Front respects traditional horse and hiking use so that conflict with motorized use is minimal. Further, the Front has no economic potential for commercial logging or hardrock mining, so these activities are prohibited under current management plans. Existing livestock grazing is mandated to continue under the Wilderness Act. Most significantly, the Front has been legislatively withdrawn from oil and gas leasing thanks to work begun by former Senator Conrad Burns and finished by Senator Max Baucus in 2006. Most of the existing leases have been bought out, with only a few remaining in the Badger–Two Medicine.

So, why is there even a question about securing the suitable federal lands on the Front as an *enduring* resource of wilderness? It boils down to local opposition to wilderness that is due, in part, to misinformation about what wilderness actually is and does. Dispelling wilderness myths is beyond the scope of this chapter. Suffice it to say that local acceptance is crucial, and this means working with Front communities from the bottom up. This approach takes a lot more time and effort, but the payoff is legislation that can actually pass. For more than seven years, the local Coalition to Protect the Rocky Mountain Front has painstakingly crafted a homegrown package for the Front known as the Heritage Act, most recently reintroduced on February 14, 2013, by Montana senators Max Baucus and Jon Tester as S. 364.

The modest wilderness component of the Heritage bill of 67,112 acres is 30,000 acres less than the skimpy Forest Service recommendation. But acres alone don't tell the whole story. One of the virtues of the Heritage bill is that it takes a comprehensive landscape approach to the entire Front and, in so doing, protects more land than could ever be achieved with wilderness designation alone. Exclusive of the Badger–Two Medicine, the bill provides for a 208,160-acre Conservation Management Area (CMA) for the portion of the Front not set aside as wilderness. These lands are roadless and will remain that way, with no new permanent roads and only temporary roads within one-quarter mile of five major roads in the Front. All existing public access will be maintained for hunting, hiking, horse use, mountain biking, grazing, and post, pole, and firewood gathering. In other words, the CMA is designed to keep the Front as it is, which is the one thing that almost all local folks agree on.

The wilderness component of the Heritage bill consists of five additions to existing wilderness, beginning with the 16,711-acre Silver King/Falls Creek addition to the Scapegoat on the south end. Then, from south to north, are the Patricks Basin, Deep Creek, Our Lake, and West Fork Teton additions to the Bob Marshall totaling 50,401 acres. To the north of the West Fork lies the wildest portion of the Front, the south end of the Badger, including Morningstar, Poia, and Scarface Peaks. The Blackfeet Nation has long been concerned about wilderness designation in the ceded strip of the Badger Two Medicine due to uncertainty about how that would affect their treaty rights. So, ironically, the wildest land on the Front is left out of the Heritage bill and placed on the proverbial back burner, for now.

From the standpoint of wilderness, we need to look at the Front as two major parts: the Badger–Two Medicine, which was ceded to the U.S. government by the Blackfeet with reserved treaty rights, and the remainder of the Front south of Birch Creek, which is the subject of the bill sponsored by Senator Baucus.

Even without the Badger–Two Medicine, passage of the Rocky Mountain Front Heritage bill would signal a societal act of humility by placing the Front off-limits to intensive human activities, with the objective of preserving the diversity of nonhuman life. Here we are deliberately slowing down our impulse to drill the last barrel of oil, cut the last ancient tree, or dam the last wild river. Our grandchildren can take pride in reaching a remote Front summit under their own power, in guiding a pack string over rough mountain trails, in seeing wild country as far as the eye can see.

Picture the first light of a new dawn beginning to filter across the open plains, spreading over a vast uncluttered landscape, and eventually lighting the serrated summits of the Rocky Mountain Front with the promise of a more enduring coexistence between people and the best of our last remaining wildlands.

BILL CUNNINGHAM of Choteau earned a B.S. and M.S. in forestry from the University of Montana during the 1960s. After a stint in the army, he taught at the UM School of Forestry and later worked for the Montana Department of Natural Resources and Conservation in Helena. He has authored several books about Montana wilderness along with numerous hiking guides. He also wrote a Wild Country series for Montana Magazine for nearly 30 years. During this time, Bill worked for a variety of conservation groups, including the Montana Environmental Information Center, The Wilderness Society, American Wildlands, and the Montana Wilderness Association as its first conservation director.

After nearly 40 seasons of guiding in the Bob Marshall country, Bill and Polly Cunningham sold their business to Dropstone Outfitting in Choteau. But they are by no means hanging up their trekking poles. They plan to explore their cherished Rocky Mountain Front even more!

---

[1] Bill Cunningham, "The Front of the Front: Where the Trees Lean East and the People Lean West," *Montana Magazine*, June 1994.

[2] Jim Stoltz, unpublished personal journal, 1987.

OLD NORTH TRAIL

Brian Reeves with John Vollertsen

Dr. Brian O. K. Reeves of the University of Calgary completed an intensive study of the Old North Trail (ONT) along Montana's Rocky Mountain Front. On June 2, 1992, he presented the results of his research to the community of Choteau, Montana, at the public library. His presentation was sponsored jointly by the Montana Historical Society and The Nature Conservancy.

Dr. John A. Vollertsen attended that presentation and penned and transcribed notes of it. This chapter is based on those notes as edited by Dr. Reeves in 2013.

National Register of Historic Places

Dr. Reeves and his crew have completed mapping and fieldwork on the locations of the Old North Trail, using photos taken from fixed-wing aircraft and helicopters and on-ground studies. He used a helicopter for two days: one day on each trail.

Three segments of the ONT have been nominated to the National Register of Historic Places. The register is authorized under the National Historic Preservation Act of 1966. The Deep Creek site is nominated. The second site is Pine Butte. The third site is Two Medicine Ridge. They are well defined.

Recorded on detailed topographic maps, the location of the trail extends from the Sun River to the Canadian border. The State Historic Preservation Office has these maps in Helena.

The Old North Trail Network

The trail from Helena, Montana, to Calgary, Alberta, was the focus of the presentation. The trail is about 95 percent intact from Wolf Creek, Montana, to Alberta. *Intact* in this context means the trail has not been totally plowed under. It also means that it may be overlaid by roads or other trails. Intact also means that the landscape is intact. You can sense that continuity and can essentially experience the 10,000-year environment.

The Old North Trail is actually a *corridor* with several trails at some locations, such as river crossings. There is evidence of three trails crossing a river.

It was previously held that trails in the area were no more than 200 years old. The Blackfeet people have been here 5,000 years. This estimate is based on oral history, genetics, and language. The Blackfeet have identified themselves as having been here for the past 2,000 years. When looking at the span of time and the occupancy of the area by indigenous peoples, there is almost no distinction between history and prehistory.

Use of the Trail

Explorer William Clark traveled a section of the trail and was the first to mention it in literature. He describes it around the Dearborn River. Another explorer, David Thompson, documents Piegan Indians fighting other tribes along the trail.

Isaac Stevens made a rather accurate map of the trail. It is in Washington and has never been published. Walter McClintock, in his book *The Old North Trail,* writes about Brings-down-the-Sun.[1] There is a detailed account of the trail. The trail description *Old North Trail* was given by McClintock.

There were three main uses of the trail. One main use was to transport between quarry sites. Native movement south along the trail has occurred for 30,000 to 40,000 years, not 2,000 years as originally believed. How do we know it was used 12,000 years ago? The Alberta digs reveal chert from Helena, Three Forks, and Yellowstone. There are collections of these rocks along the Old North Trail. The Head-Smashed-In Buffalo Jump in southern Alberta reveals artifacts from the above locations.

A second main use was for warfare. There are many accounts that the Old North Trail was used for warfare, for instance, war lodges on top of Antelope Butte and Pine Butte. In 1730, the Blackfeet got horses. The Old North Trail was used for horse raiding and also for transporting slaves. There was a large Gros Ventre, Crow, and Shoshone slave trade prior to the arrival of the horse.

A third main use of the trail was for religious purposes. The religious part refers to the creation story of Napi. There are two Napi stories, one moral and the other creation. The creation story describes Napi as walking north and creating animals and the People. He gets tired and lies down. There are Napi figures in the vicinity of the trail.

Trail Well Defined

The *Dillon Examiner* describes the trail in 1910. Why was the trail so well defined even in 1910? In a relative sense, there was constant tribal movement along the trail. First, it led to water sources. Second, it was located near wood that provided shelter and fire. It was common for Blackfeet to move camps because they would run out of wood. One documented event describes 1,200 Blackfeet and 2,000 horses at one camp in Alberta. They had to move their camp in winter.

Many archaeological *features* on the land describe the location of the trail. These include rock art sites with animal figures. River crossing sites were marked with commemorative rock piles (cairns). A number of medicine circles, not medicine wheels, are along the route (native peoples did not have the wheel). There were also trail signs (cairns) and ritual sites.

Buffalo drive lanes can be found near the Teton River west of Choteau. The Sun River crossing has lots of archaeological sites.

On the Blackfeet Reservation, the Old North Trail is active today. It is called Highway 89. Trail use has gone from dogs to horses to cars. The trail is still intact to Alberta. It facilitates the interaction of old people in carrying out religious functions.

Historic Activities

James Willard Schultz says there were activities along the Old North Trail near St. Mary and Chief Mountain.

George Bird Grinnell documented Mêtis use when he wrote for *Field and Stream* magazine. To the Mêtis, the trail was referred to as *Red River Trail* because Red River carts transported people and goods over the trail. Specific measurements of cart ruts in Canada reveal they are wider than wagon ruts and the wheels are narrower on the carts. They came *down* the mountains, not *up*.

The Old North Trail goes to the Bering Strait. The Cree call it the *Wolf Trail*. Near Edmonton, the trail splits.

An 1801 map of the Bear River (same as the Marias River) shows the OldNorth Trail.

Sun River to Alberta: Markers on the Land

Advancing from south to north, many significant markers and crossings dot the landscape. Below are some of the more significant points.

The Old North Trail runs east of Haystack Butte (southwest of Augusta). It crosses the Sun River at two locations, each a mile from the other. The upper crossing has linear marks.

The trail continues to Deep Creek. James Doty crossed on the upper crossing of Deep Creek. The creek is crossed in three or four places. One crossing is about one mile above the intersection of Deep Creek and Battle Creek. The trail also crosses Battle Creek north of Piskun Reservoir.

The Indian Burial Ground (as notated on contemporary maps) in the Deep Creek area is not a burial ground. Instead, the series of rock cairns that dot across the landscape are actually trail cairns. They were dug up in the 1920s. There were no bones and no artifacts.

Hugh Monroe crossed at the Black Reef area. There is a medicine wheel there. Boulders in the area have rock art on them.

Trail cairns in the area were two meters high. Ancient travelers needed these during whiteouts in the winter.

There is an arrow on the Salmon Ranch that points toward Ear Mountain. It was built recently. This was determined by the sod material under the rocks.

The Bellevue road has several trail crossings. There is also an early record of wagon trails in the area. Also, the Teton buffalo drive lanes are here. They are very well defined. The cairns are part of the trail and part of the drive lanes. The drive was a religious activity. Some of the cairns incorporate sacred rock in the same sense as there are sacred rocks used in the sweat lodges. Some rocks have powers. The kinds of rock used would include lava rock, volcanic rock, rock with lots of iron, white rock, or black rock. They stuck these into the cairn, but not all cairns.

Travois trails: They characteristically have three tracks, one for the horse (in the center) and two for the travois. The horse trail is straight, and the travois wiggles and leaves crooked marks.

There are three major crossings on the Teton. One is at the present bridge.

Antelope Butte: There are forty-two stone piles near the butte. All are dug out. They are well defined.

Blackleaf: The trail crosses in the vicinity of where the road crosses Muddy Creek.

Cow Creek: Many years ago, a surveyor had a good account of the Old North Trail here.

Birch Creek: There are three crossings, one near the highway and two west of there.

There are two signs describing the Old North Trail, one on the Teton and the other near Swift Reservoir.

Heart Butte: The trail passes south of there.

Badger Creek: The trail is difficult to see because of the hard glacial deposits. The trail meanders in this area.

At the Two Medicine River, there is a problem as to the crossings. Doty crossed near the county road.

In the Marias area, the trail is overlaid by county road and the golf course.

North Two Medicine River: The trail crosses above the falls.

East Glacier: There are trail scars at the graveyard.

Two Medicine Ridge: This part of the trail is well preserved. Doty documents a very steep route that goes straight up the ridge. The reason is obvious. A fully loaded travois must go straight up or it will tip over.

Middle Fork of Milk River: The trail crosses here.

In 1896, a stagecoach route from Browning to St. Mary overlaid the Old North Trail.

Duck Lake: The trail goes on both sides.

Babb: The trail crosses near Babb where the bridge and siphon are located. That area of the trail is being plowed now.

Pike Lake: The trail is well defined.

Alberta: The trail was still in use until World War I. Because of the oil and gas pipelines, the trail is interrupted in Alberta, unlike in the United States, where there is less oil and gas development.

Other Related Features

The probability of another intact trail, such as the Old North Trail, is extremely unlikely. The trail should get International Trail Corridor designation.

Medicine Wheels: The Big Horn Medicine Wheel in Wyoming is one of only two medicine wheels of its particular kind in the world. The other medicine wheel is on the Bow River in Alberta. The Big Horn wheel is 5,500 years old. It has twenty-eight spokes, symbolic of twenty-eight rafters in the Sun Dance lodge.

A medicine circle is constructed when a chief dies. Four lines (representing cardinal directions) are constructed on the spot.

Why was the medicine circle constructed at a particular site? The location was chosen probably because of a vision. Then a rock cairn was constructed. Most medicine circles

have burials associated with them. Many were dug up for that reason. Some are used as directional indicators.

The Blackfeet are known for building with rock. There are 120 medicine circles (different from medicine wheels) north of the Missouri River and only two south of it. One medicine circle located on the South Saskatchewan River in southeastern Alberta dates to 1520. The date is based on human bones and a tent peg painted blue. One circle, west of Choteau, Montana, is 120 feet in diameter. Inside are four large tipi rings, each one 30 feet in diameter. Very large tipis are painted. They are for the Sun Dance and form a circle. The 120-foot circle could be a Sun Dance location. It is remembered by laying out stone in that manner.

On a butte south of the Teton River, there is the so-called stick man. Although believed by some to be culturally significant, it is actually a geological feature. It does not look like a Napi figure.

An area near the Milk River has been used recently to truck out sand. Because human skulls have been discovered, it is believed to be a burial site, probably Blackfeet and Assiniboine.

Dogs, Travois, and Tipis

A prevalent myth is that small tipi rings indicate tipis from the dog days. However, there are 4,500-year-old tipi rings that are nine meters in diameter.

During the Isaac Stevens expedition in 1853, one man was sent north. He recounts coming across a group of Piegans with lots of dog travois. The rate of travel by either dog or horse was not much different on a per-day basis, with the factor being the time it took to load and unload.

The average size of a tipi is seventeen feet in diameter and weighing about 1,500 pounds. A large Blackfeet tipi would be made of thirty-two buffalo hides. At times, there would be two tipis strung together, as would be indicated by two very close rock circles (tipis needed to be anchored with rocks to brace against the wind).

The average family had thirty to forty dogs, both big and small. The large ones were used for packing.

Burials and Quarries

The oldest and largest known burial ground is 5,000 years old. It is located at Swift Current, Saskatchewan.

Dr. Les Davis has been studying a quarry across the Missouri from Trident, Montana. This quarry was used between 900 B.C. and 200 B.C.

Quarries are sometimes very large. An obsidian quarry in Yellowstone National Park is 100 square miles in size. The Three Forks (near Trident) was mined twenty-five feet deep. It also has tunnels sixty feet long. Boulders as large as 1.5 tons were moved. The original excavators were after a yellow chert. They extracted the rock with a small simple tool made from a buffalo rib. This was a common tool.

Buffalo Jumps

The number and use of buffalo jumps started to increase about 3,000 years ago. They really started to take off about 1,500 years ago. The buffalo jump at Head-Smashed-In is actually twelve jumps. More is described about Head-Smashed-In in Bruce Weide's book *Trail of the Great Bear.*[2] The book also describes the tribal nations of the area and the Blackfeet origin stories.

The buffalo jumps on the Sun River, near Augusta, were huge. Researchers believe the Indians harvested the herds and shipped them down the river. One theory is that the Indians most likely traded for tobacco. This was a smoking tobacco, unlike most tobaccos used in ceremony.

The most massive jumps were against the mountains. The largest ever is in the Highwood Mountains. The railroad actually built a spur into the Highwood site, where the bone deposits were mined.

South of the Missouri River, the number and size of buffalo jumps drop off. In the Powder River area, sites are rare. All the way to Texas, the sites are small. A theory about the vast number of sites in this region relates to a volcano on the Columbia Plateau (Crater Lake, Oregon) that exploded 6,800 years ago. The explosion was about forty times larger than the one at Mount St. Helens. The ash spewed this direction. Some of it layered about two feet deep in the Waterton/

Glacier area. Farther out on the prairies, it was about six inches deep, which led to increased grass productivity and, thus, large numbers of buffalo in this area. The Missouri was approximately the southern limit of the ash fallout.

Miscellaneous Accounts

One particular myth about tribal movements should be dispelled. A notion prevails that tribes, such as the Kootenai and the Salish, came east across the mountains to hunt buffalo out on the prairie. Actually, the tribes never came east until they got horses. Contrary to some teachings, there is no archaeological evidence of Salish, Kootenai, or Shoshone coming east of the mountains. They did not hunt east of the mountain front except with horses.

How long have the Blackfeet been on the Rocky Mountain Front? The Blackfeet people (as an identifiable ethnic people) go back 5,000 years. This estimate is based on points, pottery, tools, and ritual, all of which can be traced back that far. Although 1,000 years can be easily traced, it is more difficult to trace 2,000 to 3,000 years back. Further back, the oral history and tradition are very strong.

In oral tradition, there is only one story for the Blackfeet and the three Blackfeet tribes. Another story describes all native tribes and goes back 10,000 years. As the story goes, the people were crossing a frozen river. A child saw a buffalo horn frozen into the ice. When the horn was pulled out, the ice divided and separated the tribe. This division was between the Blackfeet and the Arapaho, and the Missouri River is the dividing line between the two tribes. This story is 10,000 to 15,000 years old.

Over the expanse of history and prehistory, tribes sometimes go extinct. The Arapaho, for example, had five tribes. Two are currently recorded, whereas the other three became extinct around 1400 to 1500 A.D.

The Nicholas Biddle edition of the Lewis and Clark journals described the Shoshone as being driven off by the Blackfeet.[3] This is a fabrication and is not in the actual journals. Biddle was hired by William Clark to prepare the journals. In the original journals, as edited by Gary Moulton,[4] there is no mention of this.

A chapter is devoted to the Old North Trail in Joseph Kinsey Howard's book *Montana: High, Wide, and Handsome.*[5]

BRIAN O. K. REEVES is a professor emeritus at the University of Calgary and past president of Lifeways of Canada Limited, Alberta's oldest cultural resource consulting and contracting company. He has more than fifty years of research and professional experience and specializes in northern North American archaeology, ethnohistory, and cultural resource management.

---

1 Walter McClintock, *The Old North Trail: Or, Life, Legends and Religion of the Blackfeet Indians* (Lincoln: University of Nebraska Press, 1968).

2 Bruce Weide, *Trail of the Great Bear* (Helena, MT: Falcon Press, 1992). 158-164.

3 Archibald Hanna (Philadelphia: Lippincott, 1961), 2:367

4 Gary E. Moulton, ed., *The Journals of the Lewis and Clark Expedition*, Vols. 1-3 (Lincoln: University of Nebraska Press, 1987).

5 Joseph Kinsey Howard, *Montana: High, Wide, and Handsome* (Lincoln: University of Nebraska Press, 1943). 315-329.

Chapter 4

THE "OTHER" TRIBES

John Vollertsen

When we think of historic and prehistoric American Indian occupations of Montana's Rocky Mountain Front, our awareness immediately focuses on the Blackfeet Nation. Of course, there were other indigenous populations who occupied, used, or passed through areas of the Front long before or during the time of historic Blackfeet occupation. But theirs is the dominant history and the one we think of first, and hear about the most. There is good reason for that. The Blackfeet Indian Reservation is the only reservation on Montana's East Front. The Blackfeet people are intimately connected to the history of Glacier National Park, or more appropriately, the Park is a significant part of Blackfeet history and their changing boundary designations as influenced by European exchanges. In more contemporary times, the Blackfeet people have been highly visible in natural resource issues on or near the reservation in areas considered historic Blackfeet territory.

Blackfeet history is the dominant history when examining the influences of indigenous people upon the Front and of the Front upon indigenous people. A tremendous amount has been written about the Blackfeet people along the Front, or, as they call this bountiful land, the "Backbone of the World." Darrell Robes Kipp, a Blackfeet elder, multiple degree holder (Eastern Montana College, Harvard University, and Vermont College), educator, and mentor in the revitalization of the Pikuni language, wrote, "I once estimated more than three thousand major studies had been done on the [Blackfeet] tribe since the early 1900s."[1] The recording of, and *slant* on, Blackfeet history was highly influenced by such prominent writers and historians as Hugh Monroe, Clark Wissler, George Bird Grinnell, and George Willard Schultz. Much of the effort was in the wake of James J. Hill's effort to market the newly acquired Glacier National Park. No wonder the histories of other tribes in the area have been subordinated.

There are other tribes indeed that sojourned along the Front sporadically for thousands of years, although their histories in the area are far less prominent. The land bridge theory posits that the peopling of America started when the sea levels were three hundred feet lower than today and the Bering Strait (Beringia) was crossed as people traveled southward down an ice-free corridor that included the east slopes of the Rocky Mountains.

The earliest Paleo-Indians were among the first to enter America. These people are the Na-Dene, whose likely descendants were the Haida and the Tlingit of Alaska and the Navajo and the Apache of the American Southwest.[2] It seems unconventional to consider that the Navajo were among the first to occupy or travel along the Old North Trail on the east slope of the Rockies near Choteau, Montana. They may have spent two weeks on Montana's portion of the Rocky Mountain Front, or two centuries. We really have no way of knowing.

Archaeological Information

Early tribal movements along the Front have not been revealed in any abundance of archaeological information. Part of the reason is that there have been few systematic archaeological efforts from which to make specific assertions. Most archaeological work has been motivated on a piecemeal basis, usually as a part of permitting processes for resource extraction. However, some exceptions include the archaeological excavation of the Blacktail Cave northwest of Wolf Creek, Montana, and an archaeological surface survey that resulted in the nomination of parts of the Old North Trail to the National Register of Historic Places.

A third archaeological project that received attention for several field seasons (1992 to 1995) is located along the north shore of Gibson Reservoir (Sun River) west of Augusta with several sites approximately five to eight miles inside the forest boundary. The records for the Gibson project, which are only in draft form, are located at the Lewis and Clark National Forest office in Great Falls.[3]

During the Gibson project, several sites were examined on the north shore. A narrative in the Gibson records for one of the sites states: "This site has one of the highest densities of artifacts on the Lewis and Clark Forest and represents years of utilization by prehistoric peoples." The following were discovered at the site: bison teeth and bone, lithic tools, tipi circles, a possible deer pelvis, pieces of ceramic pottery, and obsidian samples sourced to Bear Gulch (located in the Centennial Mountains west of Yellowstone National Park) and Obsidian Cliff (located inside Yellowstone National Park). Two radiocarbon dates at this site average 1100 and 1180 A.D.

Another site was labeled as a prehistoric bison kill site. It contained "thousands of large mammal bones, predominantly bison." As far as the animal bones were concerned, there were so many that the investigators could only give cursory attention in the time they had. The records contained specific mention of bison and deer, although one could expect to find other mammals represented among the thousands of bones.

Another one of the Gibson sites contains a natural springs, and the report says that the springs "has permanent fresh water emanating from the ground all year, is situated approximate to the Medicine Hot Springs, contains watercress and in general is a highly desirable camping location."

The Gibson report concludes with this observation: "Archaeological investigations in the Sun River Canyon drainage have supported the contention that the Sun River drainage was intensively used by both prehistoric and historic man through time. The distribution of archaeological sites in this drainage also indicates utilization as a travel corridor for movement between the Flathead Valley on the west and the Great Plains on the east."

One of the above sites, which had the notation that the springs "contains watercress and in general is a highly desirable camping location," caught my attention. I reflected on conversations I had in July and August 2000 with Phillip "Bud" Bisnett, a lifelong East Front resident and self-educated archaeologist. Along with his vast artifact collection, Bisnett had many stories and theories about the ancient travelers along the Rocky Mountain Front. He claimed that early users of the Old North Trail ventured up mountain canyons on the west to locate year-round springs. His theory was that the natives had a physiological need for green food material. In the *off-season,* these springs yield a very desirable food source. As early as 1907, forest ranger Clyde Fickes reported on his visit to the spring in the same area as the Gibson project: "I nearly always saw mountain sheep, especially in the winter. They seemed to love the watercress that grew there."[4] As plant experts explain, watercress was introduced to North America by European settlers. If there was no watercress at the springs a thousand years ago, then what was the desired green material Bisnett theorizes? It is possible that common watercress may be more of a colloquial description for what could apply to many other plants that grow around mountain springs. Without an actual site visit but considering the locale, wild plants devotee Myrna Matulevich clarifies that there are approximately seven edible plants that could flourish at a year-round spring and would range in identification from American speedwell *(Veronica americana)* to wild mint *(Mentha arvensis)*.[5]

The Gibson archaeological site seems to confirm Bisnett's theory. Along with other amenities at these springs, his theory simply made sense. On a biographical note, in 2000 Bud Bisnett donated his vast artifact collection to the Cascade County Historical Society and in 2001 received the Montana

Archaeological Society Conservation Award.[6] Bisnett passed away in 2003 at age eighty.

That Ah-Ha! Moment

My personal interest in knowing more about the tribes of the Rocky Mountain Front stems from the fact that I am enrolled in the Assiniboine Tribe of the Fort Peck Indian Reservation in northeastern Montana. The majority of my genetic makeup is Danish and Irish, but my Assiniboine blood quantum is enough to have that tribal distinction. Having spent most of my life in the more mountainous parts of western Montana—including living, working, and recreating in Choteau and the Front in the late 1970s and 1980s—I learned from the fragmented histories of the Assiniboine that we were at times located along the Rocky Mountain Front as well. As I have pieced together various accounts, I have been able to put together rather respectable evidence to articulate the presence of the Assiniboine along the Front, and, in fact, the presence of many other tribes as well.

It demonstrates impoliteness—at least in the Indian way—to not tell or write the histories of other tribes in any authoritative way. But I will take liberties to replicate accounts of some credible historians to build the case for the Assiniboine presence on the Front.

While in graduate school, I plowed through many history books and papers to try to prepare myself intellectually for what the country was about to do: recognize the two-hundredth anniversary of the Lewis and Clark Expedition. I select the term *recognize* rather than *celebrate* for obvious reasons, since some Native American tribes do not hold the occasion in very high esteem.

It was during that time in my studies that I became aware of a map—of which most Lewis and Clark aficionados are thoroughly aware—and I immediately had one of those *AH-HA!* moments. The large foldout map appears in volume 2 of the Dover edition of the history of the Lewis and Clark Expedition[7] and clearly demonstrates that the bands of Indians nearest the Rocky Mountain Front in today's Montana were *not* Blackfeet, but rather, Assiniboine!

The original map was sent by Captain Meriwether Lewis to President Thomas Jefferson from Fort Mandan on April 7, 1805, with a notation that "the country West of Fort Mandan is laid down principally from Indian information." Lewis and Clark spent the winter of 1804 to 1805 with the Mandan Indians near the Missouri River in today's North Dakota. The Mandan village was a hub of commerce for the northern plains tribes and French and British traders. The explorers were extremely eager for information about what was west of them because there was no map to show the way to and over the Rocky Mountains; however, there was much speculation. They interviewed every person with knowledge of routes, waterways, and tribes. This was important for commerce, indoctrination, natural resources, supplies in trade, and horses. They interviewed several traders they met along the way up the Missouri River to Mandan and then several more while wintering with the Mandans. Of course, they also interviewed tribal visitors to the Mandan village.

When examining the map forwarded to Jefferson, the nearness—the term I use—of Assiniboine Indians to the Front is specifically defined in map terminology as there being "250 Assiniboine men" at today's Milk River area of central Montana, "430 Assiniboine men" north of Milk River, more (quantity not stated) Assiniboine in today's Sweetgrass Hills area, "500 Assiniboine men" north of today's Chief Mountain (designated on the map as "The King") between the 51st and 52nd parallels, and "400 Assiniboine men" northeast of Chief Mountain between the 52nd and 53rd parallels. The map shows the nearest "Black foot" Indians even farther north than the Assiniboine and between the 52nd and 53rd parallels, or approximately 230 miles north of Chief Mountain. The "Blood" Indians are even farther north of the "Black foot."

Chief Mountain is in Montana on the border between Glacier National Park and the Blackfeet Indian Reservation and about five miles south of the Canadian border, which is the 49th parallel. Chief Mountain is considered a major spiritual focal point of the Blackfeet Nation.

The map of 1805 does not designate the presence of Blackfeet Indians on Montana's Rocky Mountain Front. However, one cannot conclude they were not present. Their strong, well-documented oral history supports their presence on the Front, and in associated mountainous areas, since time immemorial. Furthermore, the map does demonstrate Assiniboine Indians as predominantly *nearest* to the Montana Rocky Mountain Front in a very legitimate sense at that time.

Another noteworthy item in the 1805 map is that the *only* tribe actually *on* Montana's Rocky Mountain Front is the Ca-ta-na-hawas Indians, and they are located precisely at Chief Mountain. We know them better today as the Kootenai Tribe, who currently reside on the west side of the Continental Divide on the Flathead Indian Reservation in western Montana. For centuries, the hearty Kootenai have been crossing the rugged mountainous passes of today's Glacier National Park and southern Alberta (during all seasons of the year) to access the game-rich foothills and prairies of the East Front.[8]

Historian Gary Moulton has edited the Lewis and Clark journals with incredible detail. Volume 1 of his works is the atlas, which contains reproductions of the expedition's large maps.[9] The map in the Dover edition (mentioned above) is located in Moulton's volume 1. The map sent to President Jefferson before the expedition left Fort Mandan in 1805 was retraced and modified. One modified map, located on page 32a of volume 1 and labeled the "State Department Copy," clearly places the "Black foot" Indians on the Rocky Mountain Front of Montana.

We know from the journal accounts that Captain Lewis and a few of his men encountered Blackfeet Indians and camped with them on the Two Medicine River several miles east of the Front. A fight broke out and two Blackfeet boys were killed. However, one historian, Robert Saindon, has advanced a very persuasive argument that these Blackfeet were actually Gros Ventres.[10] Saindon also points out that the Blackfeet and Gros Ventre were closely allied at that time.

Tribes did not necessarily have exact territories but, rather, were more fluid with tentacle tribal bands investigating new areas and displacing other tribes. Relative to the Front, historian Colin Calloway writes "that all the lands held by the Blackfeet tribes were formerly held by the Kutenais, Flatheads, and Shoshones but that those peoples had now been 'driven across the mountains.' The Blackfeet kept up the pressure. Shoshones relinquished their hold on the plains of southern Alberta and northern Montana and retreated into the Rocky Mountain ranges of Wyoming and Idaho."[11]

More about the Assiniboine and the Front

With the advent of the horse, the northern plains were churning with volatility. Mobility meant territorial enforcement, war between tribes, short-term and long-term alliances, horse raids, and trapping and hunting prerogatives. Although not permanent occupants, many tribes, such as the Crow, warred with and stole horses from other tribal occupants of Montana and the East Front and then traded them to tribes west of the mountains.

Tribal mobility was not as vigorous in the prehorse days. Tribal movements were slower, and conflict between tribes less frequent. With the quest to obtain horses, tribes went to great effort to find them.

One account describes the Assiniboine, whose homeland was Montana and Canada, traveling to the southern United States to obtain horses: "The Assiniboines were the most renowned horse thieves in the Northwest, where horse stealing was often a tribal occupation. Many of their horses were taken in raids far to the south near the Spanish settlements, and bore Spanish brands."[12]

Emerging horse cultures advanced the technology for mobility and accelerated change. Tribes were able to reconnoiter locations for the sake of food resources, which placed them in many areas of the Rocky Mountain Front and nearby mountainous locations, even if temporarily.

In her archaeological report of the Blackleaf Wildlife Management Area, Mary McCarthy points out from her research: "Other plains tribes who frequented the front's eastern slopes and foothills in the last two centuries were the Gros Ventre (Atsina), Plains Assiniboine, Crow, and Shoshone."[13]

Sometimes the interaction between tribes of the northwestern plains was not so friendly. An episode broke out among the Assiniboine, Cree, and Blackfeet along the East

Front near the Canadian border. The following detailed account is articulated by John Ewers, noted historian of northwestern Plains Indians:

> In October, 1870, large camps of Blood and Piegan Indians were pitched on Oldman and St. Mary rivers while there occupants traded at the near-by whisky forts. They knew nothing of the plan of a large party of several hundred Cree and Assinboin warriors to fall upon them while they were occupied in the drunken carousals that usually followed Blackfoot visits to the forts. At daybreak the enemy attacked the Blood camp. When the Piegans heard gunfire and yelping dogs in the Blood village, their men quickly seized their weapons, mounted their horses, and rode to the aid of their allies. With their few repeating rifles, augmented by old muzzle-loading flintlocks and bows and arrows, the Blackfoot allies forced the Crees and Assiniboins to retreat. The Blackfeet, in hot pursuit, drove the enemy into the river. Their repeating rifles "dropped the Crees like ducks." In the ensuing slaughter, few of the enemy escaped. Their losses were reckoned (perhaps too generously) at from two hundred to four hundred. Big Brave, son of the old Piegan chief, Mountain Chief, claimed to have taken nine scalps in this great victory. It was the last sizable intertribal battle the Blackfoot tribes ever fought.[14]

The Stoney Tribe of Canada is a branch of the Assiniboine. Their home range prior to 1800 extended along the East Front from deep into Canada all the way south to the Chief Mountain area of Montana.[15] Referring to a time period from the 1860s to the 1880s, Andy Russell, a longtime southwestern Alberta rancher, outfitter, and author, writes, "The Indians here (Stonies) camped in small groups all through the mountains in the sheep, deer, goat and bear country."[16]

Another informative account of Stoney presence is in Glacier National Park. Jack Holterman authored a highly accredited book about the place names of Glacier and

Waterton National Parks. About the Stoneys, he wrote: "The marshal of Great Falls, George Treat, found the Stoneys spearing fish at Lake McDonald in 1892, staying about a week and smoking their fish for the winter. Ahern met some during his exploration for Ahern Pass."[17]

In a Discovery Channel documentary called *War against the Indian* (1994), the narrator, referring to the general Glacier National Park area, spoke about the importance of the mountains to the Stoney Indians:

> According to Chief John Snow of the good Stoney people, who is also a minister, Indian traditions and oral history say that his people were always present in his part of the Great Island, which is the native name for the North American continent. [Chief Snow talks:] . . . The mountains are very precious, sacred to my people over the years. They have gone there for vision quests; they've gone there for prayers and searching for divine guidance. The mountains have always been a sacred area. The mountain hot springs; my people went there for healing. The medicine men would send some of our people there for cleansing and for healing, for medicine. . . . It's a very special place for us.

In the early 1990s, I spoke at length with Jerome "Buster" Fourstar and Buster's son Carl Fourstar Sr. of the Fort Peck Indian Reservation. I had the honor of participating in the Assiniboine family's Sun Dance and sweat lodge ceremonies. Buster has since passed away, and Carl, a member of the Assiniboine Pipe Carriers, died in 2009 at age seventy-two. Carl Fourstar recounted that his grandfather died north of Chief Mountain. He further disclosed that his grandmother used to tell stories of the prereservation days and of traveling to the "place with the bubbling water"—today's Yellowstone National Park.

My emphasis has been the Assiniboine presence on the Rocky Mountain Front. When telling the story of one tribe, one needs to be aware of the inclusiveness and meshing of so many other tribes ancient and contemporary who were attracted to the generous natural-world diversity offered by the Rocky Mountain Front.

Familial Appeal

I've made good attempts to follow my Assiniboine roots back as far as I could. Documentation runs out in the early 1800s, and remnants of oral history helped me fill in the gaps.

The confluence of the Missouri and Yellowstone Rivers in today's North Dakota is where it begins for me. Fort Buford was in that area. The Assiniboine, Cree, Sioux, and other tribes traded at the fort and also periodically maintained encampments near the military installation. My great-great-grandmother was part of the Wadopaxnatuwa (Canoe Paddler of the Prairies) clan of Assiniboine. The contemporary spelling of the band is Wadopana (Canoe Paddlers). I learned of her relationship with this particular clan not from any kind of written record but, rather, from my friend and Assiniboine relative Ken Ryan, a tribal elder and historian who is also fluent in the Assiniboine (Nakoda) language.

My great-great-grandmother married Edward Lambert Sr., who was the post interpreter at Fort Buford. In about 1870, Lambert and frontiersman Yellowstone Kelly traveled up the Yellowstone River toward today's Billings, Montana. In his memoirs, Yellowstone Kelly devotes an entire chapter to the trip.[18] My great-great-grandfather's picture is in Yellowstone Kelly's book.

Some of the familial connection was graciously brought to my attention by Bob Saindon of Wolf Point, Montana. Saindon is a historian with a vast knowledge of Plains Indians and the Lewis and Clark Expedition. While residing on the Fort Peck Indian Reservation in the early 1990s, I had the opportunity to plunge into Bureau of Indian Affairs records, which are only available to enrolled family members. I was able to connect and verify my lineage through oral history and written documentation. I was amazed at the thoroughness of early-day reservation records. If one thinks about it, it was probably so the U.S. government could stay on top of land transfers, which over the decades became so fractionalized that the government is only now dealing with how to remedy the problem. Indian people were given impersonal identifying numbers long before social security numbers were invented. One inadvertent advantage is that a hundred years later those numbers have become key to accurately tracking one's family ancestry.

Conclusion

Many Montanans boast of being 5th- or 6th-generation Montanans. I personally boast of being a 350th-generation Montanan. My kin have been around since the beginning of time, so they say. I can further assert that I have family members who traveled the Old North Trail thousands of years ago. I really don't think anyone can disprove that claim.

Anyone who has visited the Rocky Mountain Front has their own claims to the landscape. This chapter is mine. It's private. It's personal. It's something I don't talk much about. I feel a personal connection to the many landscapes of Montana, from the flatlands of Yellowstone and Missouri country to the Rocky Mountain peaks. I consider myself lucky to have the heritage and the personal history that goes along with it.

Whereas Darrell Robes Kipp mentions 3,000 major studies on the Blackfeet, I look at my personal library and I have a total of only eight books and major studies about Assiniboine people. But if I can add just one chapter to a much grander story of the East Front, then I will feel privileged to have done so.

---

1 Darrell R. Kipp, "Completing the Circle," in *Lanterns on the Prairie: The Blackfeet Photographs of Walter McClintock*, ed. Steven L. Grafe (Norman: University of Oklahoma Press, 2009), 99-103.

2 Walter C. Fleming, *The Complete Idiot's Guide to Native American History* (Indianapolis, IN: Alpha Books, 2003), 12.

3 Richard E. Newton and Sandra French, *Gibson Archaeological Project* (R2009011500058) (Great Falls, MT: Lewis and Clark National Forest, December 2010).

4 Clyde P. Fickes, *Recollections: Forest Ranger Emeritus* (Missoula, MT: U.S. Forest Service, Northern Region, 1972).

[5] Myrna Matulevich, e-mail message to author, November 24, 2012.

[6] Larry Lahren, "Montana Archaeological Society Conservation 2001 Award to Bud Bisnett," *Archaeology in Montana* 41, no. 2 (2000): 1-3.

[7] Elliot Coues, ed., *The History of the Lewis and Clark Expedition*, vol. 2 (New York: Dover, 1997).

[8] Darris Flanagan, *Indian Trails of the Northern Rockies* (Stevensville, MT: Stoneydale, 2001).

[9] Gary Moulton, ed. *The Definitive Journals of Lewis and Clark*, vol. 1 (Lincoln: University of Nebraska Press, 1993).

[10] Robert A. Saindon, "The 'Unhappy Affair' on Two Medicine River." *We Proceeded On*, August 2002.

[11] Colin G. Calloway, *One Vast Winter Count: The Native American West before Lewis and Clark* (Lincoln: University of Nebraska Press, 2003), 300.

[12] D. E. Worcester, "Spanish Horses among the Plains Tribes," *Pacific Historical Review* 14, no. 4 (1945): 409-17.

[13] Mary F. McCarthy, *Archaeological Reconnaissance Survey of the Blackleaf Wildlife Management Area Teton County, Montana* (Helena: Montana Department of Fish, Wildlife, and Parks, October 1992), 11.

[14] John C. Ewers, *The Blackfeet: Raiders on the Northwest Plains* (Norman: University of Oklahoma Press, 1958), 260-61.

[15] John Snow, *These Mountains Are Our Sacred Places: The Story of the Stoney People* (Calgary, Alberta: Fifth House, 2005), 5.

[16] Andy Russell, *Grizzly Country* (New York: Nick Lyons Books, 1967), 97.

[17] Jack Holterman, *Place Names of Glacier/Waterton National Parks* (West Glacier, MT: Glacier Natural History Association, 1985), 127.

[18] Luther S. Kelly and Milo Milton Quaife, *Yellowstone Kelly: The Memoirs of Luther S. Kelly* (New Haven, CT: Yale University Press, 1926).

Chapter 5

MÉTIS FAMILY HISTORY

Larry Salois

My name is Larry Salois. I am the son of Stewart Salois, who was born at the "Old" Blackfeet Agency on the Badger Creek in 1928. His father, Abraham, was born at the Holy Family Mission School near Browning, Montana, in 1872 and died in 1955.

Abe's father, Toussaint, was born in 1847 in the north country of Canada near Camrose, just south of Edmonton in the present-day province of Alberta. He passed on in 1934 near Heart Butte, Montana, where he and a large number of family members are buried.

My great-grandfather, Toussaint, was a participant in the confrontation with the Canadian government, which was called the Riel Rebellion.[1] After this time, Louis Riel fled Canada along with Toussaint Salois and others.[2]

This is the beginning of my story and a limited account to this publication.

I was born and raised in the city of Cut Bank, Montana, which is just across the river from the Blackfeet Indian

Reservation. I was born on Friday, August the 13th, 1948, at the "new" hospital in Cut Bank. This was my lucky day.

Our family lived in town (Cut Bank), but my mother's parents owned a small-acreage dryland farm two miles east of town. My mother's father came from Stavanger, Norway, through Ellis Island, New York, around the turn of the century. He spent his first year in Montana on the Missouri River working for a cattle company. They would dig back into the riverbank just far enough and deep enough to cover with some sort of wood, then put some of the diggings on top of that. This would serve as home in the forty- to fifty-degrees-below-zero winter. Who said this was going to be easy? He met and married Gertrude Baker near the town of Denton, Montana, where my mother, Shirley, was born in 1926.

They then moved to Kevin, Montana, where a new oil boom was in progress. My grandfather helped to build and move wooden oil derricks in the Kevin oil patch. Later, the family moved to Cut Bank just a short distance away and bought their small farm.

My Early Years

I would spend a good portion of my growing up on this farmstead, which had no electricity, no telephone, and best of all no indoor plumbing. And it did provide the most spectacular view of the Rocky Mountain Front, all the way from Chief Mountain in the north to the mountains in the south that provided drainage for the Teton River.

During this early beginning, I was fortunate enough to experience what this natural surrounding had to offer in the formation of my being.

This direct contact with the natural environment and how it works came about both by working and by playing in this unique and special place. This close and continued contact with the real world is where it was happening.

As time went on, I would spend more time with my father hunting, fishing, and camping on the Front, all the way from the Choteau/Augusta area to the Canadian border at the Port of Piegan, which is near the gateway to Waterton and Glacier National Parks.

At this time in my life, I experienced a separation of sorts with my connection to the Rocky Mountain Front. School, one year at Adams State College in Alamosa, Colorado, almost one year at the University of Montana at Missoula and then a period in the regular army (October 1969 to July 1971), after falling prey to the draft of the Vietnam conflict, kept me occupied.

I was married in September of 1970 to Betty Hutchison, a local girl, and we eventually grew into a family of four children, all girls, two of which were twins.

During this time I was involved with all sides of family and work. Work included carpentry, farming, ranching, tombstone design, oil field work, butcher/meatcutter, delivery boy, and various other work-related activities too numerous to mention, most of which were legal.

In raising a family, and the time demands of day-to-day living, as we all have experienced, there is little time or money left for the "hobbies" of life such as fishing and hunting.

Not too long after our children were grown, educated, and gone on to lives and families of their own, I began to again involve myself in the fishing, hunting, history, and lifestyle of my youth on the Rocky Mountain Front.

This would also be a time in my life that I would start to read and record past events, especially how they related to the Salois family history.

I have always been interested in all histories. I believe history to be important and personally interesting for many reasons. By studying the past, I feel a person is able to gain a better understanding of himself or herself in the present. By doing this, one is able to gain knowledge as to what impact one may have on oneself and others in the future. I firmly believe that history does repeat itself.

A Family Member's Account

I realize that this collection of stories by many individuals is to be specific to the Rocky Mountain Front in our particular area, the "Crown of the Continent." However, I feel that it would be appropriate to present writing by a family member, Mrs. Lois Leona LaBreche Magar. I feel her writing would help to give people a better understanding of the history of our Métis (pronounced "May-TEE") people in relation to the Rocky Mountain Front.

The Métis influence and impact would cover a very large area, depending on the habits of the buffalo, a major food source. The Métis impact would be felt all the way from northern British Columbia, south to Mexico, and east to Winnipeg.[3] This area relates to Louis Riel and the Red River settlement where he was born, October 22, 1844. This area also included the western border, which was the "Backbone of the World," according to First American definition and tradition.

Lois Magar was born on December 8, 1906, in Great Falls, Montana. She grew up near U.S. Forest Service ranger stations in northwest Montana and attended high school in Kalispell and Choteau. She then graduated from Teton County High School in 1924. She would continue her education at Western Montana College and would graduate with a teaching degree in 1929.

During her teaching career, she taught school on the Blackfeet Indian Reservation, in the town of Box Elder on the Rocky Boy Indian Reservation,[4] and in Augusta, Montana, which is near the St. Peter's Mission where Louis Riel taught school. She also taught at several rural schools near the Flathead Indian Reservation.

Lois married Tom Coleman in 1926 and lived in the East Glacier area of the Rocky Mountain Front. Upon Tom's death, she married Dan Salois. She moved to Columbia Falls in 1942 and then to Kalispell in 1944. She then married Bishop M. Magar in 1950.

Lois passed away at the age of eighty-five at her home in Kalispell, Montana.

The following is a written account by Lois that she had titled *The Saga of the Métis.* This writing I have just recently discovered. I feel it is a fair and accurate account of Métis life and times on the Rocky Mountain Front. It is also an excellent record of one person's real life experience.

The Saga of the Métis

by Lois Magar

The echo of the screeching ox-drawn Red River "Charettes" has died away into oblivion, but the plight of those Métis who drove them is still an every [sic] present problem. As one reads the history of this noble people, not the Métis only but the entire red race, one is ashamed to think that we the supposedly superior, and also supposedly benevolent white race has dealt so inhumanely with them. It is a striking example of man's inhumanity to man!

I have always felt a deep sympathy for these people, but as I read "Strange Empire" and "Louis Riel" whole new truths were opened to me, their nobility, their ideals, their hopes. I learned that Louis Riel became an American citizen, a resident of Montana, living and teaching here for several years. Learning of this strange, mystical background helped me to better understand stories I had heard from the lips of men who fought with him. I could better understand their love and loyalty when I learned of his great dream, his noble character, infinite patience, deep sympathy, keen intelligence, and spiritual nature, a man who willingly gave his life for his people.

In 1932 I taught near Dupuyer, Montana. Among children attending school were those named Salois. Their paternal grandfather, Toussaint Salois had been very close to Louis Riel throughout the rebellion of 1885. Their maternal grandfather, Pierre Busha (Boushie) was also with Riel. I had the privilege of talking with those men (grandchildren interpreting) and learned much about Riel and his dream of [a] self-governing state for his people the French Scotch-Cree Métis.

Recently I have interviewed a daughter of Toussaint Salois, Beatrice Jones, a resident of Kalispell. Her father was born near Camrose, Alberta, Canada about 1847 in a settlement on "Old Man River " (a north branch of the Saskatchewan). His father, Abraham Salois, was a French trapper and his mother Suzanne Jameau(?) (Bauvis), a half Cree Métis. To them were born seven boys (two died in infancy). About 1870 Toussaint married a convent-educated French girl, fair-haired, blue-eyed Lena Brelange, who spoke no Cree until after her marriage. They had fifteen children, twelve raised to maturity. The oldest son, Solomon, married Margaret Busha (Boushie), daughter of William Busha. It was their children who came to my school.

A brother, Pierre Busha, in August 1887 appeared before the Flathead Indian Council and appealed for homes for sixty families of Métis. They sympathized with Riel's lieutenant, who told of the sufferings of these exiles, but could not grant him land. He then asked their agent to wire Washington D.C. for a grant of land. With no encouragement, he returned to Dupuyer Creek.

Beatrice, the tenth child, was born near Duhamel, Alberta, St. Thomas Parish and was but a year old when Toussaint fled with his family from Batache, Saskatchewan into Montana in 1885. Batache, Saskatchewan was the last stand for Riel and his valiant little band of Métis. There were many who came then, both Scotch and French Métis in whose veins course the blood of nobility names now in many parts of Montana: Busha, Sangray, Collins, Ritchat, Salois, LaFromboise, Dumont. Some settled near Choteau, Dupuyer, Helena, Great Falls, and in northeastern Montana. Many are now on the Rocky Boy Reservation. Though some put down anchors, most of them knowing only the hunt and trapping moved from place to place, desperate in their need after the buffalo were destroyed.

Beatrice tells how many worked for the Blackfeet for a while. Then the Blackfeet, fearing they might settle, would order them off. Yet as soon as the Blackfeet needed work done again they would call them back. Thus we find Métis names in Blackfeet settlements and intermarriage. The Cree and Métis were not lazy people and given a chance were dependable workers but they were unwelcome wherever they went because they were "breeds." Hill 57 in Great Falls is a shameful example of how our state ignored them, until gathering together in mutual misery; they reached the depths of destitution.

The Salois family, Toussaint, Gabe, and Sam wanted none of that life. Finding a country to their liking, fairly wild and productive, two of them homesteaded. Their homesteads were five miles west of Dupuyer on Dupuyer Creek. Each took up 160 acres. Perhaps it was because they were more French (only one-quarter Cree) that they were more far-sighted. Sam held script to land in Canada and returned there. Gabe later sold his 160 acres to Toussaint and returned to Canada. Toussaint's sons all homesteaded around him and later some sold their land to their father. He raised fine cattle and horses. Pictures show him a striking looking young man. He was nearing eighty when I talked with him, a proud, kindly old man. Neighbors spoke of him with genuine liking and respect, a man of honesty, nobility, a sterling character. These qualities he did his best to instill in his children. Some lived as he did, others came in too much contact with the other settlers, many of questionable character. That broke his heart. The one son I knew best, Solomon, was like his father, loved and respected by all.

I would like to relate here two stories that they told me. These stories show their belief in mysticism and their reverence for Riel.

"Once," they said, "Riel and two other leaders were being held prisoners, tied hand and foot in a locked house which was guarded. Fervently Riel prayed for deliverance. In the morning they were gone." To the mystical Métis it was the hand of God as when the prison gates opened for Paul in the New Testament.

Again Riel and about fifteen Métis were surrounded on a hill by the Canadians and many times out numbered. It was nearing night so the Canadians built fires all around the hill so near each other that by their light no one could slip through, they waited for morning when capturing the Métis would be easy. In the dark hours, one or two o'clock in the morning, when sleep was heavy upon the watchers, Riel went a little way from his men to pray. Soon he returned and told them to follow him noiselessly. Both Busha and Salois told that as they neared the fires and the guards, what appeared to be a mist descended upon them, so heavy they had to reach forth and hold each other to keep from losing contact. Soon they were safely beyond danger. "Did not God guide His children with a cloud out of Egypt?"

I asked Beatrice why if her father and his brother homesteaded why didn't the others? She smiled and said, "My father was like Riel he looked into the future the others didn't." Yet the opportunity was there for all and that is what Riel saw. He saw that they needed help and instruction. He believed with education and acquiring new skills they could hold their own. I feel that this is the key to their problem educate them to take their place in society, create in them a pride in their heritage and a desire to bring honor to it.

Acknowledgments

I would like to conclude my contribution as I reach the limit of my abilities. I would also like to thank John Vollertsen and Nicholas Vrooman for their interest in both my and my family's recollections of our Métis history and culture. These accounts are closely connected with both Canadian and U.S. history.

LARRY SALOIS lives near Cut Bank, Montana. He is a descendent of the Métis and Blackfeet people and actively advocates for cultural and ecological resource preservation along the Rocky Mountain Front.

---

1 Joseph Kinsey Howard, *Strange Empire: A Narrative of the Northwest* (St. Paul: Minnesota Historical Society Press, 1952).

2 Maggie Siggins, Riel: *A Life of Revolution* (New York: Harper Collins, 2003).

3 Herman J. Viola, *After Columbus: The Smithsonian Chronicle of the North American Indians* (London: Orion Books, 1990).

4 Hugh A. Dempsey, *Big Bear: The End of Freedom* (Lincoln: University of Nebraska Press, 1984).

Chapter 6

TAKING REFUGE ON THE EAST FRONT

Mary Strachan Scriver

On the East Front of the Rockies where the cordillera meets on the perpendicular a line of limestone peaks tall enough to have been refugia rising above the great millennial glaciers, the oldest maps indicate landmarks and valley mouths. Places to hide. Natural sanctuaries for men and wildlife. Those who had need for such places drew the maps for each other with sticks in the dirt. By the 1800s, they were sketching them onto paper and hides. In Theodore Binnema's *Common and Contested Ground* is just such a map from the Hudson's Bay Company Archives called "Old Swan's Map."[1] It is a bit disorienting until one realizes that the north/south line of the Rockies has been turned so it goes from left to right instead of up and down. More subtly, this map is more diagrammatic than analogical. The makers had no compass, so navigated by landmarks as seen from the prairie.

On modern maps, Highway 89 follows roughly along the East Front, showing access up the unpaved webs of roads up the valleys to ranches, wildlife refuges, and summer cabins. These roads must be navigated cautiously according to weather conditions from summer thundershowers that turn the gumbo to slime. Pounding hail or sudden snowfalls can hit almost any time. Distant mountain storms can swell rivers quickly.

Blackfeet Refuges

In modern times it has been literati who took refuge up the East Front valleys, notably A. B. Guthrie Jr., the Walker/Schemm family, and Joseph Kinsey Howard, the Métis journalist whose masterwork was *Strange Empire*, the story of the Red River people, "the people who own themselves."[2] Led by a mystic, Louis Riel, the Métis tried to declare themselves a country in the days when western Canada was called Rupert's Land—little more than a Hudson's Bay franchise—but were crushed by the frontier authorities in Canada, sending them into a diaspora that persists today. Many hid up the valleys along the Rocky Mountain Front.

But for thousands of years before the Métis or any Europeans, those who used the East Front as a source of salvation were the Blackfeet. Their young men chose solitary points on the eroded shale scree above the foothills, where it was possible to see to the horizon. After making themselves *dream beds* by outlining their prone bodies with a little stone wall around the place they would stay, possibly to provide a bit of wind protection, they lay down to alter their consciousness by fasting and thirsting until they had a vision that could confirm and guide them for the rest of their lives. This was dangerous enough to require a helper, often the boy's father, in case of going too far into the mysticism induced by deprivation or maybe in case of a curious predator. Successful completion meant empowering confidence in a man's ability to survive.

When the Blackfeet were forced onto reservations and the land was divvied up according to the Dawes Act, the older people chose the drainages of Whitetail Creek, Blacktail Creek, and Badger Creek where good hunting still persisted. Like grizzlies pressed back from the prairies by settlement and agriculture, they better understood how to survive in the foothills than on the flats. The winters might mean more snow, but there was plenty of wood and surely more game than on the prairies once the buffalo were gone. In most years, sarvis berries abounded.

The people remembered the valleys where the old war trails across the mountains began, traversing the divide into enemy territory. Ancient trails went up Two Medicine and Cut Bank Creeks. Walter McClintock tells the story of the warrior who stayed at the top of the Cut Bank Creek pass to block off pursuers while the rest of the party escaped.[3] He fought like a grizzly, and when he was killed, he became an actual grizzly, and when that grizzly was killed, he became a tree that reared up with reaching branches so that it looked just like a grizzly.

The people tried to keep secret the Two Medicine route, which was the Marias Pass that the Great Northern Railroad was seeking. Once the industrialists found the route, the old days were doomed. A. B. Guthrie Jr. wrote one of his late sorrowing novels about the betraying guide who showed John Frank Stevens that long-rumored access to a relatively easy crossing.

The high pass now called Logan Pass on the Going-to-the-Sun Road across Glacier National Park was a summer war trail. A Blackfeet student of mine, Galen Upham, once tried to claim it back for his own people by stealing a red Glacier National Park tour bus and driving it over the pass by moonlight. We wrote a radio play about it, fantasizing that he crashed, was knocked unconscious, and was met in time-bending fashion by a young man from long ago. Galen did not live long enough to become the writer he should have been.

It was not the Blackfeet who guided Lewis and Clark over the Rockies, but rather Shoshone, Sacagawea's people. The person who took them west over the Lolo Trail, Old Toby, was said to have lost his way, but perhaps as he came to understand what the expedition was really about—claiming the continent for the United States—he became less in sympathy with their goals. Maybe he even tried to ditch them. They were not the first whites in the country. England had been supplying the Blackfeet with guns and thimbles for a century, and French trappers, some half-Iroquois, shuttled all through the West in their canoes.

Europeans, acting on the delusion that the North American continent was empty and therefore claimable for their own ends, drew a fantasy map that at first showed France *owning* the eastern part of what we now call Canada as well as everything between the Missouri River and the Rocky Mountains; England *owning* everything west of the Great Lakes and down into what we now call the Pacific Northwest; and Spain *owning* everything as far as they could push north against the French, especially along what is now the California coast. The east slope of the Rockies was both a political and a geological marker for this schema.

The Métis

In the time after the first coming of Euros and the last of the primeval days of the tribal peoples, there arose a population through "ethnogenesis," a unique melding of interacting sources responding to the northwest fur trade. Called the Métis, they were unlike any group known before. Their origins were complex, beginning with the early French trappers on the east coast of Canada where voyageurs loyal to the Catholic Church intermarried with Iroquois women. After England captured New France (Quebec) and Anglo-Brit settlement began across the north, the fur trade moved west. But beyond the Great Lakes, the unexplored territory called Rupert's Land amounted to a giant franchise for the Hudson's Bay Company, which gradually was challenged by American companies from the northern lands of the Louisiana Purchase.

Educated English *factors*, who, in the colonial fashion, had strong ties back to England, were charged with running the trading posts and keeping their records, plus managing tough intermediaries drawn from places like the Orkney Islands, the Scots Highlands, Brittany, and other ancient Celtic lands. They took indigenous wives from whatever tribes were local *in the fashion of the country*, meaning practical arrangements rather than legally documented. Their Protestant origins were a little looser about such matters. These tribes might be Anishinabe or Chippewa or Cree or Assiniboine.

For the Frenchmen married to Iroquois who remained attached to the Catholic Church, missionaries quickly arrived. Regardless of religious rules, some men formed tender ties with their wives and children that not only preserved their intimate affections but also prevented their return to Britain, because they did not feel they could take indigenous families back to Europe or even to the East Coast. They had grown used to their newer horizons and ways.

The difference between individuals called (sometimes pejoratively) *half-breeds* and these new people was not blood quantum but, rather, cultural and familial affiliation woven together by celebrations and inheritance. This body of mixed but related people varied in degree of identification with either indigenous groups or the Euro origins. Often they could function as go-betweens and interpreters on the frontier and were greatly valued for that. They developed new ways fitted to lives divided between following the animals they harvested and homesteading with cabins and gardens.

The Métis developed the notoriously *screeching* Red River carts, modeled on European farm carts, which allowed them to move heavy loads when the fur trade transitioned from beaver and mink into the harvest of buffalo. Their methods and trails allowed them mobility that Europeans could not match until the buffalo trade moved to steamboats on the Missouri.

As their numbers and identity strengthened, the Red River people grew more and more restive. The Hudson's Bay Company was withdrawing, so that many employed trappers became free operators. Governance from Ottawa was tightened, and European settlement began to increase. Finally, the Métis rebelled under the mystical inspiration of Riel and his more earthbound cousin, Gabriel Dumont, and tried to form a government of their own. British Canada—already worried about the rebellious Irish Finians and aware of the Celtic sentiments barely under the surface in many of the trappers—decided to simply crush them. There were two surges of rebellion, separated by decades. Finally, the Métis nation was dispersed, driven over the American border, or pacified to reservations. Some found sanctuary in the east slope valleys of the Rocky Mountains where they persist today, still practicing their custom of fiddling and jigging in their joyous, defiant way.

Each mixed person or household could make a choice: Would they identify as Indian (which tribe?) or would they identify with the father and become white? Some fathers pushed their children toward assimilation by providing better housing, clothing, and an education. At one point, the Hudson's Bay Company and the American Fur Company were both run by privileged mixed-blood men. But others preferred the shelter and warmth of the mother's tribe and identified with their ways and language.

Contemporary Métis Strength

Peter Bowen has drawn vivid accounts of the Métis in a series of novels. On Halloween in Heart Butte or during Homesteader Days in Valier, the Métis are there. This enduring affinity unites the French diaspora that includes Michif, Arcadian, Creole, and Cajun groups. Many Blackfeet families have French names, though in early days when landless mixed bloods were forced onto the Blackfeet Reservation, no one was pleased. And yet Louis Riel taught at the mission school called St. Peter's, now near the town of Cascade, and the more white-identified end of the spectrum formed Lewistown.

In Choteau, one of the Métis log winter cabins has been restored, complete with a hammock above the parental bedstead so that the mother could reach up to rock the baby. Perhaps some of the strength and resilience of these people comes from being founded on binaries held in energetic tension, the original dyad having been created by white Euros coming onto the North American continent. But the shelter of the east slope valleys, which includes the eternal shelter of the small cemetery not far from Choteau, helped to save them from extinction. Al Wiseman of Choteau has continued to spearhead an annual gathering to maintain the little fenced burial ground. He is Métis and enrolled in the Little Shell Band of Chippewa, which still seeks federal recognition and land of their own.

Once the Canadian prairie stopped being either Rupert's Land (an ambiguous *country*) or a Hudson's Bay Company specific franchise, authorities had to decide what to do about mixed people. In the end, the Métis managed to make the case with Canada that they were a special group, neither Indian nor white. Once the 49th parallel was drawn and new differences in culture began to form because of immigration and politics, many U.S. Métis ended up in limbo, stigmatized and sometimes deported.

The Literati Refugia

Their recording champion of the Métis was Joseph Kinsey Howard, a journalist in Great Falls who wrote *Strange Empire*, the major accounting of the Métis struggle. Howard was at the center of a small literary colony that formed up Teton Canyon west of Choteau. It included Dr. Ferdinand Schemm, who wrote for medical journals about a revolutionary treatment he developed for edema; his wife, Mildred Walker, who wrote a series of best-selling novels, including the classic *Winter Wheat*; their daughter Ripley Schemm Hugo, a poet married to the poet and professor Richard Hugo; and A. B. Guthrie Jr., famous for writing, among many other books, *The Big Sky*. Dan Cushman, author of *The Great North Trail*, was also part of the group. Dr. Schemm, Cushman, Howard, and occasionally Guthrie enjoyed one another in Great Falls homes, but it was up the canyon that they could really relax or find the solitude to work intensively. This sophisticated group, in the mode of hard-drinking, chain-smoking, Manhattan-published authors with agents and Easterners coming for short restorative stays, were not much like local ranchers of their time. They badly needed and greatly cherished their cabins with porches and fireplaces to sit around while talking. Even that respite was not enough for Howard, who, at age forty-five, was hit with a heart attack at his Teton Canyon cabin and died at the hospital in Choteau.[4]

The next generation of writers, scattered along the Korean and Vietnam eras, grew up in the foothills or on the nearby prairie but found these to be blind canyons. Ripley Schemm Hugo and James Welch Jr. gravitated to Missoula, where the University of Montana offered a different kind of refuge. (James Welch the senior is buried on the little wild-strawberry knoll that is Dupuyer's cemetery.) Ivan Doig ended up in Seattle, where he writes about Montana. Peter Bowen came and then left again in the nomad Métis way. Dan Cushman stayed in Great Falls, where he immortalized the landless Métis who lived on Hill 57 in his novel *Stay Away, Joe*, a depiction not appreciated by those trying to be respectable. Bernard DeVoto, the respected historian, often came to visit but did not stay, nor did Wallace Stegner, who passed through Great Falls as a teenager, where he mowed Charlie Russell's lawn.

Specifically Blackfeet writers who live on their east slope reservation, mostly in sight of the Rockies, are numerous enough to deserve a chapter of their own. Percy Bullchild *(The Sun Came Down)* lived in Heart Butte. Woody Kipp, a journalist, has written about his experience in Vietnam and at Wounded Knee II. His relative, Darrell Robes Kipp, has made the move from written poetry to video scripts, mostly environmental and historical, and then, startlingly, to an opera libretto on the subject of Lewis and Clark. He is acutely aware of the Rockies as a watershed and of the status of the reservation as headwaters of the Missouri. Darrell's personal refuge is in the St. Mary's Valley, another Métis settlement once haunted by horse rustlers and bank robbers who found even more remote hideouts in the mountains along the Medicine Line (Canada/U.S. border) where they could dodge back and forth between jurisdictions.

Adolf Hungry Wolf, father of enrolled Blackfeet, has edited a four-book historical compendium of major importance that is now owned by the Browning Public Schools. Bob Scriver used his personal funds to self-publish books preserving his bronze sculptures of Blackfeet and the Scriver family's artifact collection. Many historical figures have contributed to the literature of the tribe and its historic range. James Willard Schultz, George Bird Grinnell, and Frank Bird Linderman have become legends themselves.

Less luminary and usually self-published is a host of historians and storytellers. In Choteau, Olga Monkman's husband was a county commissioner; Olga never published her many boxes of historical materials, but she grew up on a ranch not far up one of those east slope valleys and longed for that place for the rest of her life. Her nephew, Pierce Mullen, was an academic historian on the faculty at Montana State University in Bozeman. Her father, a staunch humanist, was buried by

A. B. Guthrie Sr., father of the novelist, acting as a secular pastor. Marion Trexler Brandvold was another girl who grew up on horseback but nearer to Bynum, where her son, David Trexler, would become a paleontologist and publish books about climate change. Long, long ago, the east slope was the shore of a huge but shallow inland sea, inhabited by nesting dinosaurs.

Scotty Zion's ranch adventures—and later ventures into all sorts of enterprises—began to cross over into a new medium when he was interviewed on videotape and then wrote a series of small local books. Historian Nancy Thornton, of Choteau, is the present chair of the Friends of Old Agency on the Teton, Inc., who collaborated with the Zion brothers to preserve the history of the early Four Persons Agency, the second Blackfeet agency. A visit to the location was filmed on videotape with the help of Darrell Kipp, Kipp's son Darren, and cinematographer Joe Fisher. One hardly knows how to classify David Letterman, celebrity host of a television talk show, but surely he takes refuge in this terrain.

Up a drainage near East Glacier was the George Jennings ranch, where George's brother Talbot and his wife, Betsy Jennings, came to live with him in retirement. Talbot and Betsy were screenwriters of *The Good Earth*. Betsy served as the postmaster of East Glacier for many years. In the St. Mary's Valley, which accommodated many Mêtis since it opened to Canada, was the summer art school of Winold Reiss. Artists and writers have always been potent ambassadors for wilderness. So many writers have celebrated Glacier National Park that they could also constitute an anthology. Far more than these slip quietly in and out of chosen private places. Charles M. Russell created his hideaway on the western side of Glacier National Park.

In 1990 while I was teaching at Heart Butte, it became clear to the Montana writing community that A. B. Guthrie Jr. needed to be honored with a Festschrift. In fact, when one was finally organized, he was already too ill to attend. I took four of my best writing students to the event at Choteau High School. Though Blackfeet, they were nevertheless wary of James Welch, one of the speakers. He was too well-known. They preferred to be hidden. Welch himself was warm and generous. I vividly recall Mary Clearman Blew joshing with

Ralph Beer, both from ranching backgrounds anchored by the smaller clusters of refugia.

Another writer read from his novel about small-town basketball that included the immolation of a wooden cigar store Indian at a main street crossroads. The four students fell madly in love with that storyteller. I think that's the same man who taught a writing class at the restored country one-room Bellview School up one of the east slope valleys one summer. I'm not sure his novel was ever published. So much of the east slope life is not exactly hidden but certainly elusive. Sometimes with good reason. It is a place of refuge. Sometimes writing is simply a reason for being there. And that works the other way around as well.

One summer afternoon while traveling one of those valley gravel roads, I came across Mary Sexton (of Choteau) on horseback, looking for a missing bull. We had a long leisurely talk about politics and conservation, reservations and books. It's that kind of place. Living on the east slope means that the sun comes up on the flatlands early and descends behind the mountains also early. Writers don't need daylight so much these days, but there is a psychological rhythm in the light that can be helpful. With high walls of stone nearby, one is acutely sensitive to moving shadow as well as the pools of intense sunlight that can move across the landscape. The only constant is the persisting change.

The terms *refuge* and *sanctuary* have religious meaning, formally defined and even legally defended. But it is no accident that the three peoples I have mentioned as inhabiting the east slope canyons, namely the Blackfeet, the Métis, and the writers all have close and emotional connections to the land. Their living participation is as biologically primeval as the instincts of bears and beavers. In these sheltered and watered places, humans can find meditation as constantly renewed as the meltwater still cascading down the Rockies. They are aware of the shrinking mountain glaciers yet feel safety, healing, inspiration, as well as the deep play that is the substrate of creativity and sanctity. These people have every reason to prevent exploitation, industrialization, and endless resource extraction.

MARY STRACHAN SCRIVER grew up in the rain in Portland, Oregon, and took her undergraduate B.S. at Northwestern University just north of Chicago. On the way back to Portland, she stopped in Browning, Montana. She taught English in Browning and later in Heart Butte.

The sixties were with Bob Scriver in Browning. The seventies were back in Portland as an animal control officer. The eighties after graduate theological school at the University of Chicago were a prairie ministry for the Unitarian Universalists. The nineties were in Portland again, working for the city. In 1999 she bought a house in Valier, Montana, sat down in the back bedroom, and started writing with no intention of stopping, moving, or reconsidering. Ear Mountain, Heart Butte, Chief Mountain, and the Sweetgrass Hills are all visible from this little village.

Reference materials for Blackfeet subjects can be downloaded from www.lulu.com/prairiemary. Mary blogs daily at www.prairiemary.blogspot.com.

---

1 Theodore Binnema, *Common and Contested Ground: A Human and Environmental History of the Northwestern Plains* (Norman: University of Oklahoma Press, 2001), 146-47.

2 Heather Devine, *People Who Own Themselves: Aboriginal Ethnogenesis in a Canadian Family*, 1660 1900 (Calgary, Alberta: University of Calgary Press, 2004).

3 Walter McClintock, *The Old North Trail: Or, Life, Legends and Religion of the Blackfeet Indians* (Lincoln: University of Nebraska Press, 1968).

4 "Noted Author Passes Away at Hospital," *Choteau (MT) Acantha*, August 30, 1951.

Chapter 7

ELK AND OTHER WILDLIFE

Harold Picton

The winds of the East Front have carried many stories. Many of them are of wildlife, and some are of humans. Here are a few that stretch over two centuries.

Meriwether Lewis provided the first written description of the wildlife of the East Front. His party from the Corps of Discovery crossed the Continental Divide at Lewis Pass on July 7, 1806. On July 8, the small party turned north toward the Dearborn River. They rejoiced at being once again on the wildlife- and food-rich eastern slopes of the mountains and the Great Plains of Montana. They killed a buck deer and several antelope from the large numbers that they encountered. Several bison but no elk were seen. The party passed Haystack Butte, southwest of Augusta, and descended to the Sun River, where Lewis killed a large white wolf. After camping on an island in the Sun River, they left the Front area to follow the river down to the Missouri, encountering an immense herd of bison on the way.[1]

In 1836, a party of Salish from the Colville area in eastern Washington visited the North Fork of the Sun River and witnessed an event that was to go down in tribal memory. After hunting for bison unsuccessfully for several days, they happened upon an entire herd that had stampeded over a high cliff for unknown reasons. While they killed many injured animals and salvaged as much meat as they could handle, they were appalled by the waste.[2]

In 1854, the Stevens Expedition was commissioned to explore the Northwest to find a railroad route to the West Coast. On May 8, 1854, a party from the expedition led by Mr. Doty proceeded up the Sun River until they encountered the 100-foot cliffs and waterfall at the current site of Diversion Dam. Turning north under Castle Reef, they traveled to the Teton River, encountering herds of elk along their route. Another portion of the expedition crossed to the lower Sun River, reporting numbers of deer, antelope, bighorn sheep, and an "almost inconceivable number of bison."[3] This abundance of wildlife had made the East Front and adjacent plains a popular hunting area for local tribes as well as for those from west of the Continental Divide, cementing the relationship of humans as the top predator of the area that has existed for 11,000 years.

Abundant Large Species

In the first half of the nineteenth century, Plains bison *(Bison bison bison)* were probably the dominant grazing animals of the more level and open grasslands, with relatively small groups in the rougher terrain. Some smaller herds used the higher grassy plateaus and perhaps some open grasslands back in the mountains in the Sun River drainage. Enormous migratory bison herds seasonally visited the foothills and lower portions of the Sun River and other rivers along the mountain front. Of course, the bison was honored by the buffalo nickel as the iconic American species. As mentioned by Charlie Russell, "damn little money for so much meat!"

American pronghorn antelope *(Antilocapra americana)* were abundant members of the grazing system. Mule deer *(Odocoileus hemionus)* were found in the rougher upland terrain with white-tailed deer *(Odocoileus virginianus)* using the brushy river bottoms. Rocky Mountain elk *(Cervus elaphus nelsoni)* generally were found in the rougher and more timbered areas along streams and on the mountain front. Rocky Mountain bighorn sheep *(Ovis canadensis canadensis)* were usually in the neighborhood of rocky outcrops and rougher terrain with cliffs. The climate supporting this abundance of species was that of the Little Ice Age, which did not end until the early twentieth century. Glaciation was increasing in what was to become Glacier National Park, but there is little indication of such recent glaciation in mountains stretching south. Winters were long and hard, but summer streamflows were maintained well by melting snowpacks. This area of the mountain front does not seem to have been subject to the very devastating plagues of Rocky Mountain locusts that impacted the mountain front and Great Plains from Helena south to Colorado every few years. Signs of the coming changes due to settlement began to appear with Colonel Vaughan, the first Indian agent in the area, noting in 1857 that the bison had begun to decline.[4]

Decline and Protection

The second half of the nineteenth century was a period of decline for the large species of the area's wildlife. Market and subsistence or *pot hunting* to meet the food needs of settlers took a heavy toll on the wildlife resources. Animal diseases, including anthrax, were introduced to the area by the increasing numbers of livestock. Native wildlife had little resistance to these imported diseases. Three hundred cattle brought into the area in 1862 by the American Fur Company were the first to arrive, but increasing numbers followed to populate the livestock paradise over the next twenty years. Bounties were placed on predators, leading to the deaths of four grizzly bears at Fort Shaw in 1885. Loggers and sawmills furnished lumber, firewood, and railroad ties as the new culture replaced that of the Plains Indians. Wildfires were common, burning both forest and grassland when conditions were right. The extraordinary impacts of the few tens of thousands of newcomers and their culture made wildlife a scarce commodity. Hunters were forced to go ever farther back into the mountains to find game, and even that option began to vanish. The new residents of the area became concerned with the loss of wildlife and began to organize and ask their legislators to do something about it. It was the circumstances at the end of the nineteenth century that led to making the twentieth century the *century of the elk.*

Before Montana became a state in 1889, the territorial legislature had passed some laws to protect wildlife, but these were not enforced and had many defects. The situation was somewhat similar in the first ten years of statehood, although a few counties hired game wardens. Finally, the legislature got more serious about the problems of wildlife and in 1901 established the Office of the State Game Warden, with W. F. Scott as the chief game warden, supported by several deputies. This began the long effort to educate the public on the need to protect wildlife and to gain acceptance of wildlife law enforcement as the first step in wildlife conservation. It should be noted that this state agency was formed several years before the U.S. Forest Service and other federal conservation agencies.[5] The situation for elk in the Sun River country, the state, and the continent was dire. Montana's elk herds consisted only of those in the Yellowstone Park area and a few small groups scattered over the vast forested land from the East Front to the Idaho border.

The Tale of the Elk

To begin the tale of the elk in the twentieth century, we must travel west from the mountain front about twenty miles to the Lewis Range, which forms the Continental Divide. Formed by the Lewis Overthrust, the range's tens of miles of massive cliffs that make up the Chinese Wall and similar features provided sanctuary for the last 300 to 1,500 elk remaining in the area. Perhaps it should be noted that if Sir George Simpson of the Hudson's Bay Company and David Thompson of the Northwest Fur Company had had their way in the early 1800s, this row of cliffs would have been the western boundary of the United States.[6] However, American fur trappers and settlers won the Hudson's Bay Company's *fur desert* war and the treaty of 1848 set the Canadian boundary at the 49th parallel all the way to the western sea.

The first elk census was attempted in 1910 and located 965 elk. The Sawtooth Range, which makes up the mountain front, was essentially devoid of elk. Formed by a series of up to six overthrust faults, the range provides a rugged landscape but one in which wildlife was overharvested by settlers, horse thieves of the Sun River, and other varieties of humankind. Livestock grazing along the forks of the Sun River provided competition for wildlife. Wildfires burned 72,000 acres of the Lewis Range forests in 1910. Much of this burned landscape was along the Chinese Wall in the upper Sun River drainage. In addition, a railway construction gang working in the Marias Pass area set a fire that burned the Two Medicine and Badger Creek drainages. Although unsuccessful attempts had been made to homestead on the forks of the Sun River in the mountains, the mountain portions of the drainages were made part of a national forest reserve in 1907. As the newly formed U.S. Forest Service took over management of the area, it was pressured to reduce livestock grazing on the national forest lands of the Sun River. In 1913, approximately 6,560 head of cattle and horses and 5,500 sheep were permitted to graze the Sun River backcountry. A little-discussed and obscure bill passed by the 1913 legislature created a game preserve between the North and South Forks of the Sun River and eliminated cattle grazing on 22,400 acres of marginal winter range in the new game preserve. This winter range was less than a tenth of the size of the game preserve. The Sun River Game Preserve still exists, although other, adjoining ones that were also formed have long since been eliminated. The preserve soon began intensifying competition between elk and cattle for the critical forage resources necessary to survive winter.

The first step in the creation of the Sun River irrigation project was taken in 1908 with the construction of Willow Creek Reservoir. This was followed by the construction of Diversion Dam and Gibson Dam over the next twenty years.

Elk attempting to winter on the backcountry rangeland that had been grazed heavily by livestock did not fare well in the frequent severe mountain winters along the forks of the Sun River. Winter starvation losses of elk occurred during the 1920s and early 1930s. Hunting was used in attempts to reduce the numbers of elk and the conflict with livestock. The game preserve reduced hunting access. This measure concentrated hunters along the boundary lines formed by the rivers, thus denying elk the opportunity to spread out and use all of the rangeland. Some elk attempted to solve the problem by migrating over the Continental Divide, with the first such substantial movement occurring in 1917. By 1925, an annual migration had been established across the Divide; however, the cattle and hunters formed an effective barrier to movement to the east into the Sawtooth Range.

Elk were not the only species affected by the situation. The herd of deer, estimated at 1,200, appeared to decline. A herd of bighorn sheep living in the preserve suffered a loss of 70 percent of its members in the severe winter of 1924 to 25.

Forest Service studies by T. C. Spaulding in 1915 and by C. C. Sperry in 1936 laid out the basis for action by the land and wildlife management agencies. The elk herd had grown to at least 2,000 animals. Because of the game preserve, its remote location, and weather conditions, hunters were often unable to harvest the annual increase. The U.S. Forest Service reduced the livestock grazing in the area by 87 percent between 1912 and 1930. Nevertheless, elk and bighorn sheep suffered winter starvation losses. Bruce Neal was the deputy state game warden in the area and slowly brought respect for the wildlife laws to the scene. He was a strong spokesperson for the elk and helped the U.S. Forest Service work toward more effective land management.

The big change came in 1934 when the chief forester of the United States established the Bob Marshall Primitive Area. This became the Bob Marshall Wilderness Area in the 1960s with the passage of the Wilderness Act. The prohibition against using wheeled vehicles (horse-drawn wagons) increased the costs of grazing cattle in such a remote area. Livestock grazing in the primitive area was closed out in 1934.[7]

As early as the severe winter of 1925, some elk were filtering past the hunters and moving many miles out into the prairie east of the mountains. The erratic nature of the hunting harvests could not control elk numbers, and large numbers of elk began finding their way to ranches along the mountain front. The source of the elk was not entirely clear, and some reports had them moving over the Continental Divide from the South Fork of the Flathead drainage. Now the Sawtooth Range was being colonized by the elk.

A Regulatory Structure Is Born

Bruce Neal worked with exasperated ranchers in attempts to drive the animals back into the mountains to the north. In the 1930s, it was felt that the state did not have the authority to kill elk trespassing on private lands. The situation finally came to a head in 1938 when C. H. Rathbone advertised in a Chicago newspaper to hire machine gunners to kill elk on his ranch at the foot of Sawtooth Mountain. While no machine gunners showed up, Rathbone did kill some elk and was arrested, convicted, and found guilty. The case was appealed to the Montana Supreme Court, which ruled that wildlife are a natural hazard for landowners, as is weather and other natural events, but that the state had the duty to take reasonable actions to protect landowners from undue damage and, in this case, found that efforts by the state to herd the elk into the mountains were not effective.

The wildlife management scene was changing. There had been a political controversy involving the state fish and game department in the early 1930s. A second situation developed in 1934 when the U.S. Secretary of Agriculture declared that the U.S. Forest Service would manage all wildlife on forest lands. While this never came to pass, it did indicate to the state that it should get its wildlife management act together.

In 1937, the U.S. Congress passed the Federal Aid in Wildlife Restoration Act, better known as the Pittman-Robertson Act, which imposes a tax on firearms and ammunition and then distributes the money to the states to be used only for wildlife management. It also requires the states to spend all hunting license money on wildlife management and to hire trained, competent personnel to conduct the management. This law established what has become the most effective wildlife management system existing in the world today.

In 1939, the state legislature reorganized the Fish and Game Department, and in 1940 Sam Ford, the new governor, pledged to eliminate politics from the department. Robert Cooney was hired as the first wildlife biologist for the department. The 1941 legislature made Montana the forty-seventh of the forty-eight states to accept the Pittman-Robertson Act and set the scene for a sound system of wildlife management. The Wildlife Restoration Division was established in the Montana Fish and Game Department with Bob Cooney as its head.

Immediately after he was hired in 1940, Cooney set out to get a handle on the Sun River elk situation. He had been working for the Forest Service and had knowledge of the area. He and a local rancher, Ray Gibler, undertook a survey of the Sawtooth Range, the Sun River, and adjacent portions of the Flathead River drainages for elk, grizzly bears, mountain goats, and other wildlife. They traveled over 1,800 miles on horseback and foot from July to October 1940, surveying the wildlife of these areas. More than 300 miles of this travel was in the Sawtooth Range from the southern border of Glacier Park to the Dearborn River.[8] While this survey did not solve the problem of elk on private land on the mountain front, it did provide some indications of the migration routes they were taking and started the process of refining hunting seasons.

Cooney and Gibler found that elk seemed to be heavily affecting the bighorn sheep winter range north of Gibson Lake. Even though World War II had started, they were able to have Faye Couey undertake a field bighorn sheep research project. Additional research projects were carried out as the war ended, and the details of the wildlife populations were pieced together. The reports written before 1950 often documented the snow and other winter conditions on the winter ranges, which seem to be more severe than the ones seen in recent decades.

In 1947, a major opportunity developed that was to influence the future of the entire East Front. At 11:00 a.m. on a Saturday, Mr. Brucegard, an elderly rancher, offered the Montana Fish and Game Department an option to buy his ranch, which adjoined national forest land at the foot of Sawtooth Mountain. Banks closed at 12:00, and the department did not have access to ready cash. The ranch would be sold to another buyer if a certified check for a down payment could not be delivered that day. A rancher living in the Choteau area, Carl Malone, and Tom Messelt, a Great Falls businessman, were able to come up with the $10,000 check necessary to save the land for the elk. Funds for hunters contributed through the Pittman-Robertson Act reimbursed the citizens and provided the remainder of the purchase price. Finally, elk had a place to call their own on the mountain front.

Much of the effort over the next twenty-five years was devoted to improving range conditions for the elk and reducing their impact on ranches and also on bighorn sheep. Hunting seasons and areas were adjusted to provide a sustainable future for all species using the area. The Sun River Game Range, as it was called then, was expanded as opportunities were presented. Eventually, it was renamed the Sun River Wildlife Management Area.

Like many human endeavors, this process of providing for the elk was contentious, with many citizens expressing their opinions loudly and forcibly. Citizen groups like the Sun River Conservation Committee often spearheaded the way, leading to better lives for both wildlife and humans.

Elk the Focus but Others Benefit Too

After World War II, law enforcement became better accepted. Some land uses changed, and the quality of range management improved. Responding to these and other factors, the mule deer population increased considerably followed by the white-tailed deer population. The mule deer generally winter in the foothill areas along the Front and use the mountain areas in summer. The white-tailed deer use areas along the rivers and in summer sometimes penetrate ten miles or so back into the mountains following the river-bottom habitats.

Although other species were not ignored, the primary management focus—as well as that of the hunting public—was on elk. The management practices adopted for the wide-ranging elk population provided an ecological umbrella that benefited other species as well. As time progressed, the Ear Mountain Wildlife Management Area was acquired just south of the

Teton River. Then the Blackleaf Wildlife Management Area was added even farther north along the mountain front.

The desire for elk was infectious. In 1959 and 1960, discussions were held concerning the possibility of transplanting elk from Yellowstone Park onto the Blackfeet Indian Reservation. The proposal was not carried through. This was significant because it left the elk herds in the wilderness complex stretching west from the East Front as the only native elk herds that had not received genetic input from the Yellowstone area. The introduction of Yellowstone elk nearest to the East Front occurred in 1912 in the West Glacier area. The prohibition of game animal farming in Montana has helped to protect this genetic resource. This preservation of genetic diversity could be important to the species in the uncertain future.

Another charismatic species began to discover the virtues of the mountain front. Very rarely, a grizzly bear came over the mountains in the 1950s to investigate. Then, slowly, more and more bears began to show up, and eventually they became a focus of management. The desire increased to protect habitat not only for elk but also for grizzly bears and other species as the Endangered Species Act took force and the grizzly bear was listed as a threatened species. The Nature Conservancy acquired the Pine Butte area along the Teton River, allowing bears safe use of its water-rich habitat. The Boone and Crockett Club purchased its Theodore Roosevelt Memorial Ranch north of Blackleaf Canyon, providing another site of beauty and food for elk and grizzly bears. As decades passed, it became clear that what had started as an area of contentious and strident opinions and battles was slowly becoming an area in which calmer discussions and efforts to work out compromises for the benefit of both wild and human communities could occur.

The elk population at the beginning of the twentieth century was located in the Sun River backcountry. Then it expanded to use the mountain front. As wintering areas became more secure on the eastern slopes, the elk began to spread northward. The creation of new, smaller hunting districts and more carefully regulated hunting harvests in the twentieth century permitted the elk to expand their domain and better utilize it. Hunting harvests became more evenly distributed along the Sawtooth Range.

Flourishing Megafauna and Species Conflict

Human hunters were not the only ones to find the big game of the area interesting. Although evidence of an occasional wolf in the area had been reported off and on for many decades, in 1986 it was publically recognized that wolves had established a permanent pack south of the Canadian border along the western edge of Glacier National Park. Wolves then colonized and established other packs, including one on the East Front. Although that pack's den was on the ranch of a tolerant rancher, its hunting territory included the Sun River Wildlife Management Area and even some areas north of the Sun River. As the wolves reproduced and the size of the pack increased, they began killing cattle and were invited to leave. In 1996, the ten members of the Sawtooth Pack, as it was called, were trapped and released in Yellowstone National Park as part of the wolf restoration project there.[9] Although this pack is gone from Yellowstone, others have remained. It might be noted that the relatively large multiple-pack *shock-and-awe* wolf reintroduction in Yellowstone Park had major effects on its northern elk herd. The more natural reintroduction of wolves to this northern area (Northern Continental Divide Ecosystem, which includes the East Front, and approximately 250 miles north of Yellowstone) which allowed elk more time to adapt to a new predator has seemingly not had the catastrophic effects on those herds of the East Front. Wolves continue to range through the Sawtooth Range and along the foothills.

Bighorn sheep reign on the rocky outcrops and cliffs, but they also must come down to the grassy slopes to feed. Living in small groups, they form loosely connected populations broken into ewe and lamb groups with more widely ranging small ram herds. This is where they may come into competition with elk and mule deer. The Sun River bighorn sheep herd is unquestionably one of the major and most influential ones in the world today. Until the 1960s, this competition was deadly for the sheep, and the herd was having great difficulty maintaining itself. Research projects documented the important areas of conflict among the species. Hunting seasons were adjusted to fine-tune elk and deer distribution and numbers. In the initial research project done in the 1940s, Faye Couey had found the bighorn sheep herd to be beset with disease and malnutrition and to be barely maintaining itself. Ground surveys found fewer than 350 sheep in the entire area. Even though the purchase of the Sun River Wildlife Management Area had reduced the pressure on the range produced by the elk at least a little, the sheep herd was still in critical shape in the late 1950s, with fewer than 400 being seen. The bighorns responded rapidly to new changes in management, and by the early 1980s, the population had climbed to nearly 900.[10]

This population in the Sawtooth Range is significant not just to hunters and sightseers. Genetic studies have shown that it has the most diverse gene pool of the bighorn populations that have been tested. Although one ram was translocated to this herd from a herd in the Gallatin River drainage in 1944, it is probable that the diversity is and has been native to this herd. It should be noted that there is another small but distinct herd that has historically lived in the Sun River Game Preserve a few miles to the west and has never been included in surveys. Such a situation also helps to maintain genetic diversity.

The size and robustness of the Sun River bighorn population has allowed it to be used as a source to establish new populations of this charismatic species throughout Montana and other areas of the West. More than fifty transplants have been made of sheep from the Sun River drainage to establish bighorn sheep populations in at least twenty-nine different areas in Montana. In addition, the legacy of these populations has been extended to begin new herds in Nebraska, Utah, and Washington.

The bighorn sheep population of the East Front extends north from the Sun River. Bighorns are found from the Teton River (west of Choteau) north to the Birch Creek drainage. About 150 sheep range in small bands in this area. In the 1970s, the population was given a boost by translocations of animals from the Sun River and from the Lost Creek area near Anaconda. The continuity of the species northward along the mountain front into Canada is maintained by the population in the Many Glacier area of Glacier National Park.

The historic transition area between bighorn sheep and mountain goat populations has been in the climate transition area of the Sawtooth Range west of Ear Mountain. Historically, bighorn sheep were more abundant in the drier climate south of this area, and mountain goats were more established to the north in areas that tended to be wetter.

For reasons some understood and some not bighorn sheep populations are subject to disease outbreaks. These epizootics are sometimes catastrophic, killing up to 80 percent of the herd. While some incidents in other areas have been related to contact with domestic sheep that may harbor microorganisms to which the wild sheep are not resistant, the cause of other mortalities is very uncertain. As noted by Bob Cooney in his 1940 wildlife survey, domestic sheep grazing has a long history in the Sawtooth Range north of Birch Creek. There is research that suggests that some survivors of a major die-off may be disease carriers that do not show symptoms but that can transmit the disease to other bighorns, thereby continuing the excessive mortality and making it difficult for populations to recover.

The other large mammal mentioned by Captain Lewis in his July 8 journal entry was the American pronghorn antelope. Originally more abundant on the Great Plains than the bison, it fell on hard times in the 1800s, declining to near endangered species status and becoming extinct along the plains and foothills of the East Front. Archaeological evidence from the time before recorded history suggests that native humans of the Sun River area may have made heavy use of antelope during some past eras.[11]

In 1946, the Montana Fish and Game Department developed new and highly effective techniques for trapping, transplanting, and beginning new antelope populations. This program was carried on until 1966 in Montana, but no transplants were made along the East Front. Antelope trapping was continued in Montana until 1972 to furnish animals for starting herds in other states. Once a small population was begun, it was left to colonize surrounding areas through natural processes. The introductions nearest to the East Front were made in 1947 and 1951 about sixty miles away. In 1960, a few pronghorns were present west of Highway 89 in the southern portion of the Front. Some had been noted on the eastern side of the highway for several previous years. Over the years since, this native species has spread northward and developed into a robust population.

A Persistent Struggle

The 1940 Cooney survey found ptarmigan in the highest country of the Teton River drainage. This small population has survived into recent times, but the future has become more uncertain for small populations as well as large. Warming and drying revived the more intense fire cycle as of 1988. Winds bearing smoke have become much more frequent along the Front. Longer and longer annual drought periods reduce the duration and size of green foraging patches for animals. Green vegetation is several times more nutritious than dry standing vegetation and is essential for the survival of plant-eating animals. The young of the year pay the price for shortfalls in food quality and abundance. Without the young, populations may not find migrations to be profitable, thus changing animal numbers and their use of the landscape.

Data collected in the past describing migrations of wildlife may not be adequate for future management. Irrigated lands become more attractive for wildlife in the summer drought, increasing conflict with farmers and ranchers. The living systems of the wilderness and the Front will adapt to climate change. Human society must be alert to these changes to allow them to proceed if the great current legacy of the East Front is to be maintained.

The *century of the elk* brought many changes to the ecology of the Sawtooth Range and the East Front. Funds provided by the hunters of Montana under the Pittman-Robertson Act and the active participation and support of the general public have made it possible to restore all of the native species to the area, except for the bison. The charisma and popularity of elk supported the drive to provide an ecological umbrella that has provided homes for many other species as well. For example, the conversion of Freezeout Lake from a closed saline dump basin for used irrigation water into a robust waterfowl habitat added greatly to the bird resources of the Front.

Humans interested in the area have shown an impressive amount of cooperation among agencies, private corporations, nonprofit organizations, Native Americans, ranchers and other landowners, and just plain people to build an ecological system worthy of the planet Earth.

HAROLD PICTON is an emeritus professor of wildlife at Montana State University. He received two degrees in wildlife management from Montana State University and a Ph.D. in comparative physiology from Northwestern University. He worked as a wildlife biologist, including several years in the Sun River and along the East Front. Family recreation included frequent use of the Front after joining the faculty at Montana State. He has written three books and a number of articles and has helped document Montana's wildlife history for television.

---

[1] Gary Moulton, ed., *The Definitive Journals of Lewis and Clark: Over the Rockies to St. Louis*, vol. 8 (Lincoln: University of Nebraska Press, 1993).

[2] Frank McCloed and Bon I. Whealdon, "Exterminating a Montana Buffalo Herd in 1836," in *"I Will Be Meat for My Salish" : The Buffalo and the Montana Writers Project Interviews on the Flathead Indian Reservation*, ed. Robert Bigart (Pablo, MT: Salish Kootenai College Press; Helena: Montana Historical Society Press, 2001), 39-41.

[3] Isaac Stevens, *Reports of Exploration and Surveys to Ascertain the Most Practical and Economic Route for a Railroad from the Missouri River to the Pacific Ocean: Survey near the 47th and 49th Parallels*, vol. 12 (Washington, D.C.: U.S. War Department, 1855), 1:120-239.

[4] Jack C. Vaughan, *Colonel Alfred Jefferson Vaughan, The Frontier Ambassador* ([Dallas?], 1957).

[5] Harold D. Picton and Terry N. Lonner, *Montana's Wildlife Legacy: Decimation to Restoration* (Bozeman, MT: Media Works Publishing, 2008).

[6] Jack Nisbet, *The Mapmaker's Eye: David Thompson on the Columbia Plateau* (Pullman: Washington State University Press, 2005).

[7] Harold Picton and Irene E. Picton, *Saga of the Sun: A History of the Sun River Elk Herd* (Helena: Game Management Division, Montana Department of Fish and Game, 1975).

[8] Robert Cooney, wildlife survey field notebooks 1940, Montana Department of Fish, Wildlife and Parks, Kalispell.

[9] US Fish and Wildlife Service, Gray Wolf Monitoring in Montana, in *The Yellowstone Wolf: A Guide and Source Book*, ed. Paul Schullery (Wordan, WY: High Plains Publishing, 1996), 102-7.

[10] Tom Carlsen and Glenn Erickson, *Montana Bighorn Sheep Conservation Strategy* (Helena: Montana Department of Fish, Wildlife, and Parks, January 2010), 223-41.

[11] Douglas H. MacDonald, *Montana before History: 11,000 Years of Hunter-Gatherers in the Rockies and Plains* (Missoula, MT: Mountain Press, 2012).

Chapter 8

GRIZZLY BEAR RESEARCH

Keith Aune

In my childhood years, I was always within sight of that long gray string of limestone mountains known as the Rocky Mountain Front. I formed many great childhood memories while hunting, fishing, trail riding, and hiking in the shadow of these spectacular mountains. In fact, because of those rewarding experiences, it became my childhood dream to investigate the wildlife in this spectacular landscape. Little did I know what was soon to be in my future.

While seeking my dreams of studying wildlife, I became enamored with the early work of the famous Craighead brothers who pioneered research methods on grizzly bears. It was not surprising then that I pursued my advanced education at the University of Montana, bringing me close to several of the key researchers on grizzly bears.

While at the University of Montana, I was able to secure my first job working with bears as a work-study student for the Border Grizzly Project led by Dr. Charles Jonkel. While chasing my maturing dreams, I eventually became a field technician on the Rocky Mountain Front grizzly studies, and then, after a two-year interruption to earn a graduate degree at Montana State University, I returned to the Front to conduct grizzly bear research from 1980 to 1989. This was one of the most rewarding experiences of my life, made even more meaningful because it was in that landscape that meant so much to me as a child.

Early and Recent Research

As is the case with most wildlife research, I was by no means the first person to examine the life history and ecology of grizzly bears on the mountain front. There are many early references to the sightings of grizzly bears in old U.S. Forest Service reports dating back to 1936 when that federal agency began a series of game studies in the Sun River. The first Federal Aid in Wildlife Restoration (Pittman-Robertson) program in Montana began in 1941 and provided federal funds for wildlife management and research. One of the benchmark studies commissioned under that act was a grizzly bear survey that also began in 1941. In that study, Robert Cooney conducted grizzly bear surveys throughout the Bob Marshall ecosystem, including the Sun River and Teton portions of the Lewis and Clark National Forest. Cooney used miles of trail traveled per grizzly observation as an index of grizzly density. In the Sun River, he found evidence of one grizzly per 13.5 miles of trail traveled. He found more grizzlies inside the Sun River Game Preserve, where game was protected, than outside the preserve. In the Teton area, he found sign of one grizzly per 35.7 miles of trail. He felt that the Teton was understocked for grizzly bears, and as a result, the spring season on grizzlies was closed.

Several surveys followed over the next three decades. Merle Rognrud and his survey team conducted surveys in 1955 using the same basic survey technique as Cooney. They reported seeing sign of a grizzly bear every 11.2 miles of trail surveyed. This represented a 26 percent increase in grizzlies in the Sun and Teton River drainages since 1941. Mike Frisina and Ken Hamlin reported on a grizzly bear survey in

1974. They found grizzly bears widely distributed along the Front, and they reported fairly frequent spring migrations of bears into area ranches we now know are very important to grizzly bears based on radio telemetry. This survey provides one of the earliest comments regarding bears moving beyond the forest boundary onto private ranching lands below Split Mountain and Walling Reef. At about that same time, Allen Schallenberger produced a reconnaissance survey of grizzly habitat on the Lewis and Clark National Forest. He reported that grizzly bears occurred throughout the forest, including habitat outside the forest near Elk and Smith Creeks.

All of these great field surveys established one very important point that remains relevant today: the Rocky Mountain Front has long been an important home for grizzly bears, which depend on a mix of private and public lands for their survival. What these early surveys could not learn are the details of how bears used these lands, how best to live alongside this great bear, and how to manage important bear habitat to ensure their long-term survival. That remained yet to be discovered.

By the middle 1970s, the future of the grizzly looked somewhat tenuous to many researchers, conservationists, and federal land managers. As a result, the grizzly bear was listed as threatened under the Endangered Species Act in 1975, and it was not long before serious field research efforts were launched on the Front by the Border Grizzly Project (BGP) at the University of Montana. Dr. Charles Jonkel, supported by biologist Allen Schallenberger, led this initiative from 1977 to 1979. I had previously served as a work-study student for "Chuck" Jonkel and the BGP while attending the University of Montana. Then I jumped at the opportunity to work as field technician in 1978 helping Allen Schallenberger out of Choteau. After an amazing summer work experience on this bear project, I entered graduate school at Montana State University in the winter of 1978 to 1979 to extend my research credentials. By fate or providence, I returned to Choteau in May 1980 to lead the Rocky Mountain Front grizzly study after graduating from Montana State University. I felt I was back home and pursuing that childhood dream. Over the next ten years, I was blessed with a unique lifetime opportunity to work alongside many great biologists and with the unique people along the Front while conducting important wildlife research on black and grizzly bears. For me, it was a remarkable life experience that I will never forget nor regret despite the often difficult wildlife and social issues we faced. People living with federally threatened grizzly bears is not a simple proposition!

On May 4, 1977, the very first research bear (no. 257) was captured on the Rocky Mountain Front near the Blackleaf Wildlife Management Area. An added bonus to research was that bear 257 was an adult female of reproductive age and, ever since that capture, a new era of grizzly bear research had begun. The grizzly bear research along the Front continued from 1977 to 1988 and resulted in the capture of fifty-three individual grizzly bears for research and thirteen management bears involved in human conflicts. However, only fifty-one individual bears were fitted with radio tracking devices and followed for some portion of their lives on the Front. Capturing these bears was no easy feat. We typically expended 184 nights of trapping effort to capture one bear. During the study, we experienced eighty-two capture episodes. Even now, very few people really understand the monumental task—physical and mental—we undertook each year during this study and the tremendous human energy applied to capture and track a grizzly bear.

Although it took great effort to capture these grizzly bears, it required even greater commitment of human time and energy to track them as they wandered the wildest regions of the Rocky Mountain Front. Many of the areas they inhabited were roadless and logistically very challenging to navigate. We followed these individual bears over imposing mountains and through soggy swamps, by airplane and on foot, during daytime and the dark of night, and while enduring eternal East Front winds blowing in all types of weather. In some of the most unusual conditions, we even tracked bears for twenty-four- to forty-eight-hour periods to determine their life activity patterns. A precise location was determined more than 2,700 times, but we observed the animals just 22.5 percent of the time when out in the field. Through these monumental efforts, we made many important discoveries while advancing the conservation of bears and shaping lasting friendships.

Discoveries and Experiences

One of the earliest and most surprising discoveries was that grizzly bears were living year-round on the plains and foothills east of the Lewis and Clark National Forest. The first two adult female grizzly bears captured in 1977 included bears 273 and 257, who lived mostly outside the national forest. Both of these adult female grizzlies were monitored for nearly a decade and spent much of their time in low-elevation habitats along the Front. This discovery flew directly in the face of the prevailing conservation view that grizzly bears were wilderness monarchs. Since the 1960s, the science community and conservationists had educated people to believe that grizzly bears required lands absent of humankind and that their future depended on those wildland anchors. Now we began to form a new frame of thinking and realized that grizzly bears do live and even thrive outside of wilderness lands. This discovery caused some confusion among the scientists, land managers, and members of the general public living along the Front and was not immediately accepted by all people. It raised questions and even heated public debate about where bears should be allowed to exist and whether these beasts should be permitted to occupy human-dominated landscapes. That debate rages yet today. It became evident to me that science often raises more questions than the answers we anticipate.

Early tracking of East Front grizzly bears clearly indicated the importance of two unique areas: the Pine Butte Swamp/Teton River and Antelope Butte regions of the Rocky Mountain Front. We now know these areas are not just seasonally important to grizzly bears but used year-round. This finding drew much attention to management of these special areas and opened up public discussions about how to conserve them. These conversations quickly focused on safety issues for those who lived and recreated on these lands and on land-use priorities. There emerged a serious concern among some members of the public that they were now being forced to live alongside grizzly bears on private and adjacent state and federal lands. In addition, many prominent people sought to introduce extractive industries onto these lands to boost a sagging economy. The importance of these areas to a threatened species, the grizzly bear, introduced a new and often uncomfortable variable into the land management framework for these lands.

Eventually, our studies showed that grizzly bears actually survived by using two major strategies on the Rocky Mountain Front. Although there was a segment of grizzly bears living year-round on the lowland habitats, there was another group of bears that were backcountry bears. These bears typically made short seasonal excursions to the Front during the spring then returned to mountain habitats for the summer and fall. Each of these two bear groups was applying some unique adaptations to their strategy for living on the Rocky Mountain Front. Our research identified differences in seasonal food habits and daily activity cycles. The lowland bears were using dense riparian habitats to feed on forbs, grass, and summer berries while locating many deer and elk carcasses or feeding at ranch boneyards (a place where ranchers dispose of dead livestock) and a few refuse dumps. Backcountry bears typically used these lowlands in spring, seeking carrion, grass, and forbs but returned to mountain habitats for a diet of roots, mountain berries, and pine nuts. Lowland bears were living a nocturnal existence, with which they could avoid human conflict, while backcountry bears tended to be diurnal in their activity patterns. These variable strategies illustrated the great adaptability of bears if humans can learn to coexist with them.

The wilderness bears we tracked taught us a great deal about the many wonderful and remote corners of our Rocky Mountain Front. While tracking them, we visited some impressively unique and intensely lonely places that few people will ever see. However, the real take-home lesson for all humankind was the discovery that wilderness alone, although important, will not save the grizzly bear. We had to find some way to enable even wilderness bears to use non-wilderness lands and, yes, even some private lands to sustain healthy populations of grizzly bears. Although these mountaintop bears needed and used magnificent alpine areas like the top of Rocky Mountain and Scapegoat Mountain for root digging, they also needed access to critical low-elevation spring habitats where winter-killed ungulates and early emerging grasses could sustain them until the high country became habitable for this enormous omnivore.

We radio tracked grizzly bears in all areas along the Front but found them to be more abundant in specific areas of the Front. In general, we found that bears were more abundant in the geography north of the Sun River than in areas south of the Sun River. We searched longer, worked harder, and dug deeper into the mountains to capture and monitor grizzly bears south of the Sun River. As had been previously reported, we confirmed some very important habitats along Elk, Smith, and Blubber Creeks. Over the years of research in this southern region of the Front, we found just a few females while capturing a good number of very large males. In fact, the largest male we ever captured during this study was bear 355, who lived in great wilderness haunts of the Sun River country and probably weighed in at over 700 pounds by the fall. One challenge grizzly bears face in this area of the Front is that the boundary between forest and private lands reaches much farther into mountain habitats, making the contest between the needs of man and the needs of bear a greater factor in their continued existence here. This particular area experiences more cattle grazing well into mountain country, while quality spring habitat becomes less abundant and patchier south of the Sun River. Nonetheless, there are many great areas where grizzly bears thrive in this region of the Front, and if we can tolerate these bears, the landscape can sustain wild bears.

Capturing and tracking wild grizzly bears for research taught us that, like people, bears have variable dispositions. This is probably why it is so hard to generalize about bear behavior as people often want scientists to do. Over the years, I have experienced aggressive bears, docile bears, very smart bears, and some that are just not that bright. The most aggressive bear I have faced was bear number 412 from Smith Creek, who showed intense ferocity during the very first capture episode. He would lunge repeatedly at the quarter-inch stainless cable we anchored to a very large tree and was very vocal. We witnessed that incredibly buff bear lift and toss through the air the very large logs that we had used to craft our cubby (a tipi of woody material used to guide a bear into a snare set). He was the one bear I would not want to meet in the outdoors in the dark. Eventually, he was removed through management actions because he repeatedly killed livestock in the Elk Creek area. Ironically, one of the most docile male bears I met was grizzly 355, who was also one of the largest we ever captured. We captured that bear multiple times, and each time he would simply ignore us as if we were not present and wait patiently for the capture event to end. However, based on his size, I suspect that in the right conditions he could become a formidable foe. So, despite his amiable character, we were always careful around him. The smartest bear I met was bear 346, who at the very first capture in Cunniff Basin had outsmarted us many times by carefully exposing our snare cable so that he could avoid placing his foot in that snare. Finally, I captured bear 316, the female he was traveling with. She was in estrus, so I collected some urine spilled on the soil around the capture site. I fashioned a ball of this urine-soaked soil and placed it in what is called a dip set. The next day we had bear 346 in that snare. I concluded that 346 was naturally wary and careful because he had never been captured prior to this event. After our acquaintance, he was even more educated about man's devious ways.

In some cases, these highly individual bears become either incredibly adept at busting our snare sets to get a free meal (the bait) or will become so elusive that they will not venture into a capture site again. For example, the elusive bear 218 was captured on Ear Mountain in 1978 and then quietly lived in this area without being detected by our trapping efforts until 1991, when he was destroyed after he killed livestock. To my mind, bear 218 exemplifies the ability of these great bears to remain undetected and quietly live alongside people for most of their lives.

While trying to catch and study bears, we were always inventing new ways to outsmart these bears while they, in turn, were exploring their own ways to outwit the research team and live alongside humankind. It was a remarkable game of wits and taught us to respect the individuality and intelligence of this remarkable mammal. The variable and dynamic grizzly bear behaviors we experienced and recorded during our study were an everyday part of our wild adventure on the Rocky Mountain Front.

People often ask and frequently expect that bear research involves constantly facing danger. While traveling through bear haunts in the Rocky Mountain Front, we had surprisingly few high-risk episodes with our research bears. However, there were a few notable exceptions, and it is important to share that during our research, we learned a lot about respecting the potential ferocity of this great bear. In the time I spent afield with grizzly bears in the light of day or darkness of night, no event caused me more fear than the time in 1978 when Allen Schallenberger and I were charged by a large male grizzly (271) on the top of Rocky Mountain. In that circumstance, we were traveling on foot up a very steep but barren alpine slope. We were nearing the top of a pass where we knew grizzlies, sometimes in fairly large concentrations, frequently dug roots. To our surprise, just as we approached the last steep slope toward our destination, we saw the large humped male bear 271 come up over the pass headed our direction. Just as we stopped in surprise, the bear rose up on his hind feet, whiffed the air, then woofed as he charged down the slope toward us. We were completely exposed on an open slope with no cover around us for miles. It looked as if we would be in a serious battle as Allen recommended we raised our weapons for defense. The bear was coming at us like a freight train and only a mere 100 yards away. After what seemed an enormous time, we quickly determined that we might be able to step back a bit and use the contour of the slope to disappear from the sight of this huffing and puffing bear headed our way. As we did so, and waited anxiously for what was probably only a few seconds, it was not long before 271's enormous frame appeared in our view, only about 10 yards way. To our surprise, he abruptly stopped with shale flying as he applied the brakes. As if he could not see us, he quickly huffed and broke to our left and disappeared over the slight hill in front of us. Phew, that was a close call, and he clearly let us know we had violated his space. We did continue up the slope and complete our visit to these enormous digs, but we did so quietly while thinking about what had just happened. It is always a bit concerning to be about the business of conserving a species but realizing that your efforts are not known or understood by that species. We were taught a great lesson by bear 271; despite our good intentions, saving grizzlies can be very dangerous work.

One more interesting facet of our research for me was the study of both black and grizzly bears on a shared landscape. During our study, we captured 139 black bears as it was impossible to build traps that selected only for the capture of the grizzly bear. At a critical point in our study, I felt it was very important for us to understand the relationship between these two closely related species. So, we collared and tracked 7 black bears in the area between Teton and Birch Creeks where we had already placed collars on an equal number of grizzly bears. Like grizzly bears, we found that black bears occupy all regions of the Rocky Mountain Front and that they are more abundant than grizzlies. To illustrate this fact, we captured one black bear for every 34 trapping nights compared to one grizzly bear for every 184 nights.

When we followed these two bear species in the same region, we discovered that black bears are the primary bear of the conifer forest while the grizzly owns open country (like alpine and open prairie habitats). Although black bears will also travel down into the riparian habitats like Antelope and Pine Buttes, they were more frequently using the forested habitats closer to the edge of the Lewis and Clark National Forest. Scientists theorize that black bears are strongly adapted to a forest habitat existence and can readily climb trees to avoid the larger grizzly bear or other threats. These forest bears are experts at finding interesting forest foods like ants and termites in rotting logs, forest shrubfields for berries or grass, and forbs in meadows within the dense forests. Grizzly bears, on the other hand, possess the larger digging claws and do not depend on tree climbing for protection. They use their larger size and ferocity for protection and are much better predators. Black bears on the Front denned in a wider range of elevations but almost exclusively within forested habitats. Grizzly bears, on the other hand, usually den at very high elevations and on north-facing, steep slopes that approach the alpine habitats at the upper end of the mountain forests. We also found that black bears tolerated human disturbance and roads more readily than grizzly bears. This tolerance of humans has provided a unique opportunity for black bears to exist closer to the margins of human development. Our studies confirmed that these two species, although closely related, were uniquely adapted to best exploit specific habitats within this shared geography.

One incredible long-term finding of bear research was the clear evidence of the gradual expansion of grizzly bear range over the past twenty years. I am convinced after an examination of historical data and through our own telemetry studies that grizzly bears have been moving eastward to the limits of our human tolerance over the past sixty years. Early surveys from the 1940s rarely mentioned grizzly bears beyond the limits of wilderness landscapes. By the mid-1970s, bear studies clearly show that some bears are living at least part of the year outside the Lewis and Clark National Forest. Since the first discovery of lowland bears 273 and 257 in 1977, it has become more evident that grizzly bears, if not killed by humans, can occupy habitat far from mountain habitats. They have stretched the human capacity for tolerance on the Rocky Mountain Front. What we viewed as an unusual phenomenon in the middle 1970s has now become routine and even more common. Clearly, grizzly bears are living far out onto the prairie along the Front and continue to illustrate the great adaptive nature of this creature.

Learning about Humans and Bears

During our grizzly bear research, we provided critical information about bears and their habitat needs to inform many land-use decisions. We were able to supply important data that could be applied to managing human coexistence with bears, livestock in bear country, natural resource extraction (like oil and gas), and bear populations. Although at the beginning of these studies we did not intend to transgress into the human dimensions of bear management, it was inevitable that we became involved in many management experiments to help find ways for man and grizzly to coexist.

For example, as we followed our research bears around their Front homelands, we discovered that our research bears and humans came into a variety of conflict. Using our understanding of bear biology and our new technical capacity, we were able to investigate the biological dimensions of human-bear conflicts. Because we gained intimate knowledge of each bear—and frequently located these animals—we were able to try new and experimental approaches for managing conflict. Keep in mind that at this time we developed and were applying some improved tools to capture and immobilize bears and that these had only recently become available. The first efforts to immobilize a bear only date back to the work of the Craigheads in the 1960s. Even with greater understanding of how to use these tools, better drug concoctions and improved skills really did not evolve until the late 1970s when bear research first began on the Rocky Mountain Front. In addition, new technologies in wildlife telemetry were rapidly evolving at that time and it was not until the late 1970s that a reliable radio tracking collar could be placed on the neck of a wild bear. All of these emerging tools and skills were very new during the late 1970s and were not fully perfected until the 1980s.

With the advent of many new research tools, the idea of monitoring problem bears took root in the late 1970s and early 1980s. Wildlife managers began to apply these tools in conflict situations by removing these bears alive and transporting them to a new home. With advances in telemetry also came the chance to determine if these methods would really work to resolve bear conflicts. During our study on the Rocky Mountain Front, we began tracking problem bears and widely using relocation as a management tool. Because of these efforts, we learned many things that have helped us adapt new strategies for managing human-bear conflict. Using our field study approach, we reviewed the records of 103 translocations of nuisance bears from across the Northern Continental Divide Ecosystem and found about 44 percent of these were deemed successful. Many factors determined success, including type of offense, number of offenses, and the sex and age of the bears. The success of relocating a repeat offender was only 15 percent, showing us that problem behaviors become habitual.

Females were much more likely to be successful than males. Armed with these data, we now have a much better sense of how to practice translocation as a management tool.

Extraordinary stories about our translocation effort on the Rocky Mountain Front include the adventures of adult female bear 500 and the successful translocation of subadult male bear 381. The history of bear 500 is remarkable in that she was moved twice in one month and returned rapidly each time despite best efforts to find her a new and safer home. The story begins when bear 500 and her yearling cubs started raiding apiaries in a small creek bottom west of Choteau. They were captured and relocated on June 11, 1985. She and two of her yearling cubs were moved to Bunker Creek in the South Fork of the Flathead, where they were released at the edge of the Bob Marshall Wilderness. By June 26, she was already back home on the Teton River. She and both yearlings made that trip across the full length of the Bob Marshall in less than two weeks. She returned to raiding bee hives. So again, she and her yearlings were captured using a helicopter and dart gun. On June 29, they were moved to the east side of the Mission Mountains. By July 15, she and her yearlings had again returned to the Teton River. Despite heroic management efforts, this female bear and her yearlings twice traveled across the Bob Marshall to return home in less than two weeks.

In the meantime, bear managers began using some very good electric fencing technology to successfully deter bear depredations on beehives. Bear 500 survived on the Rocky Mountain Front for several more years and avoided more serious trouble, thanks to these prevention efforts. Using modern telemetry and modern capture tools, science has learned about the great homing skills of grizzly bears. We have also learned that the entire Bob Marshall complex is not large enough to prevent grizzly bears from returning to the site of conflict. Clearly, the prevention of human-bear conflict is the most effective way to save bears and help humans live among bears.

Our work with subadult male bear 381 presents a less remarkable but contrasting story worth telling. Bear 381 was one of two yearling cubs from a very well-known adult female bear, number 335, who frequented Dupuyer Creek. Bear 381 was a young inexperienced bear and found himself in trouble by association with his mother. Bear managers determined that he should be separated from her and given a second chance. So he was translocated to Bunker Creek in the South Fork of the Flathead. In the fall of 1987, just as we were concluding the bear studies on the Front, I initiated a new bear research study in the South Fork of the Flathead, where our team engaged in intensive trapping in the spring of 1988. Surprisingly, this young bear 381 was captured in that study, and our telemetry information showed that he had carved a new home range in his adopted homeland. From my perspective, it was quite satisfying to find this bear in our South Fork Flathead study because it illustrated a rare example of how translocations are sometimes successful and result in the assured survival for some problem bears.

The stories and events surrounding management of problem bears on the Rocky Mountain Front did cause some confusion among the public about the incidence of research bears in human conflicts. When we started research on the Rocky Mountain Front, there were no bear management specialists in Montana, and often research biologists were called to help management biologists capture and handle problem bears. Because we became the public face of bear management in those early years, many people confused our research with the occurrence of problem bears that we monitored for managers. In an effort to explore the role of research bears in conflict, several research biologists in Montana shared their data from across the Northern Continental Divide Ecosystem, including the Rocky Mountain Front. With these shared data, we found that from 1975 to 1985, most (84 percent) of our research bears did not conflict with humans and generally lived long, productive lives. However, once bears came into conflict with humans, they were prone to repeated offenses and did not survive long after their first infraction.

Bears That Kill Livestock

Grizzly bears and livestock have existed together on the Rocky Mountain Front for over 100 years. In an early wildlife report, H. B. Ayers from the U.S. Forest Service reports on the abundant wildlife, including bears, on the Lewis and

Clark Forest Reserve when it was established in 1897. He also describes the large number of cattle and sheep grazing on the forest. Cattle were brought into the North Fork of the Sun River by 1890, and sheep were grazed there for many years in the early 1900s. The first official government record I can locate referencing conflict between bears and livestock on the Rocky Mountain Front dates back to 1936–1937, in a report by L. J. Howard of the U. S. Forest Service in which he notes that in the Sun River "the bear season should be closed to stockmen and sheepmen: stock killing bear or no stock killing bear. If they want to put their livestock in the mountains, they have to take their chances with the bear." This rather progressive comment for that time in history suggests that the dialogue about conserving bears on public grazing allotments is not a very new one.

While we were studying grizzly bears on the Rocky Mountain Front, conflicts between bears and livestock ranchers were fairly common. I found that it was very difficult for livestock producers to adjust to the situation that emerged in the 1970s when multiple bears existed on their ranches at one time and grizzlies became protected under the Endangered Species Act. For the many decades prior to our study I believe that only a few bears existed on these ranchlands along the Front, and removing a particular bear that killed livestock could be quickly accomplished. However, as grizzly bear populations increased, it became very common to find not just one but several grizzlies on a ranch property. In addition, previous management practices resolved livestock conflicts quickly and immediately without question. It was easier to kill an offending bear since it was not protected by federal law. The new legal status of bears required a much more limited and careful response by government agencies. During our research efforts, we also became aware that more than one bear was often within range of a depredation site, and the task of determining which grizzly bear killed livestock became much more difficult. These changing conditions led to increased distrust of government and an increased frequency and complexity of conflict between ranchers and grizzly bears.

A recent example of how the changing conditions affected the relationship of people and bears on the Rocky Mountain Front is illustrated in a series of stories about cattle-killing bears west of Augusta from 1987 to 2001. As we were winding down our field research, grizzly bears killed numerous cattle on several ranches and, from my perspective, emotionally charged philosophical debates raged. Confusion reigned among wildlife managers and the public about the appropriate response to livestock depredations on the Front. Prior to that time, our research had identified a suite of bears west of Augusta, including female 316, young male 326, and three large older males 355, 412, and 346. These bears periodically visited private ranchlands from the Dearborn River to Smith Creek. We also knew there were additional unmarked bears in the region. As livestock kills occurred, intense social pressures mounted, demanding a rapid response to livestock losses. Due to this social intensity during a time of change, several bear legends and myths were born. Three bears were eventually destroyed, cattle killings continued, and helpful long-term solutions could not be fully considered.

The story begins with the legendary antics of a young female bear, number 316. The first in a series of depredation events in 1987 seemed to involve young female bear 316 because she was radio tracked near several depredation sites. Heroic efforts were made to save her from the final solution, but once she was publicly labeled a cattle killer, the die was cast. It became clear that every dead cow for miles around would now be attributed to bear 316 no matter where she was located by our research team. She was eventually killed using an experimental grizzly bear damage hunt program that was highly controversial. In this case, even the hunter's story, published as a book, crafted a legendary story about a notorious cattle killer who he claims had taught an older male bear to kill cattle despite the fact that she was the younger of the two, and female. The reality was bear 316 was one of only two adult females found in the entire geography south of the Sun River and represented a significant blow to the local population. Despite the removal of bear 316, livestock killing in the region continued, and in July 1988 a second research bear, number 412, was killed at another depredation site. Bear 412 was a large male about nine years old and—as mentioned earlier in this chapter—was the most aggressive bear I met. We had suspected that he might be a livestock killer but lacked solid evidence to make that conclusion during our study.

Finally, as time advanced, cattle killing in this region still continued and another legend of a livestock killer emerged: the story of the so-called Falls Creek Bear. This bear, number 346, was the six-year-old bear that I had captured in May 1985 in Cunniff Basin and was naturally wary and very much a wilderness bear. Based on our tracking evidence, his adventures into the foothills were typically seasonal and associated with breeding season. Interestingly, during that year we did not find 346 in Falls Creek often, and he spent very limited time outside the Lewis and Clark National Forest. His radio collar slipped off his neck (which is not uncommon in large males) in October 1985, and he was actually never radio collared again. Despite our knowledge about his movements, he somehow acquired a legendary status as a livestock killer and was given a geographic namesake that was not supported by our radio tracking evidence. I presume it is part of human nature to do so, but again, people in the region began to attribute every dead cow to the notorious behavior of bear 346—and without a shred of real evidence that he was involved in these infractions. Some people argued that the track measurements were indicative, but I can show data that many adult male bears have feet with similar track measurements. Science has long ago shown us that track measurements are not a very reliable indicator of individual bears, unless there is some clear anomaly (like missing toes) in the print. Even more ironic, I had long worked in this region and we had captured other large male bears in this geography and knew of unmarked bears that could easily have been involved in some or all of these depredations as well. Eventually, government agents in a helicopter darted grizzly 346 at a cattle depredation site where most certainly he was involved in cattle killing. Bear 346 was transported to the Montana Fish, Wildlife, and Parks research laboratory in Bozeman, Montana. By then, I had moved on to a new position at the laboratory and, by coincidence, I had to administer the euthanasia drug that killed the so-called legend of Falls Creek.

While at my office in the laboratory, I kept a cast of the skull from bear 346, and I believe that the rest of this story has never been told. Bear 346 may well have lived peaceably in this region of the Front for many years, and he was, by my standards, a quite respectable bear with no clear record of killing livestock. When he arrived at my laboratory, he was twenty-two years old and well past his prime. More than once we have witnessed the fact that old male grizzly bears begin to suffer from poor dentition. When living out their last years in a landscape filled with cattle, there is an increased likelihood they will begin killing them to survive. I remain baffled by attempts to link bear 346 to killed cattle—especially in Falls Creek—without a shred of telemetry evidence or clear observation of a marking on the bear near these sites. I am convinced that he was labeled a cattle killer because he was the bear people knew because of our research. So it became easy to attribute killing to him despite many alternative explanations. From my perspective, the legend of the Falls Creek Bear is simply a good story created more by humankind's need to explain nature than from any remarkable evidence based on good science.

As I have examined our long-term data and from my own experiences related to livestock-killing grizzly bears, it has become apparent that as the bear population increased on the Front and their ranges expanded, the easiest solution to understanding livestock killing has defaulted to legends and stories that justify the destruction of grizzly bears. While I admit that destroying some bears often delivers a temporary solution for the rancher experiencing depredations, I believe we need longer-term sustainable solutions that ensure a future for grizzly bears on the Rocky Mountain Front.

Conclusion

Grizzly bears and humans represent two dominant mammal species on the North American landscape. Both are very intelligent beings, desire to use the same lands, and expect the other to yield when conflict arises. It is no real surprise then that since the beginning of time, bears and man have faced off in an ancient battle for food, space, and life. There is also no doubt that modern humans have acquired the capacity to conquer this great bear if they so will. Fortunately, some unique features of our own intelligence include our capacity to conceptualize the future, learn from the past, explore and understand complex relationships with other humans and nature, and share our world with other life. Unlike the grizzly bear, which only applies its intelligence to survival, humans can choose and devise ways to reasonably ensure the future of other species. Our grizzly bear research on the Rocky Mountain Front during these past decades has been incredibly important for teaching humans about the needs of grizzly bears and for raising the hard questions about how to live with them. I am convinced that by applying the knowledge we acquired through this long-term research, and by shaping our human will to live with grizzly bears, we can ensure their future on the Rocky Mountain Front. The only task before us is crafting enduring human cultures that value nature, seek to live sustainably on the land, and are willing to ensure a future for people and all wildlife on the Rocky Mountain Front.

KEITH AUNE, MS.C., is a senior conservationist with the Wildlife Conservation Society (WCS). He grew up in Dutton, Montana, and completed his master's degree in fish and wildlife management from Montana State University in 1981. Keith came to WCS from the Montana Department of Fish, Wildlife, and Parks (MFWP), where he served for thirty-one years in various capacities. He conducted field and laboratory research on black and grizzly bears, wildlife diseases, wolverine, lions, and bison. Keith worked on the research and management of Yellowstone bison for ten years. While at his last post with MFWP, he served as the chief of wildlife research and directed multiple research projects across Montana as well as supervising the annual harvest survey and the Wildlife Research Laboratory staff. Since coming to WCS in 2007, Keith has worked on several issues, including the WCS Wildlife Corridors Initiative and the American Bison Society Initiative, and as senior advisor to the

Wildlife Action Opportunities Fund. In 2011, he became director for the WCS-North American Bison Program and the American Bison Society initiative. He is currently chair of the International Union for Conservation of Nature's Bison Specialist Group for North America. He is WCS liaison with the Blackfeet Confederacy on the Iinnii Initiative and is conducting conservation outreach among tribal communities in Montana and South Dakota.

Chapter 9

TWENTY YEARS OBSERVING BEARS

John Vollertsen

"We need places where we have the liberty to get utterly lost, frozen, starved, or mauled by a grizzly."
—Reed Noss[1]

FIVE! I couldn't believe it. My twenty-power spotting scope—locked tight to the tripod and braced against a brisk East Front wind—captivated my eyeballs with the most incredible sight: five grizzly bears . . .

Twenty years and hundreds of hours of seasonal observation, and I'd never matched such a sight. Yet, the more I persisted at observing East Front bears, the more I appreciated the development of patterns, such as where they were and what they were doing.

As a solo hiker in grizzly country, I regard my experiences as an intimacy of sorts between myself and nature, and to recount my experiences would only be in the most respectful way.

I am a lifelong Montanan, and I avidly hunted my favorite high country areas of western Montana until roughly twenty-five years ago. My energy to hunt morphed from a philosophy of hunting big game to observing nature—especially bears. I retained the culture of most outdoor sportsmen, and I still respect the cardinal rule that a hunter does not disclose her or his favorite hunting spot or fishing hole. I've continued that same philosophy with observing bears. My adventures have been my own, with limited disclosure, mainly to family members. I'm a rather private person, and I suspect many people that have known me for a long time will be surprised at the contents of this chapter.

Although I've pondered the temptation for many years to write of my experiences, I was always concerned at just how to do it. I don't mean *how* in terms of cranking out sentences and paragraphs but, rather, *how* in terms of context. When it comes to bears and bear stories, I have mixed emotions about attaining a happy medium between dry—although highly educational—research-based journal articles and the rote grizzly bear attack books in sporting goods stores that depict bears in the attack posture with gnashing bloody teeth. The latter image is not necessarily for the consumer's edification as much as it is for promotion and media sales.

Then there are the profuse magazines and books about bear hunting with which the reader is left wondering whether the focus is more about venerating the hunter than about revering and respecting the hunted. Somewhere in the magnificence of the author's experience, reverence for the animal is far outweighed by the prowess of the hunter.

The Context of It All

Several years ago, I subscribed to the Grizzly Commons listserv on the Internet and became privy to a multitude of postings by a very sharp bunch of people in the bear world. These folks contribute heartily by sharing research, experiences, personal philosophies, and respect for conservation and education. It is there that I found a comfort zone that helped stylize *how* I wanted to write about bears and my experiences observing them. I read a posting by a researcher/activist expressing frustration about the popularity of bears being sensationalized by the blood-and-gore theme. She posed the question, "Why doesn't someone write something that is simply educational about bears?" Seemed like a fair question to me. A number of really good authors came to mind, and I thought, "I can do that." So I'm taking the self-challenge and will see if this chapter hits the mark.

I've not had any violent run-ins with bears. I haven't been scuffed up by a grizzly and—with maybe a few benign exceptions—have never had an encounter with a bear. But I have had some keen observations—in fact, many of them. And I think some are unique. I caution people when I talk about this chapter: "If you are looking for an adrenaline rush, skip this chapter." It's raw, it's real, and it's truthful. But it won't give you a rush.

My approach is to give an abbreviated rendition as I recount my experiences. Then, as risky as it may seem, I give my interpretation as to what I think was going on. I think *risky* is a good word to use here, because I have read and listened to so many *interpretations* of bear stories that I am sometimes left wondering about the informant's knowledge base or experience level, or if the person just relishes being a good storyteller. I hedge against definitive interpretations, because the professionals will tell you no two bears are alike. To make predictions about bears can also be risky. On the ground, they may be flat-out life-threatening.

Even though my renditions may fall some distance from established plateaus of research, they are nonetheless educational. And I think good educational value is best grounded in experience. I intend to share both.

Systematic Observation

Hike high, look low. That's my basic premise for viewing bears. I believe springtime is a premium time of year for viewing bears on the Rocky Mountain Front. In the spring, grizzlies emerge from their dens in high-elevation areas of the western perimeter of the East Front. As grizzlies emerge from these high-elevation den sites, they move into the lower-elevation areas to consume winter-killed carrion or to forage the early *green-up areas* of the lowlands. Directionally, the Front runs north to south, and predominant bear movement at emergence is from west to east. The spring snow cover divulges bruin track information as you hike or snowshoe north or south along the Front. Plus—and here is the big benefit—very few people are in the woods. In twenty years of snowshoeing, I've never seen another set of human tracks or snowshoe tracks in the core areas I visit. It is solitude at its finest.

When I say *systematic observation*, I'm really talking of doing things over and over again and watching and recording patterns. Information from tracks is very helpful. That's why spring snowshoeing is so much fun. When most people are done with recreational snowshoeing, I'm just getting started. The almost daily thawing, freezing, and wind loading makes snow conditions ideal for snowshoeing. I've walked over six-foot-deep frozen snowdrifts in the early morning hours as though walking on a sidewalk. Then, in the afternoon, as the warmth softens the snow, the work begins as those same drifts on the return trip suck your snowshoes deep.

With relative certainty, I can say that cutting bear tracks is not necessarily a haphazard enterprise. Bears are creatures of habit and, unless disturbed, will repeat their avenues to enjoyable habitat. Some areas are better than others for cutting tracks. I have uncovered what I call three reliable travel routes. For lack of a better term, I call them *corridors*. Without question, there could be a hundred so-called corridors up and down the Front. But for my purposes, I pay particular attention to three of them. One is about two miles wide, another about one-quarter mile wide, and a third one—believe it or not—is about twenty feet wide. Not too often does a season go by when I don't find bear tracks in one or more of these corridors. Again, a hunter does not divulge her or his haunts, and this bear observer does not divulge his.

I believe the bear biologists have a good idea of where bears den and where the bears go for nourishment. But I suspect that the route bears take to get there is a little bit of a mystery. In some areas, my records may fill that informational gap. But that knowledge probably hasn't been that important to the biologists. With the advent of global positioning system

(GPS) collars, biologists can now follow bear movement on an almost continuous basis with readings recorded every few hours.

Wildlife biologists have worked hard to develop technology for locating and tracking bears. Imagine how primitive the information base would be if there was no baiting, no trapping, no radio or GPS collars, no aerial flights, no four-wheel-drive trucks? If you strip technology from the quest, then you minimize your tools. But that is what I—along with the cadre of bear aficionados—am left with. My technology boils down to a pair of binoculars and a cheap 1970s-vintage pawnshop spotting scope. The rest of my contribution to the information base comes from lots of miles in the high country and lots of hours behind the spotting scope.

I suggest that observing bears along the East Front is not an easy task. I say this because they are probably a bit fickle about who they mingle with. By comparison, Yellowstone National Park has approximately 1.3 million visitors per year. Yellowstone has vast open areas rich in wildlife, including grizzlies. It is not uncommon to see bears near roadways as people stop to watch and take pictures. It is not uncommon to see bears feeding on ungulate carcasses or foraging at distances where they can hear and see people and cars.

The National Park Service does a commendable job of keeping space between people and bears. But when bears lose fear of humans, or tolerate humans or human activity within their presence, this is habituation, and it can even occur without a food reward.[2] Wildlife managers will argue that Yellowstone bears are not habituated. However, I'm a little skeptical. I think it varies considerably within the Yellowstone ecosystem, but of the purported 600 grizzlies in the ecosystem, I suspect many of them do not exercise the *flee* instinct when in the proximity of humans. One seasoned hiker, Tim Rubbert, shares concern about habituation in Yellowstone and Glacier National Parks and sees problems with habituation as more and more people visit bear country.[3]

Along the Rocky Mountain Front, I surmise it is a different story. I do not think the same opportunities for habituation exist, and I surmise that one major reason is that East

Front bears don't see the same level of visitors as do Yellowstone or Glacier. With the exception of occasional infractions, such as livestock depredation or rummaging through livestock feed, garbage, or pet food, East Front bears pretty much stick to themselves. I guess that's what makes the Rocky Mountain Front so special. The bears you see are, in most respects, truly wild. And that is something unique in the lower forty-eight states.

Below are my firsthand stories about those bears, followed by my afterthoughts.

A Sight to Behold

FIVE! I couldn't believe it. My twenty-power spotting scope—locked tight to the tripod and braced against a brisk East Front wind—captivated my eyeballs with the most incredible sight: five grizzly bears. I was a good mile or so away and a thousand feet above them. Bear activity occurred among sparse limber pine intermixed with brushy areas and small open grassy meadows. I could not distinguish one bear from the other. All five were grizzled gray and all about the same size. It was May 7. It seemed early in the year, but what I suspected soon became obvious. One bear mounted another, enthralled with romance. The mating lasted about twenty minutes.

One bear emerged from a large patch of brush and walked across a meadow in a nearly straight line to a thicket of Douglas fir. Then, out of sight. A second bear emerged from the same spot as the first bear, and trailed it, using the same route and about 200 yards behind. Then a third bear . . . same route, same distance from the preceding bear. Then, all out of sight.

A little later, two bears exited thick timber and walked close to each other as they approached a lone Doug fir in a small open park. One bear stood up and rubbed its back against the tree. When that bear was done, the other bear walked to the tree and—remaining on all fours—rubbed its shoulder and its side against the tree.

About a quarter mile away, two grizzlies emerged from the tall brush. They seemed at comfort with each other as they ambled up a sparse brush-covered hillside. They were joined by a third bear. Then I saw it—the proverbial cowboy walk.

The viewing of the five grizzlies was the longest I ever experienced at one sitting. It lasted from about 11:00 a.m. to 1:00 p.m. What a sight!

The first thing that occurred to me is that it seemed too early in the year for bears to be mating. I witnessed mating activity on May 7 and again on May 14 of the same year. I scanned the literature on the subject and found that bears generally will mate in June and that mating season can last two or three weeks.[4] Yellowstone bears were reported in 1969 to be mating as early as May 14.[5] However, when comparing breeding seasons in twelve ecosystems in North America, the grizzlies of the Northern Continental Divide Ecosystem, and the Rocky Mountain Front in particular, breed the earliest. These *courtship associations* range from April 21 to June 28.[6]

Springtime in the Rockies means romance is in the air for bears. The sight of grizzlies following each other is a strong sign of courtship. I've seen track evidence of that procession in fresh snow—two opportunistic male grizzlies following the lead of a female bear, each track almost perfectly placed on top of the female's track.

Even the experts concede that they do not know exactly why bears rub against trees. Bears probably rub for many reasons. They may be *scent marking* the object—which could also be a fence post or a rock outcrop, or even a telephone pole—to signal their presence to other animals. Who knows why? Maybe their hide just itches! Some biologists have speculated that female bears intentionally *do not* mark these objects in the springtime when they have newborn cubs so as *not* to signal their presence, thus escaping detection by a male bear who may be tempted to kill the cubs.

The cowboy walk is somewhat of a fascination. We've all seen the old Western movies where the two gunslingers slowly walk out on the street with hands at the ready, hovered over their holstered six-shooters. The body posture is a *dead* giveaway that something is going to happen as bowed legs slowly step into the fight position. Two male bears will do similar body posturing as they walk broadside to each other in a slow semicircle with heads held low, elbows outstretched, remaining a few feet apart, sizing each other up before the attack. I was not close enough to see every detail, but Dr. Stephen Stringham, a bear behavior expert, describes the cowboy walk very well and further states that bears will similarly do the *stomp walk*.[7] More common to black bears, the stomp walk is also a form of broadside display that involves slight elevation of the forepaw before it is slammed onto the ground, step after step.

But in my experience, the attack did not occur. They simmered down and slowly parted company. Stringham states that is the usual outcome.

A Creepy Feeling

I cut two sets of grizzly tracks in a timbered area I had snowshoed through just twelve days prior. The tracks were not fresh. A very light snow fell in the area, covering the tracks about 12 hours before I arrived there. I backtracked their trail to see where they came from. I always get a little bit of an adrenaline rush when seeing tracks. I go into the alert mode. The two sets were of different size, possibly indicating a female grizzly and a one- or two-year-old cub.

I proceeded a couple hundred yards and then found something . . . a slightly elevated round frozen pile covered by the light snowfall. As I brushed the snow aside, I could see raw bones with bloodied sinew still attached and compacted in the frozen heap of snow. I got that creepy feeling and quickly knelt down, looking below the Doug fir bows in every direction. It was awfully quiet. My reasoning surmised that the bears had been present at this kill site or scavenge site (whichever it may have been) somewhere between twelve days and twelve hours ago and there was nothing to worry about. But my instincts hammered "BEWARE" deep into my skull. I pulled my canister of Counter Assault bear spray. I wanted to be ready. I've never wanted to put myself in close proximity to a bear. But as cautious as I've been for so many years, I wanted to hedge against the inadvertent consequence of having done something stupid.

The slowly vanishing layers of winter snowfall still left discernible tree wells at the base of the Doug fir trees. One tree well close to the carrion pile had a concave indentation, suggesting a day bed, perhaps for many days—but just one, and not particularly large at that.

I took notes and snapped a few pictures. I wanted my visit to be brief, and I remained vigilant in every direction. There was no incident. No hint of a critter anywhere in my vicinity. I headed out, camera and notes packed securely in my backpack. I hadn't gone forty feet before I came upon a huge circular depression in the drifted snowbank . . . perhaps ten or twelve feet in diameter. That had to be Mama's bed. I didn't want to take time to retrieve my camera or do further note-taking. I was out of there at a vigorous snowshoe pace for the next three miles back to my vehicle.

When bears are feeding on carrion, they can remain in the same area for days at a time. Often, they will cover the dead animal with whatever debris is available, including dirt, forest duff, branches, or snow. They will eat their fill and—if not disturbed by another intruding bear or scavenging predator—will bed down nearby or even on top of the carcass. I surmise that what I saw was the result of a bear's body weight on top of a partially covered carcass. The compaction of bone and snow probably resulted from the weight and body heat of a bear as it rested atop the nearly fully consumed animal. I could not determine what the dead animal was because I was a bit nervous about spending much time in the area to search for bone or body parts that may have identified the animal. The bones I saw were about the size one would expect to find in an average-sized ungulate carcass, possibly deer, bighorn sheep, mountain goat, or young elk. I've seen all these animals over the years in this general area.

When on foot in bear country, it is important to be vigilant at all times. Even the slightest distractions can lead to undesirable circumstances. All senses need to be alert.

I caution novice hikers to pay attention to smells. Even the most subtle odor of something rotten or decaying may signal winter-killed carrion in the area—an excellent food source of bears. Watch for birds, especially ravens and crows. They also scavenge carrion and will alert you to the possible presence of bears on a dead animal.

Hunters need to be particularly aware of bears. Bears have been known to be drawn from miles away to a fresh kill or a gut pile to scavenge. Hunters may or may not be present. The excitement of hunting and taking an animal has a multitude of inherent distractions.

One Montana big game hunter had the misfortune of becoming a victim of a grizzly attack while field-dressing an elk.[8] Timothy Hilston of Great Falls was hunting elk during the 2001 season. Powell County coroner reported that Hilston was bent over, field-dressing an elk, when he was attacked from behind. The hunter did not have time to reach for his weapon and was not carrying bear spray. The hunter lost his life, and a female grizzly and her two cubs were captured and destroyed three days later. The incident occurred at the southern end of the Northern Continental Divide Ecosystem—far west of the Rocky Mountain Front but still part of the same general ecosystem.

Always carry pepper spray. It is useful on bears and other large predators.

The Smiling Grizzly

I anchored my backpacking tent near the crest of a 6,400-foot ridgetop. Rocky Mountain Front winds are humbling. All night long, the wind blew with incredible force. Mimicking the wave-shaped escarpments of the Front, the wind surged in waves all night long. I could hear the wind gather its momentum a thousand feet below me in the timbered narrow valley to the west. As it ascended the forty-five-degree angular mountainside, the velocity of the invisible force cracked like a whip as it exited the ridgetop above my tent. I didn't sleep much, wondering if the next wave would take my tent with it.

The next morning, I scoped two grizzly bears as they emerged from the dense quaking aspen onto a low-growth brushy peninsula that jutted into the aspen for a quarter-mile. The bears were on the perimeter of the brushy area about 200 yards apart and slowly walking parallel, westward. One bear soon went back into the aspen. The other continued its slow westward trek, exiting the peninsula with aspen protection and onto the expanse of a beautiful, still-brown grassy plain. The bear continued to the middle of the 400-acre open plain. With magnificent confidence, it sat down on its haunches and gazed to the south, and then very slowly turned its head to the north. From my mountaintop perch, my scope revealed what I swear was the grandest smile of bearish contentment. Maybe my brain was playing tricks, but that bear seemed like he had not a care in the world and was enjoying the cool Rocky Mountain Front spring breeze and all the lovely smells it carried.

It seemed like quite a while but it was probably only a few minutes before the bear swaggered northward on his way to the limber pine in the distance.

I relish watching large mammals interact with other species that share their habitat. This was one of those great occasions to witness something special. A cow elk stood motionless, watching the bear approach. Oddly, the elk began to approach the bear. As they neared each other, they respectfully maintained a distance of about fifty yards between them—elk walking south, bear waltzing north. No racing or chasing like you see in National Geographic depictions—just raw respect for each other.

But it was a different story with the deer. As the grizzly approached a herd of fifteen deer, they spooked. Fifteen muleys bulleted across the flat land at top speed, not stopping to look back for a good half mile. The bear hardly broke his half-lazy stride. He just remained on his northbound course, not seeming to care one way or the other about anything.

The little valley of the bear doesn't have a designated map name, but I call it Happy Valley.

When camping along the Front—whether in a valley floor or a few thousand feet above on a mountaintop—one needs to be prepared for severe winds. They can come at any time. Number one warning: don't pitch a tent where a tree can be blown on top of you.

Species interaction is puzzling sometimes. I suppose the disposition of the predator species is regulated by its appetite. Perhaps the elk that walked toward the grizzly could sense minimal danger and thus did not display the *flee* mode. Maybe it is not common for East Front grizzlies to pursue a cow elk or calf elk like they do in the Yellowstone ecosystem.[9] I've never gotten a firm answer as to whether anyone has actually watched a grizzly catch or even pursue elk on the Front. Again, it was a common occurrence, one well documented through extensive field observations and videotaping in Yellowstone Park by Dr. Steve French and his wife, Marilynn French, back in the late 1980s.[10] In the past ten or so years, the elk population in Yellowstone has dropped significantly, and observing grizzly predation of elk calves has become a far less frequent event.

As for the Front, I've only read one instance of a grizzly taking an elk calf. Paul Hazel is a legend when it comes to Sun River history. Hazel was interviewed by Fish and Game official Bob Cooney, and the interview was published in a magazine in 1979. Hazel spent sixty years in the Bob Marshall Wilderness. He recounted an incident on the West Fork of the Sun River where a grizzly bear chased, caught, and fed on a calf elk.[11]

In 1999, a more recent informal report was published in the Choteau newspaper. Quentin Kujala, a Montana Fish, Wildlife, and Parks wildlife biologist, addressed the question, "How many newborn elk calves do bears eat in the Sun River area?"[12] Kujala indicated they "made forays into the backcountry during the elk calving season with the specific objective to find direct evidence of elk calf mortality." He reported that he hadn't found any dead elk calves. He further reported examining a half dozen or more bear scats every spring and did not report finding evidence of elk remains in bear scat.

He did report watching a grizzly that was "clearly looking for elk calves."

I've also talked to many men and women who hunt and hike the Rocky Mountain Front. They report that elk do prey on elk calves, but I've never heard any of them report actually seeing it happen.

Death from Natural Causes?

The black bear carcass was severely deteriorated. No smell. No fleshy meaty material. I figured it had been lying near the tiny spring in the quaking aspen sidehill for at least all winter. Some of the ribs were still attached to the backbone. Detached bones were not scattered particularly far from the main carcass. The skull and lower jaw were close by. The hide and hair were still about 50 percent present, but shrunk and shriveled. The hair was a pretty reddish brown, nearly cinnamon. It must have been a beautiful bear during its lifetime. I was curious about how it may have died. Did it die of natural causes? Was it from predation by another bear? Was it poached? Was it shot legally during hunting season and got away just to die later? Curious. Very curious indeed.

I examined the skull and teeth. The back molar identified the animal as a black bear. One incisor was missing, yet bone growth nearly closed the recess in the lower jaw. Overall, the teeth were worn considerably. The back of the jaw had a slight bulge. Again, it was probably bone growth to heal an old injury. I surmised the adult bear simply died of old age.

But there was something else. No claws. I could not find one single claw.

I got a good educational overview of bear skeletal anatomy when I took a three-day course at the Yellowstone Institute in Yellowstone National Park. Students were instructed on predator skull identification. We learned other identifiers associated with predator anatomies as well. The course created awareness but certainly not expertise. It added a few tools to my tool chest of wildlife knowledge.

The black bear carcass had a complete skull. All the creepy crawly little forest critters had done a good job of removing all fleshy material. Teeth were easy to identify. The back upper molars were a giveaway as to its being a black bear skull. The molars were significantly under an inch long, much less than a grizzly. That is about as far as my field guide[13] took me, and I am confident that it was a black bear.

I was puzzled as to why there were no claws. A bear has twenty, and I did not find one. The possibility of the animal being poached and its front and hind pads being removed is not out of the realm of possibility. There is a black market for such bear parts, but my lack of experience certainly could not confirm this as being a case of poaching and removal of body parts. The last time I read about the taking of bear body parts in Montana appeared in a newspaper article in 2010.[14] Grizzly bears are a poacher's trophy and carry strict penalties since they are a federally protected species. Black bears probably rank rather low, but an opportunist during hunting season may take a bear just for the claws and then abandon it.

Experiences like this makes one appreciate the raw nature of the Rocky Mountain Front. The Front provides ample opportunity to bring into play a lot of the primitive senses, alertness, and intelligences we all possess. If the black bear encountered a natural death—which is the likely scenario—then it is in the witnessing of this special cycle of life and death that makes the Front an extraordinarily rich resource. There is a spiritual dimension to the Front, and sometimes we enter it by accident, and sometimes it can be harsh.

Wow, That Was Quick!

I was driving up a narrow access road through the Blackleaf Wildlife Management Area. I didn't see the grizzly in the dim dusk light until it bolted. It was only fifty yards from the road and it was really hauling, kicking up fresh new snow that had fallen the night before.

At first it was running almost parallel to the road toward me. But then it planted a sharp left turn and sprinted straight away. It was out of sight in no time as it sliced through the dead limber pine at lightning speed.

For some reason, I felt an odd compulsion to measure the length of its stride. Thankfully, I dissuaded myself from stepping out of my rig—at least for now. It was a warm spring day, and I knew if I waited too long the snow would be gone. The wildlife management area was open at that time of year, so trekking across would not be a problem.

I continued three miles to Blackleaf Canyon and spent part of the day hiking around. I came back to the site of the grizzly six hours later. The snow had melted out somewhat, but tracks were still discernible. I headed out with a tape measure in my pocket and bear spray on my side. The dead limber pine afforded good viewing a half mile in every direction. I didn't want to get too close to the taller, thicker Doug fir in the distance. There could be a surprise over there, and I didn't need that.

The grizzly's stride averaged from eleven to thirteen feet. The bear kept that same pace for a good 400 yards. I was impressed.

I looped back to my vehicle, choosing more open country for my return route. I looked down and spotted tracks from another grizzly. This second bear was walking on fairly open ground. The tracks were fresh, and the impressions in the snow and dirt clearly indicated this bear was BIG. The front pad measured six and one-eighth inches in diameter. I was impressed.

The sight of my vehicle looked mighty good.

Viewing a large track does not necessarily imply a large bear. That is the conclusion of at least one author on the subject, Enos A. Mills.[15] Mills concluded this in 1919, and it probably still stands the test of time. I haven't seen anything in the literature that would help me determine the size of the bear by the measurement of its track, at least not with any reasonable accuracy. Rocky Mountain Front grizzly biologist Mike Madel once reported the foot measurement of a large bear trapped on the East Front. The record-size 850-pound bear had a front pad diameter of over seven inches.[16] However, one variable to consider is the methodology of measuring tracks.

I took a short course from the Yellowstone Institute taught by Dr. James Halfpenny. Halfpenny described the proper way of measuring tracks. But one has to remember that there are a multitude of conditions to consider, such as the substrate, or the surface on which the animal walks. Ideal track measurements would be analogous to my walking barefoot in the mud and then tracking the mud on a linoleum floor. Measure the width of your track on the floor and then compare it to, say, measuring the outside diameter of your foot at the shoe store. You will quickly note a significant difference. Halfpenny discusses the importance of using the *minimum outline* method for consistent measurement in his popular *Scats and Tracks* books.[17] As an anecdote, Halfpenny noted in his course that measuring the pad of a tranquilized bear does not necessarily equate to the measurement of the track left by the same bear as it walks.

Record Number

I snowshoed eight miles by the end of the day and tallied nine sets of bear tracks—seven grizzly and two black—and one mountain lion track. Sure, some of the bear tracks could be a repeat of the same bear. In fact, I'm convinced one grizzly track was the same as another track I'd seen a couple miles back.

The one grizzly track stuck out from the rest. "Stuck out" is a good term because the track was characterized by the outside claw on the left front pad sticking out at a cockeyed angle. Instead of leaving a nice straight claw impression, it was longer and in the shape of a nearly complete question mark. I figure it sustained an injury at some point in life and had just healed oddly.

The lion track offered evidence of the athleticism of the animal. The cat was walking on a relatively flat gradient next to a steep shallow embankment when—for whatever reason—it jumped to the top of the embankment. There was a good snow cover that left good track impressions, and I was able to make a fairly good estimate that the distance of the jump was about twelve feet. But the impressive evi-

dence is that it was about seven feet vertical. It appeared the cat did that from a standing position.

It was one of my better days in twenty years of tracking.

I felt privileged to see so much on one outing. Lots of bear sign, including rub trees. Having been through the area many times over the years, I know where many rub trees are located. I never fail to find hair lodged in the sap of the trees that are scraped by clawing.

I also felt fortunate to not have an encounter. I spent most of the day in timbered terrain where the probability of surprise encounters is relatively high. Although the system is not foolproof, I am constantly making loud sounds. Snowshoeing on hard-packed spring snow with aluminum snow shoes can be a noisy experience. There is a lot of clattering going on at foot level from the metal of the shoes hammering against the solid surface of the snow. It's amazing how noisy that can be. I'm sure animals hear me long before I see them. I would probably be amazed at how much I've missed by being so noisy. But I have no problem with that. Noise in bear country is something you want. No surprises, please. And it is up to me to make sure they don't happen.

For years, I rented snowshoes and then finally settled on buying a good pair of Atlas shoes with bindings that are easy-on and easy-off. That is important, because spring snowshoeing means deep snow on the north-facing slopes and bare ground on the open south-facing slopes. So, I can remove my snowshoes in seconds and, without taking my pack off, carry them for a quarter mile across open ground and then slip them back on again when I reach the heavy snow.

The grizzly with the odd-shaped claw kept me wondering as to how that could happen. It's sheer speculation, but it may have been from a natural circumstance or it could be from trapping. Leghold snare traps are probably the trap of choice for experienced wildlife biologists on the Front. I've listened to presentations by government trappers and am impressed at how dangerous a situation can be when approaching a grizzly bear with a cable around its ankle. Of course, in order to deal with a bear in a leghold trap, a tranquilizer dart from a gun needs to be administered. Sometimes bears can be docile and at other times they will charge repeatedly until the tranquilizer takes effect. Another common method of trapping is through the use of a culvert trap (also called barrel trapping) with bait inside. If the bear needs to be handled, then a tranquilizer is administered in a less dangerous situation. Helicopter darting is effective as well. Depending on location, purpose, and expense, the leghold trap is probably the more practical choice, and helicopter darting is rare.

It is not uncommon for bears to sustain serious injury and trauma from various trapping procedures.[18] The leghold snare trap can result in a condition known as *exertional myopathy* (EM).[19] EM "is a noninfectious disease of animals characterized by degenerative or necrotizing damage to skeletal and cardiac muscles associated with physiologic imbalances after extreme exertion and stress."[20] In extreme cases, death can occur from trapping. In less extreme cases, it would not be uncommon for animals to sustain injury and possible deformities from those injuries. It is common for bear trappers to report that the trauma of the trapping episode is so impressive on the bear—especially a problem bear—that the bear may become quickly conditioned to associating the bad experience with humans, thus effecting a behavioral change in the bear to not get in trouble again. But I suspect those kinds of reports are more anecdotal than research based.

The UFO Bear

On this particular day, I was snowshoeing on a Forest Service trail. I sifted across an east/west canyon, narrow and thinly timbered with a quiet shallow creek. The south-facing slope of the canyon had numerous open areas with bare ground from the spring thaw. The base of the canyon was 75 percent covered with snow, and certain stretches of the stream had mud on its perimeter.

I shoed to the north side and immediately encountered deep snow on the shaded north-facing side of the canyon. The trail sliced through thick Doug fir, and I had plenty of work ahead of me. The snow was thick, the temperature in the low 50s, and my Atlas shoes were picking up additional weight with every step up the mountainside.

I decided I had had plenty of fresh air and sunshine for one day and made a U-turn and chugged back over my tracks. It was downhill, and the compressed snow from my existing tracks made for a quick descent back to the floor of the canyon. Perhaps it was a little too quick.

I discovered there were grizzly tracks on top of my existing snowshoe tracks. I had been at that spot—only sixty yards after crossing the stream—just two hours prior. I could see where the bear had been following my tracks on the trail and then made a quick right turn and headed straight uphill at a running pace.

My head was churning with all kinds of possible scenarios, all of which spelled danger. But two things were convincingly evident: one, the bear was on my tracks, and two, it could have been two hours ago or it could have been two minutes ago!

I was at a decision point. I needed to leave the area, but which way to go? I decided to wait in the thick timber, assuming I knew which way the bear went but not being absolutely sure. I figured the bear knew where I was and that it would be wise to let the bear neutralize its own circumstance before I made a move. So I waited—pepper spray in hand and remaining vigilant.

About an hour passed, and I decided to continue my return trip, which was opposite of where I thought the bear might be. I "backtracked" my and the bear's tracks to the creek. I crossed the creek, but there were no bear tracks on the other side. Where did the bear come from? My curiosity persuaded me to check areas up and down the creek. It must have crossed that canyon, but where?

I checked both sides of the creek for about a quarter mile in each direction from the last known tracks. Nothing. I checked the sparse timber in the canyon floor, which was about three quarters covered with snow. Nothing. There was mud. There was snow. There was plenty of opportunity for the bear to leave evidence of where it came from before it entered the timbered mountainside with several feet of snow depth.

> *Maybe an expert tracker would not be puzzled, but I sure was. The only logical conclusion I could formulate—given my vast experience (interspersed with occasional ineptness)—is that the bear stepped out of a UFO at the point where the trail crossed the creek. As fantastic as the interpretation seemed, it helped me giggle off a little bit of nervousness on my trek back to the trailhead, knowing there was a grizzly in the area.*

If there is a lesson to be learned here, it would that bears are far more aware of our presence than we are of theirs. In this circumstance, if there had not been snow on the ground, I probably would have been completely oblivious to the bear's presence.

I respect bears and their intelligence and senses. Bears are extremely polite and will neutralize the potential for encounters in countless ways. Most of the time, we humans most likely have no idea this happening. In fact, the scenario probably applies to most of the large critters in the forests and foothills of the Front. They sense our presence long before we do theirs.

In the above circumstance with the grizzly, I have toyed with the hypothesis that the bear wanted to cross the narrow canyon without leaving any trace of its route. It may have selected its footing strategically so as not to leave pad impressions in snow or mud at least minimally. Perhaps it stepped in brush or grass and picked its way across the canyon until it entered snowfields where it could not avoid leaving tracks. Back in the years when I did a lot of elk hunting, I remember tracking a spike bull for a couple hours through about three inches of snow. The mixed conifer forest had a lot of bear grass, and the broad, rounded clumps stuck up through the snow. The elk would step straight down on top of the bear grass, making it a challenge to figure out where the tracks led. They seemed to just disappear at times. Obviously, the crafty young bull knew it was being tracked and was going to make the job difficult for the hunter. He succeeded.

To the UFO bear, I wish him well . . . and a long life.

What Happened to the Bears?

The years roll by and things change. But I never realized change could happen so quickly, at least, not in a relative sense. There became fewer and fewer bear tracks and fewer and fewer bear sightings. Odd, because bears are a very slowly reproducing species and I wasn't seeing or hearing anything from the professionals that would point to a collapse or displacement in some regional population, at least not in the areas with which I was familiar. After about four years of dwindling bear activity, I finally recorded no bear sightings in my spring outings in 2011 in my favorite spots. Even the bear corridors only produced one set of black bear tracks. What happened to the bears? I am particularly puzzled as to why I was not coming across anything at a time when the bear biologists were telling us the grizzly population in the Northern Continental Divide Ecosystem (NCDE) was increasing annually. They were elated to report in late 2006 that 545 individual grizzly bears were counted.[21] This was based on a bear hair study by the U.S. Geological Survey. With the application of sophisticated software packages, the estimated numbers climbed each year. By late 2011, a newspaper account claimed that biologists estimated 1,000 grizzly bears in the NCDE.[22] The principal researchers on the project published a journal article that concluded there was a growing population of more than 1,000 bears in and adjacent to the NCDE.[23] I am amazed at how professionals can almost double the population of bears in six years using statistics. I have a high degree of respect for the seasoned professionals who conduct grizzly bear research and management, but I remain mystified at how field-hardened biologists can return to their offices and grow grizzlies with software. I was always under the impression that growing grizzly bears required habitat.

I haven't conferred with biologists about the specific dilemma I was experiencing with fewer and fewer bears, and I certainly don't have long-term population trend data to substantiate my assertion that something is going on. As I observe and read, I've decided to posit three possible reasons I am seeing less and less bear evidence and there are fewer bears in the areas I've visited or viewed.

First, natural events and human-caused events may be going on. One thing that comes to mind is fire. There have been naturally occurring fires along the Rocky Mountain Front. There have also been prescribed burns set by the U.S. Forest Service to control relatively small acreages in key areas to hedge against the spread of much larger wildfires, should they happen. Such prescribed burns are almost always done in unison with public comments and in consultation with all the appropriate biologists of various agencies.

I don't find fault in prescribed burning, but I don't think the data are available to determine possible displacement to bear movement. As I mentioned earlier in the chapter, biologists have a good handle on den site locations and where the bears go in the spring to feed, but I'm not sure they have a good handle as to the movement patterns from point A to point B, if such patterns exist. I maintain they do.

Second, bear management activities have changed. In the past, bears were generally trapped and radio collared after they had become a problem bear. These *problem bears* were released and monitored with the hope they would not become repeat offenders. Now, bear trapping policies have been modified to include trapping a certain number of bears each year to record their existence and their movements. Female grizzlies are the main target. These *research bears* of the East Front are trapped as part of a larger study of population trends in the NCDE. They are baited, trapped, tranquilized, weighed, measured, syringed, marked, and radio collared. Then they are released back into their familiar domain.

Biologists of the East Front are very experienced at trapping bears. I have no doubt they want to do it in a manner that is least invasive to the bear's physical or emotional well-being. But trapping has a certain amount of trauma associated with it, especially when Aldrich leghold snares are employed, compared to less invasive methods, such as darting from a helicopter or using barrel traps.[24] We humans probably don't understand the level of trauma a trapped or handled animal experiences, but I would suggest that bears communicate with other bears and what once were their favorite areas and pathways are now zones of punishment. Thus bears are avoiding such areas as much as possible.

My third theory to explain these changes is the basic precepts of climate change. As a generalist, I can't point to specific cause-and-effect circumstances. The issue of climate change and how it affects bears is in its infancy. In time, as the research catches up, specifics may become more obvious. Some research is being conducted with polar bears, but in my search of the professional literature, I've not seen anything oriented to the Northern Continental Divide Ecosystem, though I have seen some speculation in a newspaper article and some related research.

A wildlife biologist has seen a pattern of grizzly bears emerging from their dens along the Front earlier than they did twenty years ago.[25] Apparently, the reason is a trend toward warmer and drier weather. The biologist, Mike Madel, suggests that they're responding to an earlier loss of snow and probably less snow over those den sites. Factors may be positive or negative. On the positive side, certain bear foods, such as chokecherries, may become more abundant. On the negative side, there may be fewer areas for army cutworm moths to congregate. Moths are an important source of fat for bears.

A researcher in Glacier National Park is noting changes in grizzly habitat due to climate change that may affect populations.[26] David Butler claims that evidence of climate change is affecting grizzlies in several ways. Tree seedlings are invading mountain meadows, thus crowding out burrowing animals that grizzlies feed on. Additionally, snow avalanche paths are reduced in size. This affects plant habitat on the edges of snow paths as well as the availability of carrion in the margins of snow paths.

As for answering the question of what's happening to bears, I have not advanced my opinion beyond experience-based speculation. However, I'm also skeptical of the notion that an *expanding* population of grizzly bears may be indicative of a *growing* population. This is a popular expression among wildlife biologists and managers. It is on this notion that I think the public needs to see long-term evidence that discerns the opinion of biologists from biological opinions. There is a difference, and I encourage citizens to press hard for that distinction. If grizzly bears are expanding their range to areas they haven't inhabited for a hundred years, is that really a sign that the population is growing? It may be an indicator, but I have not seen the science behind it. In fact, the influence of climate change may explain the question in part. Are grizzly bears moving out of old haunts because of a loss of habitat? Again, I think science-based data are in its infancy to adequately explain the answer. I further think that before we accept the assertions of wildlife biologists and managers, we should concurrently examine the agendas of the agencies for whom they work.

Conclusion

I get about 400 miles out of a pair of hiking boots. I would put my pile of worn-out hiking boots up against that of any other outdoorsperson. I've hiked a lot, I've read a lot, and I've thought a lot. Anyone who has spent much time on the Front has done the same. If piles of worn-out hiking boots represent experience, then I think enthusiasts for the Front could build a formidable mountain of advocacy for this marvelous place of world-class splendor. It needs it.

---

[1] Reed F. Noss, "Sustainability and Wilderness," *Conservation Biology* 5, no. 1 (March 1991): 121.

[2] Katherine L. Jope, "Implications of Grizzly Bear Habituation to Hikers," *Wildlife Society Bulletin* 13, no. 1 (Spring 1985): 32-37.

[3] Tim Rubbert, *Hiking with Grizzlies: Lessons Learned* (Helena, MT: Riverbend, 2006).

[4] Erwin A. Bauer, *Erwin Bauer's Bear in Their World* (New York: Outdoor Life Books, 1990).

[5] John J. Craighead, Jay S. Sumner, and John A. Mitchell, *The Grizzly Bears of Yellowstone: Their Ecology in the Yellowstone Ecosystem*, 1959 1992 (Washington, DC: Island Press, 1995).

[6] Albert L. Harting, and Maurice N. LeFranc, *Grizzly Bear Compendium*, sponsored by Interagency Grizzly Bear Committee (Washington, DC: National Wildlife Federation, 1987), 43.

[7] Stephen F. Stringham, "Aggressive Body Language of Bears and Wildlife Viewing: A Response to Geist (2011)," *Human Wildlife Interactions* 5, no. 2 (2011): 177-91.

[8] Daryl Gadbow, "Elk Hunter Killed by Grizzly," *Missoulian*, November 1, 2001.

[9] Glen F. Cole, "Grizzly Bear-Elk Relationships in Yellowstone National Park," *Journal of Wildlife Management* 36, no. 2 (April 1972): 556-61.

[10] Steven P. French and Marilynn G. French, "Predatory Behavior of Grizzly Bears Feeding on Elk Calves in Yellowstone National Park, 1986–88," in Eighth International Conference on Bear Research and Management, *Bears: Their Biology and Management* 8, pt. 1 (1990): 335-41.

[11] Bob Cooney, "Paul Hazel: 60 Years in the Wilderness," *Montana Magazine*, September/October 1979.

[12] Quentin Kujala, "Bear Predation of Elk Calves in Sun River Area Status Quo in Recent Years," *Choteau Acantha*, June 23, 1999.

[13] Kenneth R. Greer and Vernon E. Craig, *Bear Hunting in Montana* (Helena: Montana Fish and Game Department, June 1971).

[14] Karl Puckett, "Wildlife G-men on Patrol: Outdoor Scofflaws Keep Agents Busy, " *Great Falls Tribune*, February 21, 2010.

[15] Enos A. Mills, *The Grizzly: Our Greatest Wild Animal* (Sausalito, CA: Comstock, 1919).

[16] Sonja Lee, "Front Grizzly Mauls Size Record," *Great Falls Tribune*, May 24, 2003.

[17] James C. Halfpenny, *Scats and Tracks of the Rocky Mountains: A Field Guide to the Signs of Seventy Wildlife Species* (Guilford, CT: Falcon, 2001).

[18] Marc Cattet et al., "An Evaluation of Long-Term Capture Effects in Ursids: Implications for Wildlife Welfare and Research," *Journal of Mammalogy* 89, no. 4 (2008): 973-90.

[19] Marc Cattet, Gordon Stenhouse, and Trent Bollinger, "Exertional Myopathy in a Grizzly Bear *(Ursus arctos)* Captured by Leghold Snare," *Journal of Wildlife Diseases* 44, no.4 (2008): 973-78.

[20] Cattett, Stenhouse, and Bollinger, "Exertional Myopathy in a Grizzly Bear," 973.

[21] Jim Mann, "DNA Study Tallies 545 Grizzlies," *Daily Inter Lake* (Kalispell, Montana), November 16, 2006.

[22] Jim Mann, "Six Grizzlies Caught, Two Put Down," *Daily Inter Lake*, November 29, 2011.

[23] Richard D. Mace et al., "Grizzly Bear Population Vital Rates and Trend in the Northern Continental Divide Ecosystem, Montana," *Journal of Wildlife Management* 76, no. 1 (2012): 126.

[24] Cattet et al., "An Evaluation of Long-Term Capture Effects in Ursids."

[25] Karl Puckett, "Most Grizzlies Still in Mountain Dens: Long-Term, Front Bears Appear to Be Emerging Sooner," *Great Falls Tribune*, March 27, 2013.

[26] David R. Butler, "The Impact of Climate Change on Patterns of Zoogeomorphological Influence: Examples from the Rocky Mountains of the Western U.S.A." *Geomorphology* 157/158 (2012): 183-91.

Chapter 10

EXTREME NATURE: BEAR ATTACKS

John Vollertsen

The definition of environmental history has many dimensions. The relationship between humans and nature is commonly slow and deliberate. But on other occasions, history can occur quickly, and by accident—for example, through forest fires, floods, or windstorms. But there are some aspects of that relationship between humans and nature that I place in the *extreme nature* category. Such history can evolve so quickly that it lasts only seconds. Events of extreme nature in this chapter are in the form of encounters between humans and grizzly bears *(Ursus arctos horribilis)* and, in a couple of possible cases, black bears *(Ursus americanus)*.

Six bear attacks are highlighted in this book. Five of the six are encounters occurring in what would be the Rocky Mountain Front, east of the Continental Divide. One of those encounters—occurring in 1956—did not occur on the Front by the traditional definition. As I point out later in this chapter, however, that encounter has an interesting irony that I consider Front-related.

This chapter discusses four grizzly bear attacks and a fifth *likely* grizzly attack. A separate chapter discusses a single bear encounter that occurred in 1974. That chapter developed from a single article appearing in the *Great Falls Tribune* and—as far as my research took me—had never been reported anywhere else. My literature search and investigative interviews became so expansive I decided to develop a separate chapter around it. I've titled the chapter *Bear Attack, Fox Hunt*. The *Tribune* story typifies what an award-winning *Tribune* writer, Bob Gilluly, once said about news reporting: "Newspaper stories are the first draft of history."[1] In this case, not only is the bear-encounter story the first draft, it is likely the only draft—until now.

One thing that makes environmental history in the American West so exciting to read is its stories about bears. Hundreds of books and articles are written that cover the gamut from casual black bear encounters to vicious, slashing grizzly attacks. The Rocky Mountain Front had its share of encounters. Many of these are subtle and buried in the family histories of regional history books, such as "Beyond . . . The Shadows of the Rockies" and "Bynum—A Roundup of Memories."[2] However, two stories stood out to command their own separate sections within these books. The bear attacks of 1947 and 1948 are memorable in their respective communities.

The grizzly mauling that occurred in 1956 has an interesting twist of irony, and a search of newspaper accounts brought to the forefront some unrecognized outcomes.

The attack of 2007 was by a grizzly that ventured far out onto the flatlands of the Rocky Mountain Front. In recent years, the number of sightings of grizzlies east of the mountains and foothills has increased.

The attack of 2013 is curious. The woman was literally blindsided.

Bear Attack 1947[3]

Known around Great Falls as Coffee Pot Joe, sixty-five-year-old Josif Chincisian herded sheep on the Mosher ranch west of Augusta.[4] It was September 1947 when a grizzly bear became a nuisance—a sheep killer.

The herder's sheep wagon was in a coulee near Cunniff Creek about sixteen miles south of Augusta. In the black of night, Chincisian took his flashlight and rifle and headed out the door of his wagon to check a disturbance. Two sheep had been killed. In pursuit of the bear, the herder rounded a clump of willows and was twenty feet from the animal. He fired one shot and missed. There was no time to bolt in another shell. The bear struck him and knocked him to the ground, rendering him unconscious. The bear raked leaves and rubbish over the man then left.

Chincisian regained consciousness and, although severely injured, started to crawl across the creek and up the ridge toward his wagon. But he only made it about 100 feet from the attack site and—instead of going to the wagon—holed up in a fallen-down homesteader's shack until he could regain strength.

He waited a while and continued crawling up the steep ridge to the wagon. Making it to the wagon, he lay on the bunk until his wounds clotted. Chincisian decided to try for the Heydweiller ranch 1.5 miles away. Likely staggering and falling, he attempted the slow, painful trip, crossing two fences.

On September 27, 1947, Henry Heydweiller, a rancher living on the North Fork of the Dearborn River, discovered Chincisian lying half-conscious on the ground. "The bear had torn away most of his scalp and one ear, and they hung now in a dried, bloody flap over his face. He also had a deep cut at the corner of one eye. His body and legs were untouched, and there were no claw marks on his arms. High on the right arm near the shoulder, however, were four deep tooth punctures, as if the bear had picked him up to drag him . . . a piece of skull about the size of a silver dollar had been smashed out and torn away. He [Heydweiller] was looking at exposed brain."[5] Subsequent investigation of the scene concluded the damage to the herder was caused by a single blow from a forepaw.

A small, wiry man, the unconscious Chincisian was taken to Deaconess Hospital in Great Falls for brain surgery.[6] The doctor said only *toughness* had kept him alive. Ten days later, on October 7, Josif Chincisian died without having ever regained consciousness.

Reading Mosher's account leaves the reader with certain empathy for the victim and attributable heroism for some of the main players in the bear attack incident. But there was a turn in the story that acclaims the bear with unusual intelligence and cunning.

The day after the attack, the sheep were moved to a location farther out from the mountains to a corral with a small shack. Theodore Olsen, an experienced sheepherder, tended the sheep and was left with orders to not leave the shack at night. The grizzly found the new location and paid a visit around midnight. Olsen did not go against orders and remained in the shack, ignoring the commotion made when the grizzly killed a ewe. The bear did not touch the sheep again but, rather, made himself a bed near one corner of a shed thirty feet away.

Bruce Neal was the area game warden and had dealt with bears for almost fifty years. During his investigation, he was convinced the grizzly killed the sheep to bait Olsen out of the shack. The grizzly waited in ambush. Following orders, Olsen did not leave the shack. Around daybreak, the bear departed.

Naturally, the community was aroused by the long, painful struggle and subsequent death of the herder. A hunt for the bear lasted through the fall but to no avail. No bear was ever killed. Winter passed. The next spring, sheep were taken back into the hills. There was no more bear trouble. It's speculated the culprit bear may have been shot by an unknowing hunter miles away from the attack site.

I visited the grave site of Josif Chincisian in the Augusta Cemetery. A quiet March squall had deposited a one-inch blanket of fluffy snow on the Rocky Mountain Front. As I stood there, appreciating the gentle falling snowflakes on a gray day, the dark tombstone with dark letters whispered a shadowy, cool—and humbling—message.

Bear Attack 1949

The story of E. Broadhurst "Broadie" Smith and his encounter with a grizzly bear near Heart Butte appeared in *Western Sportsman* in 1950 and was later written as an abbreviated version in "Bynum—A Roundup of Memories" in 1986.[7] The cover of *Western Sportsman* labeled the encounter as "One of the dad-gumdest bear stories you ever read!" I'm entertained by grizzly depictions. The front cover of the magazine illustrates a man shooting at an enraged grizzly. The grizzly is bearing its prominent, white canine teeth and sharp, pointed claws. The entertaining part is that the artist was apparently not familiar enough with grizzlies to illustrate the bear with five claws on each front paw. It shows four. Nor do grizzlies have sharp, pointed claws. They are rather blunt.

However, the substance of the story is—agreeably—one of the *dad-gumdest* in the annals of the Rocky Mountain Front.

"Broadie loved his sheep . . . Sheep were No.1," according to Al Wiseman.[8] Wiseman worked for Smith in the 1950s and was interviewed by *Choteau Acantha* reporter Nancy Thornton in 2010. When reading about Smith's dedication to his sheep—as described by one who knew him—it partially corroborates why Broadie Smith ventured out in the dark of night to face two grizzly bears.

Smith, a lifelong bachelor, homesteaded property seventeen miles west of Bynum in the Blackleaf area, where he raised cattle and sheep.[9] In July 1949, Smith's sheep were grazing the foothills on Hungry Man Creek six miles from Heart Butte. On July 30, Smith decided to move his sheep to higher ground after discovering his hired herder had left the sheep in one spot for two weeks. Disgruntled with the situation, Smith grabbed two blankets, his dog, a Winchester Model 94 (.32 Special) rifle—which the hired herder used to scare bears away since the caliber is too light to actually take down a grizzly. Smith headed up the mountain ridge with the band of sheep.

The sheep were settled on the slope for the night. Smith and his dog—a vicious, one-eyed old Australian blue—were bedded down on a small green knob. The moon went down and the night was pitch-black.

Then the sheep stirred and the dog barked. Smith rose and grabbed the camp gun—the caliber of which was hardly enough to deal with a big animal. In the darkness, he could make out a female grizzly with a good-sized cub coming up the trail. She "stood up, growled to the cub to keep back, and circled around to meet him [Smith]."[10] Smith fired his Winchester, hitting the bear in the chest. The bear rolled down a steep swale and remained motionless. Smith dashed to the spot and was going to finish her off with a close-up head shot. The hammer came down on an empty chamber. The grizzly scrambled to all fours and attacked. Smith swung the gun like a club, having no effect as it struck her head.

She slapped Smith to the ground and began raking her claws and teeth over his head. His dog, Old Blue, left the field of battle. The grizzly continued, sinking her teeth into his arms, shoulders, and thigh. Then the bear left him for dead.

Sensing a chance to escape, Smith stood up. The bear returned and again delved out more biting and clawing. Smith figured she left him for dead or else she was spent from the injury inflicted by the bullet. Either way, the grizzly departed and did not return.

Smith struggled to his feet and headed for the base camp at the bottom of the valley, leaving his rifle behind. Smith reached the camp, and Frank Sabados—startled by the bloodied Smith—wrapped him in blankets and fired up the stove. Sabados got on his horse and headed for the Chenault Resort, five miles away, where Pat and Virginia Kenyon lived. Virginia was a nurse and had served in World War II.

After Sabados informed the Kenyons, he and Pat headed back to the base camp and shuttled Smith via horseback and then pick-up truck back to the Chenault Resort, where Virginia administered to Smith's wounds. Broadie Smith ended up in Deaconess Hospital in Great Falls, 100 miles away.

Blackleaf rancher Anne Dellwo—thirteen years old at the time of the attack—visited Smith when he was in the hospital. In a 2010 interview, Dellwo recalled, "He had a terrible wound on his head. He was very lucky to be alive."[11] *The Great Falls Tribune* carried a story about the mauling of Broadie Smith.[12] The accompanying picture illustrated Smith with most of his head, as well as his shoulder and forearm, thickly wrapped in bandages. Dola Fitzpatrick's story reported that Smith had large holes in his thigh and could see the bone in a number of spots.

At the beginning of this story, I stated that Smith's dedication to his sheep "partially corroborated" why he went out in the dark of night to face two grizzlies. It seems reasonable to wonder why Smith took such risky action. Three circumstances really do not point to the likelihood of an eminent bear attack from which he would need to protect himself or his sheep. First, there was no word of a grizzly attacking or killing sheep in the area, even though bears were known to do so. Second, the bears were walking up the trail. They were not attacking animal or man. Third, the female grizzly circled. As Fitzpatrick noted, she stood up, growled at her cub to keep back, and then circled the man. Fitzpatrick continues, "In the dim light he could make out a big mouse-colored sow bear coming up the trail."[13]

Obviously, Smith felt threatened and probably scared. He possibly decided to be proactive, rather than reactive, to the situation so he would have better control over the outcome. So he took up his rifle to *head off* the bear. Why didn't he use the light-caliber rifle for its intended purpose—to scare off a bear? The bear then *circled* Smith. Noted bear authority Stephen Herrero writes: "A bear suddenly confronted with a person may stand on its hind legs, not as a spoof of the biped it faces, but to better smell, see, or hear a person." Herrero continues: "Usually a bear that acts like this will flee once it has caught scent of a person."[14] It's not likely that Smith—or even wildlife professionals of the day—knew much about bear behavior and how to act or react to a bear encounter. Today, sportsmen, recreationists, and wildlife professionals have available to them a battery of information and media on how to act or react to a bear encounter.[15] But at night, a bear encounter or outcome is much more unpredictable.

I stated at the beginning of this story that the Bynum history book contained the abbreviated version of the original story that appeared in *Western Sportsman*. It is about two thirds the length of the original. One sentence edited from the original possibly suggests additional information and motivation as to why Smith would want to *head off* a big mouse-colored sow bear. That one sentence states, "BROADIE HAD ALWAYS WANTED TO BAG A BIG GRIZZLY."[16] Perhaps he did, because he claimed the bear eventually died from the one shot he got off.[17] And it was costly.

E. Broadhurst "Broadie" Smith recovered from his wounds and continued his sheep business. He died ten years after the grizzly attack, on September 19, 1959. The newspaper reported: "His body was discovered on the rolling prairie of the Blackfeet Indian Reservation in the East Glacier area where he had been moving a flock of sheep. He apparently died of a heart attack."[18]

Bear Attack 1956

The grizzly attack that led to the death of twenty-nine-year-old Kenneth Scott occurred on Basin Creek about four miles west of the Continental Divide and about forty miles west of Augusta, Montana.[19] Basin Creek drains into Danaher Creek near a Forest Service cabin and emergency airplane landing strip. It's in the heart of the Bob Marshall Wilderness.

When thinking about this incident and how it would apply to the Rocky Mountain Front, it is clearly something that occurred west of the Divide, and thus west of the traditional definition of the Front's boundary. But I decided to include the incident for a couple reasons. First, considering that home ranges for grizzly bears can be up to 300 square miles, it is entirely possible the attacking bear could be considered as having some of its home range east of the Continental Divide. A pioneering study of Rocky Mountain Front bears[20] illustrates several grizzly home ranges extending to—or including—such habitat areas as the Middle Fork of the Flathead River, Spotted Bear River, Danaher Creek, and Landers Fork—all west of the Divide.

The second reason comes at the end of the story as a caveat illustrating the eastward expansion of grizzly bear territory in the decades subsequent to the attack.

Kenneth Scott and his hunting partner Viv Squires departed Benchmark (twenty-three miles west of Augusta) on horseback with three other hunting companions, all from the

Fort Benton area. The first morning, Scott and Squires rode their horses two miles from camp to hunt elk.

They were hunting a thickly wooded ravine when Squires was charged by a grizzly bear at full speed. Attempting to sidestep the grizzly, Squires fell on his back. He put his foot toward the bear, and the enraged grizzly bit through his boot. The bear dropped his hold and headed toward Scott. Scott fired two shots at the bear with his 30-06 rifle, turning the bear downhill.

The bear left a blood trail, and the two hunters decided to track the wounded animal to prevent it from possibly attacking others in the area. They followed the bear through timber for over an hour until they spotted it again. Squires started shooting his 30-30 at the bear. Scott came alongside Squires and shot three times before his gun jammed. Squires kept shooting until he emptied his gun. Scott shouted that the bear was charging.

Squires jumped over a nearby bank, thinking Scott was close behind. In his scramble through the timber, he lost his gun. He could hear Scott shouting. He knew the grizzly had caught him. Knowing it would be futile to attempt anything without a gun, Squires ran back to his horse and headed to camp for help.

The rescuers found Scott badly wounded. They moved him off the mountain down to a creek bottom. While administering first aid, one of the party heard a twig snap. The huge grizzly mounted another charge. Morris Embleton was standing with a gun and shot the bear dead. The 800-pound grizzly dropped within ten feet of the group.[21]

Kenneth Scott was conscious but injured severely. He had wounds to his face, scalp, and neck. Squires and Frenchy Mayer rode sixteen miles to Benchmark to get the word out.

The next morning, Sunday, October 21, 1956, an airplane landed at the Basin Creek Forestry Service emergency landing strip. *The Great Falls Tribune* reported: "Dr. C.E. Magner, Great Falls, . . . said Scott, fully conscious through a long night of suffering, died about five minutes before the doctor arrived at the scene. Scott suffered scalp, facial, and throat lacerations. His hands and arms also were injured."[22]

Snow and high winds necessitated that the pilot leave two hours after landing. Scott's body was packed back to Benchmark, where an ambulance took him to Fort Benton.

At the start of this story, I saved the second reason for including Scott's story as a Front-related mauling until the end—the caveat being that grizzly bears have expanded their range from the Rocky Mountain Front down the drainages of the Marias, Sun, and Teton Rivers.[23] A stunning discovery was made in 2009. A grizzly bear traveled 150 river miles from the Front, down the Teton River, to Loma, Montana, where it was trapped after killing a sheep.[24] Fifty-three years earlier—and just prior to Kenneth Scott's going elk hunting—he and his young family moved to . . . Loma, Montana.[25]

Grizzlies hadn't been reported in the Fort Benton and Loma area since 1880, according to Jack Lepley of the River and Plains Society. In fact, the first reported grizzlies to visit the Missouri River in 130 years occurred fifteen miles upstream from Fort Benton near Floweree, Montana.[26]

The tragic ending of Kenneth Scott's life was memorialized by the town of Fort Benton. The *River Press* newspaper recognized him as one of Fort Benton's finest athletes.[27] Scott was an all-around high school athlete. His football and basketball talents were stellar. In 1945, he "turned in one of the finest individual track performances ever witnessed in the state."[28] He entered five events and placed in all five with firsts in the 100-yard dash, 220, shot put, and broad jump, and a third in the discus throw.

Two of Scott's former teammates, Steve McSweeney and Jack Lepley, along with other townspeople at Fort Benton, initiated a plan to name the football field Scott Field and to erect a flagpole and monument with a memorial to him. I contacted Jack Lepley in 2013, and he affirmed that the plans had been completed in 1957.[29]

The 800-pound grizzly bear that killed Kenneth Scott was skinned out near Basin Creek, where it had been shot. The hide, which measured eight feet, was to be tanned and sold, with the proceeds going to Scott's wife and three daughters.[30]

The news made the local papers, as expected. In 1956, it would likely be impossible to know what other media outside

Montana would have picked up the story. Today, a quick Internet search reveals that a brief article appeared in newspapers around the country and Canada, including in Salt Lake City, Pittsburgh. Hopkinsville (KY), Ocala (FL), Spencer (IA), and Windsor, Ontario. There were probably many more.

Two days after the mauling, a story came out in the *Tribune* about grizzly bear numbers in the Bob Marshall Wilderness and other areas of Montana.[31] Robert F. Cooney, director of the Wildlife Restoration Division of the Montana Fish and Game Department, reported the wilderness as "one of the last footholds of the almost extinct species." The newspaper referred to a *recently published* article by Cooney.[32] The newspaper does not specifically cite the article; however, it is likely a 1955 report by Cooney that states the number of grizzly bears in the wilderness outside Glacier and Yellowstone Parks as 439. The numbers of bears in Glacier and Yellowstone, respectively, were 100 and 125. At the conclusion of the report, Cooney asserts: "This wilderness area, accessible only by trails, represents the most important single factor in the maintenance of the largest grizzly bear population left in the United States."[33]

Bear Attack 2007

The complete story of Wednesday, October 17, 2007, is reprinted here with permission from the *Valierian.*

Bird hunter mauled by grizzly bear

Bird hunting season is underway, and hunters from all over the state, as well as surrounding states, are flocking to the Valier-Dupuyer area to get in on the great hunting available here. Not only are there great hunting opportunities on the private ranches on Dupuyer Creek, there are also many opportunities to observe local wildlife, but there is always danger lurking around the corner, as Dupuyer Creek has a very healthy population of grizzlies.

Unfortunately for one bird hunter, his hunting experience turned into a nightmare when he got too close to one of the bruins.

According to Bruce Auchly of Montana Fish, Wildlife and Parks, Brian Grand, of Stevensville, was mauled by a grizzly Monday afternoon on the Doug Henneman ranch, 15 miles southwest of Valier.

"Grand, along with three others, were bird hunting on private land along the thick brushy bottom of Dupuyer Creek when he apparently surprised a lone grizzly," Auchly said.

"He probably walked upon a bear in a day bed," surmised Gary Olson, Fish, Wildlife and Parks wildlife biologist. "This is really thick brush with willows, cottonwoods and buffalo berries along a beaver dam."

John Miller, one of Grand's fellow hunters, does not share this opinion.

"We didn't wake it up," Miller said. "That bear laid and waited there. We had been hunting in that area all morning," he continued. "We were having a good day, shooting a lot of birds."

Miller continued, "He had plenty of opportunity to go the other way. That bear was just waiting for his moment."

Miller said the attack was over in seconds, leaving Grand bleeding on the ground with numerous injuries.

"All I could see was a flash of fur," Miller said. "From the time Brian's dog ran by me with his tail between his legs, the screaming, the growls, to the crashing through the creek, it was probably ten seconds."

"It was horrifying the sounds the bear was making," he added.

Miller explained that he was only 35 yards from Grand, but couldn't see him due to the dense brush, and had talked to him just 30 seconds before the attack.

The attack was so quick Grand did not even have time to lift his gun, and only after being knocked to the ground did he get a shot off, unfortunately missing the bear.

Grand was driven to Pondera Medical Center by Miller, Todd Ahern and Rick Adams, then was taken by ambulance to Benefis Hospital in Great Falls, where he underwent surgery. His injuries included puncture wounds in his leg and head, a fractured right hand, and puncture wounds and fractures in his arms.

The bear also was apparently not injured or shot during the brief encounter.

FWP, in coordination with the Pondera County Sheriff's Department and a federal trapper, will set culvert traps to try to capture and move the bear.

This time of year, bears are in a constant search for food before their winter sleep. Bird hunters should be careful around dense cover, where bears may be bedding during the day. Sportsmen should make sure they make plenty of noise and not hunt alone.

Bear Attack 2013

Excerpts from the complete story of Tuesday, July 16, 2013, in the *Great Falls Tribune* are presented here. Credit goes to *Tribune* staff writer Karl Puckett.

Bear attacks near Duck Lake

Woman in good condition, dog dead after mauling

A bear attacked a woman north of Duck Lake on the Blackfeet Indian Reservation late last week after she and two dogs inadvertently walked past an area where it apparently was feeding on a horse carcass, according to the U.S. Fish and Wildlife Service and an area resident.

Chris Servheen, the grizzly bear recovery coordinator for the service, said the woman told tribal wildlife authorities that the bear was a grizzly but its species has not been confirmed . . .

The woman was walking past an area where the bear was near a horse carcass, Servheen said . . .

"The bear mauled the person and ran away," Servheen said.

David Walburn, a Duck Lake resident, said the woman was walking two small dogs at the time, and one [of] the dogs was killed . . .

"I don't know anything other than she's in a Kalispell hospital, and I think she's going to be OK, but she got chewed up pretty good," Walburn said.

After the attack, which occurred on Thursday or Friday morning, one of the woman's dogs showed up near Walburn's home with a leash on it. The dog had a Florida tag, and its fur was discolored . . . The discoloration on the fur turned out to be blood.

There was a dead colt on the north shore of the lake, he said.

Walburn was told that the bear had one or two cubs with it, he said. The woman had bear spray but was attacked from behind, he said . . .

Walburn said the woman remained on the scene for a few hours before two anglers found her.

Servheen did not directly investigate the incident. He received his information from tribal authorities . . .

Excerpts from the complete story of Wednesday, July 17, 2013, in the *Great Falls Tribune* are presented here. Credit goes to *Tribune* staff writer Karl Puckett.

No management action planned against bear that mauled woman on Blackfeet Reservation

Tribal authorities do not plan any management action against a bear that attacked a woman walking her dogs north of Duck Lake on the Blackfeet Indian Reservation on Friday.

Dan Carney, tribal wildlife biologist, said the bear was feeding on a dead colt about 50 yards from where the attack occurred at about 7:30 a.m. As a result, the case is being treated as a natural defensive act by the bear.

The area is eight miles east of Glacier National Park and is considered good bear habitat, Carney said.

Carney said the bear did not kill the horse. Carney said he's been told that the bear was a grizzly sow with two cubs. He hasn't confirmed the species but doesn't dispute that it was a grizzly, either.

Carney did not release the name of the woman who was attacked . . .

---

1 Bob Gilluly, "These Stories," *Great Falls Tribune*, December 27, 1995.

2 Augusta Area Historical Society, *Beyond . . . The Shadows of the Rockies: History of the Augusta Area* (Augusta, MT: Anderson Publication, 2007); Bynum Centennial Committee, *Bynum A Roundup of Memories: The Story of Bynum, Montana, and Its People* (Bynum, MT: Bynum Centennial Committee, 1986).

3 Dick Mosher and Ben East, "Dark Tragedy," in Augusta Area Historical Society, *Beyond . . . The Shadows of the Rockies: History of the Augusta Area* (Augusta, MT: Anderson Publication, 2007), 70-75.

4 "Sheepherder Clawed by Bear near Augusta, Injury Critical," *Great Falls Tribune*, September 29, 1947.

5 Mosher and East, "Dark Tragedy," 71.

6 "Sheepherder Clawed by Bear Dies," *Great Falls Tribune*, October 8, 1947.

7 Dola Fitzpatrick "Two Rounds with a Grizzly," *Western Sportsman*, 11, no. 1 (November/December 1950); Dola Fitzpatrick, "Two Rounds with a Grizzly," in Bynum Centennial Committee, *Bynum A Roundup of Memories*, 124-26.

8 Nancy Thornton, "Bear Attack," *Choteau* (MT) *Acantha*, October 20, 2010.

9 Bynum Centennial Committee, *Bynum A Roundup of Memories*, 177.

10 Fitzpatrick, "Two Rounds with a Grizzly," 12.

11 Thornton, "Bear Attack."

12 "Sheepman Loses 2-Fall Bout with Grizzly in Weird No-Quarter-Given Night Battle," *Great Falls Tribune*, August 1, 1949.

13 Fitzpatrick, "Two Rounds with a Grizzly," 12.

14 Stephen Herrero, *Bear Attacks: Their Causes and Avoidance* (Guilford, CT: Lyons, 2002), 138.

15 Safety in Bear Country Society, Wild Eye Productions, AV Action Yukon Ltd, and International Association for Bear Research and Management, *Staying Safe in Bear Country: A Behavioral-Based Approach To Reducing Risk* (Atlin, British Columbia: Safety in Bear Country Society, 2001).

16 Fitzpatrick, "Two Rounds with a Grizzly," 12.

17 Fitzpatrick, "Two Rounds with a Grizzly," 30.

18 "E. Broadhurst Smith, 72, Dies while Tending Sheep," *Great Falls Tribune*, September 21, 1959.

19 "Kenneth Scott Died Sunday following Grizzly's Attack," *River Press* (Fort Benton, MT), October 24, 1956.

20 Keith Aune and W. F. Kasworm, Final Report: E*ast Front Grizzly Studies* (Helena: Montana Department of Fish, Wildlife and Parks, April 1989), 54-56.

[21] "Grizzly Bear Victim's Body Returned to Benton," *Great Falls Tribune*, October 23, 1956; "Elk Hunter Dies after Mauling by Grizzly Bear," *Great Falls Tribune*, October 22, 1956.

[22] "Grizzly Bear Victim's Body."

[23] Karl Puckett, "Grizzlies Home on Range Again," *Great Falls Tribune*, November 1, 2009.

[24] Karl Puckett, "Wayward Bear Trapped in Snare," *Great Falls Tribune*, July 1, 2009.

[25] "Kenneth Scott Died Sunday."

[26] Travis Coleman, "Bears Break into Shed on Ranch North of Carter," *Great Falls Tribune*, June 13, 2010.

[27] "Benton Group Would Name Athletic Field for Ken Scott," *River Press* (Fort Benton, MT), October 31, 1956.

[28] "Benton Group Would Name Athletic Field."

[29] Jack Lepley, personal communication with author, March 6, 2013.

[30] "Bob Marshall Wilderness One of Last Grizzly Strongholds: Estimated 440 Bears Live in Rugged Montana Area," *Great Falls Tribune,* October 23, 1956; Funeral Rights Conducted for Grizzly Victim, *Great Falls Tribune*, October 25, 1956.

[31] "Bob Marshall Wilderness One of Last Grizzly Strongholds."

[32] Robert F. Cooney, "The Grizzly Bear: An Endangered Species" (November 14, 1955), in *Grizzly General 1955–1972*, microfiche (1955), 1. Available at Montana State Fish, Wildlife, and Parks, Helena, MT.

[33] Cooney, "The Grizzly Bear," 5.

Chapter 11

BEAR ATTACK, FOX HUNT

John Vollertsen

A story about a bear attack in the Bob Marshall Wilderness was brought to my attention by a friend, Renee Pipinich, in Helena, Montana, a few years ago. Knowing I had an interest in bears, she recounted the story and explained how her late husband, Kurt Pipinich, was involved in a bear attack incident back in 1974. Renee stated that the incident was reported in the newspaper at the time and her husband claimed the story differed significantly from his actual experience with the attack scenario.

Renee had never read the story in the newspaper, but the incident was deeply embedded in her memory, having heard it numerous times over the course of twenty-seven years of marriage. Kurt's story—recounted to friends and family many times over—was always consistent in content and sequence. So when Renee retrieved the newspaper story from the Montana Historical Society Research Center's microfilm archive of the *Great Falls Tribune,* she knew why her husband was so concerned about the accuracy of the bear attack.

I encouraged Renee to write down Kurt's rendition of the attack. She provided many details of events that led to the incident and the actions and reactions between both the bear and a sixteen-year-old Youth Conservation Corps (YCC) worker by the name of Russell Fox. The young man was working for the YCC in the wilderness east of the Continental Divide. The youth group and adults were headquartered at Cabin Creek Forest Service Guard Station, about twenty-three miles northwest of Augusta, Montana. The young man encountered a bear; the bear pursued him up a tree and pulled him from the tree, inflicting injuries that included bite wounds to his legs and heel. The youth also received cuts and bruises from being yanked through the tree branches.

The complete story of Thursday, July 18, 1974, is reprinted here with permission from the *Great Falls Tribune* with credit to reporter Wayne Arnst.

'Don't blame the bear,' youth says after wrestling match in wilderness

By Wayne Arnst

Tribune Staff Writer

Wrestling with a bear is one part of Youth Conservation Corps (YCC) environmental education that Russell Fox, 16, says he would rather do without.

Fox, 825 4th Ave. SW. was attacked Tuesday about 8 p.m. by a large cinnamon (chestnut-colored black) bear sow while returning to a Forest Service YCC camp in the Bob Marshall Wilderness.

The Great Falls youth had been fishing with other YCC workers at Cabin Creek, about 15 miles from the end of the road at Gibson Reservoir on the north fork of the Sun River. Fox said he was alone at the time of the attack, had made little noise and apparently surprised the bear when she was about 20 feet away.

"Don't blame the bear," Fox emphasized at his home, Wednesday.

The sow, who had three cubs, was between Fox and the Camp when he walked over a small hill and met her face to face, he said. The bear growled at the cubs. They scampered up a nearby tree. Then the sow charged after Fox who was racing for a tree of about 9-inch diameter.

The tree had no branches for about 15 feet up. Fox said, and he used a small sheath knife as a pick to gain a handhold. As he reached the first branches the bear was right behind him, bit his lower left leg and tore off his moccasin slippers.

Fox was up the tree about 40 feet before the bear could reach him again. He had run out of branches to climb further. The bear swiped at him and knocked off a large limb he had been standing on.

Fox showed the sheath knife but said it would have been too small to do the bear any harm and he would not have had a chance to use it.

"For the enormous bulk of that bear she was very agile." He said. The bear, previously seen in the area, was estimated to weigh about 400 pounds.

The bear, hanging onto the tree and unable to slash with her claws, sank her teeth into his lower right leg and started to pull backwards.

"Rather than let her tear my leg muscles all up, I went with the bear," Fox said.

The sow had pulled him down through the branches to about 20 feet above the ground when both fell from the tree. Fox said the fall may have knocked the wind from the bear because she did not immediately get at him again.

"I didn't wait around to see how she was," he said. In his bare feet he made another 200 yards down the trail before the sow caught him again.

She made a swipe with her claws just as Fox stumbled, he said, and it sent him rolling. He got up and ran again, but when he looked back the bear and the cubs had disappeared.

Fox again emphasized that he did not blame the bear for the attack.

"I surprised her and she only reacted naturally," he said. "I was just lucky she quit when she did."

The cubs were in a tree about 50 feet from Fox's at about the same height. Fox said he could look across and see them. His being that close to her cubs may have further angered the bear, he speculated.

The entire episode took only five to seven minutes, Fox estimated. The chase had taken him about 400 yards from camp.

Other members of the YCC crew doing trail maintenance work in the area and counselor Bernie Yednock reached Fox moments after the bear left the area. Yednock applied first aid to the puncture wounds in Fox's legs and the scratches he received when being pulled from the tree. The group then carried him back to camp.

Fox said his doctor told him it would be three weeks before his wounds healed but he would like to return to the YCC activity before that.

"It took me three years to get accepted for the job and I don't want to mess it up now," he said.

The youth said he wants to enroll in a forestry career at University of Montana when he completes high school and the YCC camp is giving him valuable experience.

A Malmstrom Air Force Base helicopter, piloted by Lt. Col. Robert Peisher and Lt. S. J. Anderson and crewed by base hospital commander Lt. Col. (Dr.) Charles Signorino and medical specialist A. 1 Richard Brimer, arrived at the Cabin Creek camp Wednesday morning to evacuate Fox to Deaconess Hospital for outpatient care. Forest Ranger Robert Duncan, Augusta, accompanied the crew to the camp site and hospital.

Lawrence Olsen of the U.S. Forest Service and Jack LaValley of the Montana Department of Fish and Game will investigate the incident. No previous bear trouble had been reported in the area.

Fox's father, Richard, said Wednesday he believes the authorities should not harm the bear which was only doing what was natural.

"The area is bear country and humans are the intruders," he added.

The caption below a photo of the injured Russell Fox reads:

> *SURVIVES BEAR ATTACK – Russell N. Fox, 16, 825 4th Ave. SW, is shown recuperating at his home Wednesday after being attacked by a bear in the Bob Marshall Wilderness area Tuesday evening. He suffered puncture wounds in both lower legs and scratches and bruises when the bear pulled him from a tree. (TRIBUNE PHOTO)*

Investigation

My interest was piqued because I had never read or heard the story and I've been following current events and reading history about the Rocky Mountain Front for over twenty years. I figured the differences in stories could be reconciled by visiting with the state and federal agencies with wildlife and resource jurisdiction in the area. The newspaper account reported that two officials of Montana Fish, Wildlife, and Parks and the U.S. Forest Service would be investigating the incident. Upon inquiry, I discovered neither agency had record of the event, and in fact—upon circulating my request through the respective agencies—I learned there was no memory of the incident, just a couple of referrals to people who may know something. I found this surprising and yet not so surprising because the bear attack occurred thirty-nine years ago; things were different in reporting then, and, obviously, agency memory vanishes over time.

The entire *cold-case* scenario was just too enticing to pass up, so I decided to offer myself a challenge and do my own investigation. I've done documentable quantitative and qualitative investigation in the past, having produced a master's paper and a doctoral dissertation.[1] In the late 1990s, I worked as an investigator for the Montana Board of Outfitters and was trained and experienced in investigative procedures.

In late 2012 and early 2013, I started my search for people. I engaged the resources at the Montana Historical Society and got off to a good start from newspaper archives and city directories. The Internet white pages were extraordinarily helpful as well as, of course, Google and a couple of paid-for Internet people-locator sites. In all, I interviewed twelve people by phone and contacted or conferred with another five people via e-mail, postal mail, or in person. Fortunately, I was able to locate and interview five of the original YCC youth and four of the original YCC adults at the Cabin Creek YCC camp.

Of the people I contacted, all agreed that they did not actually see the bear attacking Russell Fox. Their versions of the event were taken from the sixteen-year-old's account. There were some variations in the amount of information they retained after thirty-nine years, and some slight variation in the sequence and location of the parties involved. But there were also some other observations and opinions from informants that raised some question about the veracity of the printed story. Of particular concern was the suggestion that the black bear may have actually been a grizzly bear. Three of the adult informants (adults in 1974) based their recollection or agreement on the "fact" that grizzlies do not climb trees.

I continued my investigation by chunking down the story and examining the various parts. I decided to label the first phase as the attack scenario (actions of bear and human), the second phase as the black bear versus grizzly bear determination, and the third phase as the treatment of informants' recollections.

Attack Scenario

First was the attack scenario. When it comes to bear attacks, the premier source is Dr. Stephen Herrero's book *Bear Attacks.*[2] There are many bear attack books on the market, and Herrero's is highly regarded for its foundation in quantitative and qualitative examination of recorded bear attacks spanning decades throughout the United States (including Alaska), Canada, and the Yukon.

I would suggest that in the case of a complete attack/contact sequence in a *treeing* scenario, four elements need to exist: (1) The bear responds to human presence (approach/attack or flee), (2) the bear makes a second response after reaching the tree with the human in it (retreats or ascends tree), (3) the bear climbs the tree but does not make physical contact with the human, and (4) the bear makes physical contact with human (biting, clawing, and possibly pulling the human from tree). If a bear *decides* to pursue a human (element 1), it may abort the other three elements at any time. It may pause at the bottom of the tree and observe the human or chomp its jaws and then retreat, satisfied that it has neutralized the threat of human presence. It may pursue the human up the tree, stop, not make contact, and then retreat. Conversely, as the attack/contact elements increase (from element 1 to element 4), the probability of them actually happening decreases.

Using the Fox example and Herrero's research, a clearer picture unfolds as to how attack/contact elements and probabilities play themselves out. Herrero examines three field studies of 414 female black bears with cubs being approached by humans. The studies revealed that female black bears with cubs retreated from human presence at least 98 percent of the time.[3] This means that, at most, 2 percent of the time a female black bear could display aggressive behavior and proceed beyond element 1 of the attack/contact sequence. Interestingly, one researcher reported that "contrary to the popular belief . . . most female bears did not display strong maternal protective instinct, and quickly abandoned cubs when danger was imminent."[4]

In the literature I've reviewed, I've only found two instances where a female black bear with cubs pursued a human up a tree. The first occurred when David Rust, an Idaho resident, was mapping a road near the Montana/Idaho border.[5] He encountered a female black bear with cubs. The mother bear attacked (element 1). Rust went up a tree about sixteen feet. The bear advanced to the tree, stood on her hind feet, and placed her paws on the tree trunk (element 2). The bear stared up at Rust. She then ascended the tree. After reaching only a few feet from Rust's boots, the bear stopped and retreated back down the tree, never making physical contact with Rust (element 3). She aborted element 4 (making physical contact with the human) for whatever reason, rejoined her cubs, and left the area.

The second instance occurred in 1955 in Yellowstone National Park.[6] A female black bear with cubs pulled a young teenager, Delamar Normington, out of a tree. The youth and his fourteen-year-old friend were gathering firewood at Fishing Bridge Campground. All four elements of the attack/contact scenario were fulfilled, leaving young Normington's legs badly chewed and clawed. The bear was subsequently destroyed.

The latter scenario occurred in a national park at a campground. The author did not mention anything about the bear being habituated to human presence or food conditioning at a time when park regulations were much more relaxed compared to today.

When considering a female black bear with cubs attacking and pulling a human out of a tree in a *nonpark* setting, one ponders the odds of that happening. It is quite possible that the reported black bear attack at Cabin Creek in Montana's Bob Marshall Wilderness could be ranked as extraordinarily rare, if not the first ever reported outside a national park.

Black Bear or Grizzly: Size Counts

The second phase of my chunking down is to try to determine—based on size—whether the attacking bear was a black bear or a grizzly. The newspaper article contains very little information other than two references indicating "enormous bulk" and "estimated to weigh about 400 pounds." A quick check of the Montana Fish, Wildlife, and Parks website indicates that the average adult female black bear in Montana weighs between 120 and 180 pounds.

The bear attack occurred in the middle of July. This would be approximately eight to twelve weeks following normal den emerge, when female bears with cubs will awaken from their long winter's sleep. The demands on a mother bear's energy reserves to nurture three cubs would appreciably drain her body weight from spending six to seven months in a den, and with newborn cubs for about four of those months. The middle of July certainly would not be the time a healthy female black bear with cubs could be expected to be beyond the range of average weight.

Substantial weight gain normally would not occur until bears enter a phase of *hyperphagia*, during which they step up their food intake and gorge themselves on the fresh berry crop and other edibles starting around the middle or end of August. If they stay healthy, they bulk up in the fall of the year and are ready to enter hibernation, ideally with a full energy reserve.

If the attacking bear were a female black bear, it would likely be, according to the news article, two to three times the size of an average Montana female black bear. Again, one has to ponder the odds of that size of female black bear even existing. It is not beyond the realm of possibility, but it certainly would be a rarity.

Informants

The chunking down continues to a third phase, the informants. I wanted to know about the presence of both black bears and grizzlies in the area. I talked to four adults who were in charge of the youth or assisting with other details of the YCC camp and the immediate tasks of trail maintenance and fence building. Activities were headquartered at or near the Cabin Creek Guard Station and the associated tents were erected temporarily near the guard station (cabin) to house YCC youth.

Bernie Yednock was the YCC camp director. Bernie mentioned that he had seen several black bears in the area, many of which had cubs with them. Some bears were close to camp, but they did not have any problems and—as affirmed by one YCC youth interviewed—they maintained a clean camp to discourage bears.

Gene Sentz also recalls black bears in the area. He was at the Cabin Creek cabin when the bear attack occurred about a quarter to half mile away. Gene was getting gear "mantied-up" for the horse trip out the next morning.

Sharon White was the camp cook. She rode her horse into Cabin Creek from Benchmark (approximately twenty miles to the south). She recalls seeing lots of black bears with cubs. She reported, "It was a cub year."

Bruce Bourne was on his fourth summer in that area. He had made the trip many times from the Gibson Reservoir trailhead to Cabin Creek. He said he would occasionally see a grizzly on the ridges to the east after leaving Klick Ranch (approximately six miles south of Cabin Creek).

I was also interested to know what education or training adults and youth received. In a formal, structured sense, there really wasn't any. However, adult leaders stressed the importance of everyone being part of a group, not hiking alone, making noise, wearing bear bells, and keeping the camp clean. These were commonsense approaches and no less an emphasis with today's National Outdoor Leadership School, which touts only one bear attack after forty years and 10,000 youth. Their emphasis: "To minimize risk, group size in brown bear country is generally four persons."[7]

Five of the YCC youth informants were interviewed. Their responses are woven throughout the chapter, with specific recognition to three of the youth of 1974.

Definite Bear Country

The YCC camp at Cabin Creek was definitely in black bear and grizzly country. In fact, in 1992, a couple of grizzly bear incidents at Cabin Creek and the surrounding area led to boilerplate food storage regulations throughout the Northern Continental Divide Ecosystem that apply to this day.[8]

In July 1992, there were reports of problem grizzlies raiding camps in the Cabin Creek and Pretty Prairie areas. Seth Diamond, Forest Service wildlife biologist, said: "This is a very unusual and strange experience that we have not had with grizzly bears on the Rocky Mountain Front until now."[9] Anna Beug, a summer volunteer from Ireland, was staying at the Cabin Creek Guard Station when she was visited twice in one day by three grizzlies.[10]

In August 1992, two women were camped in a tent at Indian Point camp, some twenty miles southwest of Cabin Creek. Mary Van Gilder and her daughter Samsara Chapman were awoken that August morning by three grizzly bears,[11] apparently the same female grizzly and two cubs that had harassed Beug a couple weeks prior.

No human injuries occurred from the incidences. Wildlife officials implemented area closures and eventually euthanized the female grizzly.

Legend and Fact Intermingled

Further query of informants resulted in discovering that nobody was specifically trained in bear identification or in what to do if approached or attacked by an aggressive bear. When considering the time period, there wasn't much training of any kind in 1974. Bear spray was not yet available. A lot of people's reactions to bear attacks were grounded in long-held folklore. As one wildlife official in 1955 described: "Legend and fact are inseparably intermingled in the history of this great bear."[12] It was not surprising to learn that when a person was treed by a bear, that very act was one identifier that distinguished a black bear from a grizzly bear. This was based on the long-held supposition that grizzlies do not climb trees. In fact, the notion is so deeply ingrained that one of the pioneer outfitters in the Bob Marshall Wilderness, Howard Copenhaver, bluntly stated, "A grizzly can't follow a man up a tree."[13] Copenhaver, along with his family and clients, either hunted or had killed both black bears and grizzly bears for sixty years.

Another Bob Marshall Wilderness packer and guide, Bob Wilkerson, had a rather convincing episode with a female grizzly with two cubs in 1959. After being chased up a tree, Wilkerson figured he had the grizzly "licked." He thought to himself, "Grizzlies can't climb trees." Then the bear started up the trunk and pulled Wilkerson from the fifteen-foot tree by the ankle. Without further injury the bear departed."[14]

Critical Analysis

Considering secondhand accounts, interesting comparisons, and traditional knowledge about bears and bear attacks, it would be nice to have a clean and clear wrap-up to the Russell Fox bear attack investigation. I return to Kurt Pipinich's accounting of the bear attack. You see, Kurt Pipinich's story is not secondhand. He was an eye-witness to the bear attacking Russell Fox. He too climbed a tree, and watched everything. The account is compelling, and it comes reinforced by some astute observations and critical thinking by one of the other YCC youth, sixteen-year-old Jeff Curtis.

Kurt Pipinich was one of the older members of the YCC group. The eldest of five siblings, Pipinich learned responsibility early on. He was accustomed to manual labor as a young teenager growing up in Great Falls. He was quiet and responsible. He was well over six feet tall, and his athleticism gained him respect. He enjoyed weekends and summers hiking, hunting, and fishing at the family cabin on the Smith River outside of Great Falls. Having had such experiences at an early age, it seemed suitable that he was designated as YCC's "Youth Leader."[15] The exact number of boys in the youth group is not known, but informants indicate somewhere between fourteen and twenty-one members.

When I interviewed Curtis in 2013, he recalled details with extraordinary keenness. He verified much of the Pipinich rendition. Curtis saw things in a different light than other youth informants and with a different memory. Curtis credited one of his adult leaders, Gene Sentz, with instilling a desire to "get one of my degrees in botany." Teenager Jeff Curtis enjoyed working for the YCC and learned a lot from his experience in the wilderness and from his association with the adult leaders.

The first telephone interview with Curtis went well. I followed up with an e-mail and, at his request, attached a copy of the newspaper article. He hadn't seen the article since he was sixteen. I wasn't expecting a response from him but received an e-mail soon after. Furthermore, I wasn't expecting what I read. His first sentence grabbed me. "I had forgotten how bad the article was and would like to comment further," he wrote. He attached a photo of a topographic map with notations inscribed on it. He noted the "Fox route," the "Evacuation Route," the "Swimming Hole," and the "Attack."

The second telephone interview was revealing. Curtis was not an eyewitness to the attack, but following the attack he walked to the site where Fox was pulled from the tree. He was pretty sure he was at the right spot. He could see where tree branches had been broken off quite a distance up the tree. The attack site was at the base of a steep embankment, exactly as Pipinich described. There were a couple of things Curtis thought were a little curious. In one segment of the reported attack, Fox used his knife to help him scramble up the tree. According to Pipinich—who was also up a tree—Fox didn't use his knife at all. The knife remained in its sheath.

Curtis found it a little questionable that Fox ran so far (200 yards, according to the article) after being pulled from the tree and was then attacked a second time. The Pipinich account differs from the newspaper article on this point as well. The bear pulled Fox from the tree. They both tumbled to the ground, with the bear landing on her back, and Fox on top of the bear. The bear fell hard and emitted an "Oof!" The bear was stunned and motionless for only an instant. Fox appeared to be unconscious. In one motion, the bear rolled over and Fox was on the ground, bloody and looking lifeless. Pipinich speculates that because Fox was motionless, it probably saved his life. There was no further punishment by the bear.

Another YCC youth, Gary Larson, was also in the attack area. He did not witness Fox being treed, but he recalls watching the brown-colored bears retreating in the distance. He further stated that Fox did not run from the attack site. Several individuals helped move Fox back to the cabin from where the attack occurred.

The three cubs remained on the thirty-foot ridge as the female bear barreled off. The cubs were not in the tree as Fox reported. The angry bear ran down the trail toward Pipinich—who was prayerfully hugging the top of the tree—and then retreated to her cubs. As she passed under his tree, Pipinich reported later, "she was huge!" She and her cubs ran until out of sight.

The newspaper article noted that Fox estimated the "entire episode took only five to seven minutes." According to the Pipinich report, "It lasted about twenty seconds."

At the conclusion of my interview, I asked Curtis one last question: "In our first interview, you indicated you always had the understanding the attacking bear was a grizzly. Is that correct?" He confidently replied, "Right." Again, Curtis' reply is consistent with the Pipinich account, which describes the bear as being much bigger than any black bear Pipinich had ever seen. She was different. She had a hump and was cinnamon colored with silver-tipped hair. The cubs were silvery and light in color. In all his years of recounting the story, Pipinich always spoke in terms of its being a female grizzly bear.

Since 1974, the recreating public has become far better educated about bears, bear biology, bear management, bear recognition, and bear attacks. The notion that grizzlies do not climb trees is antiquated. As Herrero points out, black bears are better adapted to climbing trees but grizzlies are just as capable. When reviewing the Pipinich account of the bear attack, one can pick up on the most subtle of assertions. Pipinich agreed: bears don't climb trees—they leap up them! He further stated that when the bear was pulling on Fox, he likened it to a dog playing tug-of-war. In the book *Bear Attacks: The Deadly Truth*, James Gary Shelton devotes an entire chapter to grizzlies climbing trees to attack humans. He describes the *leaping* technique in his conclusion to the chapter: "Many adult grizzlies can climb trees by lunging up a lower limbless trunk, by climbing on strong limbs, or by hugging the tree."[16] Additionally, regarding the tug-of-war analogy, Shelton states this about one Wade Sjodin, who was treed by a grizzly in 1994: the grizzly *lunged* forty feet up the tree in less than four seconds! Shelton continues: "The bear's teeth locked into the boot heel, the front paws were released, and the bear was now using its whole body weight in a jerking motion to dislodge its next victim."[17]

Illustrative movie clips of grizzlies climbing trees have advanced to easy-to-find Internet sites. A quick YouTube search will reveal several videos of grizzlies climbing trees. A Google search will result in photographs of grizzlies in trees. My favorite is a series of pictures of an adult grizzly climbing an apple tree just outside Yellowstone National Park. The photographer is none other than Kerry A. Gunther, bear management biologist for Yellowstone National Park.[18]

The Fox Hunt

The Fox attack story is intriguing. At the outset, I referred to it as a *cold case*. But unlike the television shows, there is no villain nor culprit, nor hero. I personally am satisfied with the cooperation of all those who allowed me to interview them. They dug deep into their memory banks after thirty-nine years and helped affirm or reject rudiments of the bear attack scenario. To conclude, I was particularly pleased to speak with *Great Falls Tribune* writer Wayne Arnst. When I first read the article, I thought there might be some ambiguity in the physical description of the bear. But Wayne clarified it for me. What emerged from his interview of Russell Fox—which occurred in the Fox residence in 1974—is that the attacking bear was indeed a black bear.

I have spent many years hiking in grizzly country. I have been to all the areas mentioned in this chapter from Benchmark to Cabin Creek and beyond. I cranked out a doctoral dissertation dealing with ranchers on the perimeter of the Northern Continental Divide Ecosystem and their tolerance—or intolerance—for grizzly bears. I've read extensively about the Front and bears. When I examine the responses of informants to the Fox bear attack story . . . when I read the numerous bear attack stories written in the past thirty-nine years . . . when I examine various attack scenarios in the professional literature . . . when I read the Pipinich eyewitness account . . . when I hear YCC camp director Bernie Yednock state, "I don't know for sure that it wasn't a grizzly" . . . I can only conclude that the bear that attacked Russell Fox was not a black bear. It was a female grizzly bear protecting her cubs. In fact, as qualified or unqualified as my assertions may be, I would say that the scenario of a female bear with cubs attacking a human and pulling that human from a tree in a *nonpark* setting is far more indicative of the actions of a grizzly than a black bear.

Lastly, the burning question in the entire investigation is, "What does Russell Fox have to say about the newspaper article thirty-nine years down the road?" This chapter wraps up with a disclosure of the results of that challenging and illusive *Fox hunt.* After utilizing the more easily accessible public records, Fox essentially falls off that proverbial radar screen about four years after the 1974 bear attack incident. The Great Falls city directory provided scant but crucial information about his parents. That helped. An Internet search revealed that his father, Richard Fox, passed away in 1999. The obituary provided general, but more current, contact information, along with the names of relatives.

I telephoned Russell Fox's stepmother and mother. Both responded they had not heard from Russell in years but thought he might be in Nevada. At least that helped tighten the focus area, and my Internet search continued once again. I located a phone number common to a Russell Fox and two women, perhaps his wife and stepdaughter. I called the number twice and left a message each time.

Days later, a woman called, identifying herself as Russell Fox's daughter. Her words were slow and minced with hesitancies; the message, surprisingly brief. She affirmed her father was the one attacked by a bear at the YCC camp in 1974. She said he had told the story to his grandchildren many times. It became readily apparent Mr. Fox did not want to talk to me directly, for whatever reason. After having such marvelous cooperation from all informants, his response was dispiriting to say the least. Regarding the bear attack, the only message her father had for me was, "The details are in the article." I encouraged her to ask her father to call me. She assured me she would. I have yet to hear from Russell Fox.

In Memory

Of all the interviews conducted and all the names gathered of the YCC youth who were at Cabin Creek in the summer of 1974, I am aware of two who have since passed on.

Kurt Pipinich, owner/operator of Montana Sheet Metal for twenty-five years, passed away from cancer in 2009 in Helena, Montana.

Mike Cory, Great Falls High School All-American and educator, died of a heart attack in 1998. He lived in Neihart, Montana.

---

1 John Vollertsen, "Political Activism and Sacred Land Issues Involving the Blackfeet Traditional Religion" (master's professional paper, Montana State University, 1992); John A. Vollertsen, "Using Multiple Regression Analysis to Associate Education Levels and Financial Compensation with Livestock Producers' Tolerance for Grizzly Bears in the Northern Continental Divide Ecosystem" (Ed.D. diss., Montana State University, 2005).

[2] Stephen Herrero, *Bear Attacks: Their Causes and Avoidance* (Guilford, CT: Lyons, 2002).

[3] Herrero, B*ear Attacks: Their Causes and Avoidance*, 86–87.

[4] Albert W. Erickson, John Nellor, and George A. Petrides, "The Black Bear in Michigan," Research Bulletin No. 4, Michigan State University, Agriculture Experimental Station, East Lansing, Michigan, 1964. In Herrero, *Bear Attacks: Their Causes and Avoidance*, 86.

[5] Michael Lapinski, *True Stories of Bear Attacks: Who Survived and Why* (Portland, OR: West Winds, 2004).

[6] Bob Murphy, *Bears I Have Known* (Helena, MT: Riverbend, 2006).

[7] Craig Medred, "Alaska Bear Attack: NOLS Kids Did a 'Phenomenal Job,'" *Alaska Dispatch*, July 26, 2011.

[8] Wendy Clark, U.S. Forest Service, e-mail message to author, January 9, 2013.

[9] Mark Downey, "CLOSED! Grizzlies Trap Irish Volunteer," *Great Falls Tribune*, July 21, 1992.

[10] Mark Downey, "Irish Volunteer Thrilled by Brush with Grizzly Trio," *Great Falls Tribune*, July 22, 1992.

[11] Marie Hoeffner, "The Bear Raid," *Helena Independent Record*, August 22, 1992.

[12] Robert F. Cooney, "The Grizzly Bear: An Endangered Species" (November 14, 1955), in *Grizzly-General 1955–1972* microfiche (1955), 1. Available at Montana Fish, Wildlife, and Parks, Helena, MT.

[13] Howard Copenhaver, *They Left Their Tracks: Recollection of 60 Years as a Bob Marshall Wilderness Outfitter* (Stevensville, MT: Stoneydale, 1990), 186.

[14] "Grizzlies Can't Climb Trees? State Man Tells of His Battle With Bear," *Montana Standard*, October 12, 1959.

[15] "Youth Conservation Corps Accomplishes Many Projects in Teton Forest District," *Choteau (MT) Acantha*, August 15, 1974.

[16] James Gary Shelton, *Bear Attacks: The Deadly Truth* (Hagensborg, British Columbia: Pogany Productions, 1998), 92.

[17] Shelton, Bear Attacks: *The Deadly Truth*, 98.

[18] James C. Halfpenny and Michael H. Francis, *Yellowstone Bears in the Wild* (Helena, MT: Riverbend, 2007), 52.

Chapter 12

LIONS IN THE SUN

Jim Williams

Montana's Rocky Mountain Front and wind are one and the same. Buffeting wind gusts off the mountains are common. Everyone who lives and works on the Front expects wind. Surprise gusts, however, while flying at an altitude of 7,000 feet in a Piper Supercub are cause for concern.

As we listened to faint electronic beeps in the headsets and bounced up and down over the parallel limestone reefs west of Augusta, retired Air Force fighter pilot Jim Lowe pointed out, "That isn't my flying making these air bumps."

Jim has over 14,000 hours of flying experience and is a skilled mountain pilot.

"Can you get me closer?" I said, realizing that it was pretty bumpy this morning.

"I will try. Just hang on," Jim said.

In a matter of moments, we were circling down below the upper ridge of Sawtooth Mountain and drifting toward the rocky face. Jim throttled back, and we were almost gliding. All of a sudden, they appeared on a precipitous ledge, all four of them. "There they are!" my pilot shouted over the headsets as we flew by the cats.

Mountain lion families stay together for up to two years, and this family was made up of an adult female and three subadults. The lions were lying on a narrow ledge below the summit of Sawtooth Mountain, flicking their tails nervously as we passed over them.

Montana State University

Finding and studying mountain lions in remote wilderness country was part of an intensive mountain lion research project by Montana Fish, Wildlife, and Parks (MFWP) that took place in the Sun River area of Montana's Rocky Mountain Front twenty years ago. I was a Montana State University–Bozeman MSU graduate student. I studied under the esteemed Dr. Harold Picton of Sun River elk fame.

Being a graduate student in the fish and wildlife management program at MSU was a dream come true. I was surrounded by talented graduate students studying everything from migratory white-tailed deer and grizzly bears to native prairie fish. I couldn't believe that I was now among them as a peer.

Bozeman is almost a mile high and surrounded by high peaks that beckon climbers, skiers, and hunters. On top of it all, the professors would join the graduate students every Friday at the Haufbrau pub for libation and discussion. Of course, they would typically depart after the first round, but the rest of us grad students would often engage in fish and wildlife philosophy late into the night.

I will never forget when Dr. Picton first drove me from Bozeman to Augusta to show me the study area and to meet John McCarthy, the local MFWP wildlife biologist. John and his wife, Nora, had mentored many graduate students in the field over the past twenty years.

When we were heading north and crossed Highway 200 in the foothills near the Dearborn River, the landscape opened up with an incredible view of the abrupt ending of the prairie at the base of these giant limestone cliffs. I was immediately both mesmerized and a bit nervous. At that point, I realized that this was not going to be easy.

John McCarthy had spent most of his professional MFWP career working in the Sun River area and would become a mentor and friend. A state wildlife biologist position like the one John held represented the Holy Grail as a career choice for a Montana wildlife graduate student.

John also had been a graduate student at MSU a generation prior to my arrival. After a good lunch inside John's Augusta home, I nervously watched as he discreetly nodded his approval to Dr. Picton. I was in. Furthermore, I didn't realize it then, but I would enjoy many gourmet meals around that kitchen table in Augusta while talking about lions and life.

Houndsmen

For the next three years, John and I, and our two houndsmen, Rocky Heckman and Kelly Hirsch, were all over the East Front chasing and living with mountain lions. Houndsmen—or hound handlers—are a hardy lot. They are extremely proficient at woodcraft and mountain survival. Most of all, they love their hounds.

Training and feeding these canines is a year-round affair. Rocky always said, "Following hounds can take you to places you would never normally see in the mountains." Once you turn them loose on a lion track, you are committed for an hour, a day, or sometimes even longer.

Mountain lions evoke a wide range of emotions in those who enjoy Montana's wildlife and wild places. Some people revel in the knowledge that mountain lions still stalk our wild reaches, while others view them as a threat to livestock and human safety.[1] Others relish the opportunity to chase them with well-trained hounds and harvest these seldom-seen big game animals.

Regardless of the confusing welter of beliefs and emotions surrounding these large predators, one undisputable fact remains: their populations are secure, and hunter-funded conservation efforts have helped the mountain lion on both the Rocky Mountain Front and throughout their range in Montana.

What's in a Lion?

Mountain lions are powerful animals in relation to their weights.[2] Large masses of muscle in the shoulders and the hind quarters enable mountain lions to attack their prey explosively and maintain tight grips with their retractable front claws. The claws have evolved so that the harder a prey animal struggles the more firmly they grip. I watched this story unfold many times as evidenced by tracks in the snow. The massive jawbone has no backward or forward motion, enabling the lion to absorb the shock when it attacks its prey. The teeth of a lion, complete with shearing carnassials, are well suited to the slashing and tearing of meat.

The rear limbs of a lion are longer than the forelimbs. This, along with a long tail that may function for balance, is probably an adaptation for jumping and for occupying topographically rugged habitats. I was going to soon find out how rugged their mountain home was.

Lions in Montana History

Mountain lions had little protection in the past. Prior to 1971, when the Montana legislature classified the mountain lion as a big game animal, its status was that of a predator.[3] From 1879 through 1962, Montana paid a bounty on each lion killed. The bounty was lifted in 1962, and the mountain lion remained unprotected until 1971 when it was afforded big game animal status.

Cecil Garland, a lion hunter, wilderness advocate, and business owner from Lincoln, Montana, suggested that if mountain lions were given legal status as a game animal, they could be controlled by recreational hunters. This, Garland thought, would allow lion numbers to increase to where they were not in conflict with agriculture and humans.

Les Pengelley, wildlife extension specialist and professor at the University of Montana, took Garland's suggestion one step further. He evaluated it as a wildlife management tool, partnered with Eldon Smith at Montana State University, and began sharing this idea in university courses they instructed. This new concept developed a considerable following from mountain lion hunters and the general public. Bounties were terminated in 1962.

How to Catch a Cat

To study mountain lions, you must first learn how to find and catch them. This is not an easy proposition as they usually prowl around at dawn and dusk and are practically invisible to most people. My first experience with mountain lion hounds was afforded by international wild cat expert Dr. Maurice Hornocker's research effort in Yellowstone National Park. Dr. Picton sent me down to meet Kerry Murphy, now a noted mountain lion research biologist himself, who was leading the project.[4]

We arranged to meet near Chico Hot Springs and were going to then try to catch an old male lion and replace its radio collar. When Kerry got out of his truck with one small redbone hound, I was taken back. "She is one of the best," Kerry explained and off we went, straight up Emigrant Peak with radio tracking gear in hand and hound on leash. Steep country—I was to learn throughout my research project—was synonymous with Montana mountain lions.

Soon the signals from the big Tom lion were getting louder, which meant that we were getting very close. Kerry turned the little redbone loose and off she went, barking excitedly as she went. It was not more than ten minutes when the distant barking signaled that the lion was at bay or in a tree. Now we had to hurry, as big males sometimes come out of the tree and injure the dogs.

Sure enough, as we crested a ridge we saw a 180-pound mountain lion coming down a short Douglas fir toward the hound. He immediately stopped when he noticed Kerry and me running uphill toward him. I will never forget that first look into the eyes of a huge cat that weighed more than I did. The tranquilizer dart hit its mark, and it wasn't long before the big cat was under. Kerry and I then replaced the radio collar and made sure the cat was in good health. Given their secretive nature, it's always amazing to actually hold and observe these *ghosts of the mountains*.

Everything went as planned, and soon we were watching the male cat amble into the forest, sporting a new radio collar. All the while, we could see people soaking in the hot springs down below us at Chico. Little did I realize then how important good hounds and hound handlers would be to our cat research in the Sun River.

The Need for Research

Throughout Montana, conservation initiatives—as well as changes in prey abundance—have allowed mountain lions, grizzly bears, and wolves[5] to recover to population levels not seen in decades. Mountain lions are now found from the remote Yaak River Valley in northwestern Montana to the prairie breaks and mountains near Miles City, Montana.

Although populations are stable and exist at levels that can easily sustain hunting,[6] questions about their ecology and management remained. What were they eating? What was their impact on other big game animals, such as deer and elk? What habitats did they prefer? How many were there?

To answer such questions about such a secretive carnivore, we first enrolled the help of local Choteau area outfitter Rocky Heckman, owner of Montana Safaris, and his good friend and woodsman Kelly Hirsch of Bynum. Both were avid hunters and proficient hound handlers. Rocky outfitted Montana Safari trips for dudes from all over the country. He specialized in summer and fall horse pack trips into the remote Bob Marshall Wilderness. He also was quite charismatic and could spin a good yarn. That, along with his skill as a horseman and hunting guide, is the reason he is still in business today. We would have failed miserably without him.

Capture and Handling

In addition to their extensive skills, biologist John McCarthy had trained Rocky and Kelly to use the tranquilizer system and to safely handle the mountain lions. When I arrived for my first field season, Rocky and Kelly had already captured and radio-collared several cats.

When I first tried on the climbing spurs and other tree climbing safety equipment, it was awkward. What makes a lion capture different from other animals is that the researcher must climb the tree and lower the sedated animal safely to the ground once tranquilized. It wasn't long, however, until Rocky and Kelly showed me the ropes, and we were busy prowling the Rocky Mountain Front study area for fresh tracks, on foot, on snowmobiles, and by vehicle.

By capturing, radio-collaring, and tracking the large cats, we were provided a brief glimpse into their secretive world. In the end, we captured twenty-five mountain lions with no injuries or mortalities to the lions. That was not true, however, for the capture team.

During one capture event, we were changing the radio collar on an adult female that had climbed over thirty feet up a Douglas fir tree. After darting her, I thought that she was sedated and proceeded to climb up the large fir. About five feet below the branch where she was located, I paused to clip into my safety belt.

As I always did, I used a stick to gently nudge the cat to make sure she was tranquilized before I fixed a rope to the hind legs. Just as I approached her, she swung her head around and lunged at me with her front paws. Instinctively, I let go, and the only thing that saved me from a dangerous fall was the safety harness and belt. Her front paw made it as far as my thigh and ripped open my wool pants before she went under. Needless to say, we always used the safety harness in the future.

It's a Bighorn!

It's always exciting to locate a fresh lion track in the snow. It is the only way you know a lion has passed, and you are only afforded this hint during the snowy months of the year. One morning, just after a fresh snowstorm, Rocky and I were driving the known bighorn sheep, mule deer, and elk winter ranges when we noticed something odd.

There was a fresh snowy lump just to our right with tracks leading down to it and then back up onto Ford Creek Plateau. We quickly parked, and upon inspection, we observed a freshly killed bighorn sheep ewe that was buried in snow. There was no material to cache the bighorn, so the cat had covered her with snow at sunup.

The black and tan hounds were baying from their boxes, and in a couple of minutes we turned them loose and up the powdery slope they went. What we thought was going to be a quick chase ended up being an all-day affair that ended near the top of Cyanide Peak. It was worth it, however, as we now had a resident adult female radio-collared in the center of prime bighorn sheep habitat.

One-Eyed Male

One of the most interesting cats we captured was an old resident Sun River male. He frequented the Willow and Beaver Creek areas near the Sun River Wildlife Management Area (Sun River WMA) west of Augusta. His capture was not all that different, but his appearance was.

When I climbed up close in the Douglas fir, after he had released pungent urine that rained all over my hat from fear and from being tranquilized, I noticed his face looked different. When I was close enough, I realized that he had only one eye. This was incredible. For a stalk and ambush predator, he probably had no stereoscopic vision or depth of field.

We would learn later by following him through the winter that he compensated by hunting bighorn sheep in predictable rugged and vulnerable habitats. In fact, several of his kills were made in a bighorn migratory route that took the sheep through a narrow opening in a rocky limestone reef. He relied upon and specialized in sheep predation more than any other study animal.

Crooked Tails

Another memorable capture occurred at the end of our winter season when the snow had all but melted in the deep parallel valleys of the overthrust belt. Rocky and I were driving south out of the Benchmark Cabin area and were both quite sleepy as the warm sun shone through the windshield.

At about the same time, we looked up and saw an adult-sized mountain lion run in front of us across the gravel road. Who needs tracks? As if on cue, the hounds in the dog boxes in the back of the truck lit up with high-pitched bays. As Rocky quickly slowed the truck down to release the hounds from their boxes, I swung the door open and leaped from the truck as we slid to a stop.

The dogs flew off the bed and frantically ran directly toward where the cat had disappeared in the trees. Within five minutes, they had her up a tree. She was an adult female with a permanently kinked tail in the shape of the letter Z.

This lion was our last capture on the project, and she revealed something quite interesting. I could never find her again during my telemetry flights and wondered what had happened to her. A year later, some houndsmen treed her in Monture Creek. She was with kittens in the Blackfoot River Valley. She had successfully dispersed from the East Front and established a reproductive female home range across the Scapegoat Wilderness and in the famed Blackfoot River area.

What We Learned

So what did we learn about Sun River mountain lions?[7] First and foremost, we learned that mountain lions can teach us about local prey species and their behavior. On the East Front, virtually all of the mountain lions are closely tied to the resident and migratory herds of prey animals that inhabit this spectacular landscape.

Second, Montana's Rocky Mountain Front lions exhibited similar ecological traits as compared to other mountain populations that have been studied in Montana and throughout the West. There were some exceptions, however, and they were quite interesting.

Habitat Use

Habitat selection by mountain lions was very important to our team.[8] Throughout his tenure as the local biologist on the East Front, John McCarthy often wondered just what habitats were important to mountain lions. We tried to answer that question first. In order to do this, we needed many locations and that required regular aerial reconnaissance to locate the study animals in a vast wilderness landscape.

Then we had to hike or climb to the locations to quantify the habitat characteristics. Keep in mind that from 1989 to 1992 it was a presatellite tracking era. It was also pre-global positioning system (GPS) technology as well. Traditional VHS telemetry was the norm. However, due to high-wind periods—sometimes lasting weeks—we went for long periods between finding the mountain lions because we could not get the bush plane up in the air safely. It did not take long for us to figure out that living and walking with East Front mountain lions was going to be an excellent fitness program.

Our study area was bounded on the south by the Dearborn River and by the Teton River to the north. We followed mountain lions from the Scapegoat Plateau and Chinese Wall in the Bob Marshall Wilderness to the short-grass prairie near Augusta. The limestone reefs of the East Front run north and south and are a product of overthrust geology.

As a result, these reefs have very little soil and are quite rocky. This arid, windswept region is excellent mule deer and bighorn sheep winter range. Small, linear forested areas are limited to the valleys that lie between these parallel reefs and ridges.

Farther west, beyond the South and North Forks of the Sun River, lie the large river valleys and mountains of the Continental Divide. This interior area supports vast Douglas fir forests and spruce bottoms at higher elevations. Many deer, elk, and bighorn sheep herds summer in this interior landscape.

Back out on the Front, one habitat type that is unique to the east slopes is the limber pine wind forest or savannah. It was here that the forested landscape transitioned to prairie grasslands.

Limber Pine Savannah

We learned that the limber pine savannah provided the easternmost stalking cover for mountain lions as they searched for wintering migratory elk and mule deer on the Sun River WMA. Elk migrated to the Sun River WMA from as far as the Continental Divide. In fact, it was my graduate advisor, Dr. Harold Picton, who first documented this elk migration spectacle in the late 1950s.

Similar to elk, bighorn sheep also migrate similar distances to reach the windswept East Front. Based on past research, mule deer—especially bucks—can migrate to winter ranges on the East Front from as far as the Spotted Bear River and

Flathead River west of the divide. All three of these ungulate species were vulnerable to lion predation in forested habitats.

During daylight hours, as long as the 2,000 or more wintering elk stayed out on the prairie and away from the limber pine on the wildlife management area, they were relatively safe from mountain lion predation.

Mountain Lions in the Forest

Overall, Sun River mountain lions selected forested habitat types over all others.[9] It was clear to us that the ability to approach prey closely, using forested cover, was important for lions. Forested areas also provided habitat security for both solitary lions and family groups. This was more important than topographic diversity or rugged habitats.[10]

Mountain lions did, however, use forested habitats that were often close to rocky ledges and ridges. Given that most of our flights were during the morning hours, this data could have been partially biased. It is possible that mountain lions use the rocky habitats more at night, when relocations were difficult to nearly impossible to obtain.

One new factor on the landscape that we could not measure at the time is the impact of wolf predation on mountain lions and how that could potentially shift lion habitat use to more rugged habitat types that wolves have more difficulty traversing. Toni Ruth, a mountain lion expert working in Yellowstone National Park, actually documented this type of habitat shift impact from wolves.

Prairie Cats

We also documented mountain lion use of prairie habitats during our research. Up to three different lions were observed at various times out on the prairie and away from the mountains. These mountain lions used the cottonwood gallery forest and willow complexes along the prairie creeks and rivers as cover during daylight hours. They also preyed on white-tailed deer in these habitats.

Prairie stream complexes probably serve as secure movement areas for mountain lions along the East Front. In fact, the possibility exists that lions could use these linear river habitats as disposal corridors to reach the Little Belt and Highwood Mountains and even the Missouri Breaks far to the east, although we did not document this phenomena.

Kill Sites

Overall, mountain lion kill sites in this study were located in closed conifer, open conifer, and mixed aspen-conifer types more than any other habitats. Although kill sites were not predominately located in prairie grasslands near the limber pine wind forest, there were occasions where mountain lions attacked bighorn sheep in the grassland cover type and then dragged the carcass into nearby cover. Most deer and elk kills, however, were located in timbered areas. Lion kills were also located close to water and drainage bottoms, often near a trail or a road.

Caves, Skulls, Bones, and Pioneer Trail Cameras

Caves were also used by mountain lions in the Sun River. One particular adult female lion had a penchant for a large cave in Big George Gulch. I will never forget the first time I climbed up to the opening of the cave, at least thirty feet up a steep scree slope but still below the limestone reef, and peered into the large hole.

I had located this cat from the air and noticed the cave from the window of the plane as we circled to get her location from the beeping radio collar. I couldn't wait to hike in and explore what she was doing. So, as I climbed into the cave, the first thing I noticed was a graveyard of bones and skulls that carpeted the cave floor. I located deer and sheep skulls, small mammal parts, and lots of scat piles. It was a treasure trove of food habits information.

I gathered up all I could and brought it back to my field station in Augusta for identification. One day, noted field biologist and *National Geographic* writer Doug Chadwick came by on his way to survey harlequin ducks in the wilderness. He noticed all of the skulls and bones on a tarp that were neatly displayed for analysis. He jumped right in and was just as enthusiastic as I was when I told him where they came from.

Back in those days, there was no such thing as digital film, only print film. However, I was quite excited to have a pioneer trail camera system referred to as the "Manley Camera System." MFWP grizzly bear biologist Tim Manley was the first person to wed motion- and heat-sensing devices to trigger a remote photograph.

Tim used a military ammo box and a car battery coupled with an Olympus Infiniti camera that he had protected with a special cover. I proceeded to haul one of the heavy rigs into our study area to set in the female's cave. Once the system was set up, I could hardly wait to check the film.

Upon retrieval a week later, I noticed that all thirty-six photos had been snapped. Mark Walters, a good friend who was a pharmacist and was volunteering for me that day, helped me lug out the camera and car battery. I had developed a stomach illness, and Mark saved the day. We drove straight to the Choteau drugstore to get the film developed after we hiked the five miles back to the trailhead.

It was to take three days to receive the developed photographs, but I left the store full of anticipation and hoping for great pictures of this female mountain lion in the cave. You could have heard me groan all the way down to Augusta when I reviewed the photos. There were exactly thirty-six pictures of a pack rat running back and forth across the cave floor. The little devil used up the film in fifteen minutes.

What Lions Eat

Another aspect of mountain ecology that we investigated was food habits and prey selection. This was also accomplished by mountain flying followed by old-fashioned boot work. After locating the cats from the air during monthly aerial flights, we also hiked into the locations to attempt to find lion kills.

The Montana Rocky Mountain Front area is unique in that it contains all mammals historically present with the exception of bison. Large numbers and concentrations of resident and migratory elk, mule deer, white-tailed deer, and bighorn sheep are limited both climatically and topographically to certain migratory routes and winter ranges.

Selection of prey by Sun River mountain lions coincided with seasonal availability and vulnerability of prey populations, stalking cover present, and individual mountain lion reproductive status. Overall, Sun River mountain lions preyed on ungulate species in an approximate ratio to their availability on the landscape (see Table 1). This was our hypothesis going into the research, and in the end we validated this paradigm.

Deer

Members of the deer family were the most common prey item in our study, with deer species making up 41 percent of the kill sample. White-tailed deer were dominant in the kill sample during summer.

The summer-fall period represented a difficult foraging period for lions because elk, mule deer, and bighorn sheep were not concentrated on winter ranges. White-tailed deer, however, remained available to lions and were relatively concentrated during summer in drainage bottoms.

During winter-spring, both resident and migratory mule deer primarily occupied the moderately steep limber pine cover types interspersed with Douglas fir. This provided good stalking cover for mountain lions. Consequently, mule deer were concentrated and generally more vulnerable to lion predation during winter.

Interestingly, mule deer bucks were taken by mountain lions more than does and fawns. The solitary nature of mule deer bucks and their preference for rugged, forested habitat have been cited as behavioral factors that increase buck vulnerability to the stalk-ambush attack strategy of a mountain lion.

Rocky Mountain Elk

Elk were killed by mountain lions most often during winter and early spring. Elk cows were killed more frequently than bulls or calves. During winter in the Sun River area, elk used the limber pine forest and the open prairie grasslands. These migratory elk on the Sun River WMA often exceeded 2,000 in number.

It was immediately clear to our research team after one season of living with lions that where the Sun River elk herd winter range area overlapped limber pine and Douglas fir stands, lion kill sites were common. These edge habitats on the prairie represented a dangerous area for elk to linger for any period of time during winter because the stalking cover afforded to lions was perfect.

Table 1. Composition of Mountain Lion Diet Based on Kills Located and Scats Analyzed for the Sun River Study Area.

PREY	Kills (n=53) % of total	Scats (n=27) % of total
Elk	27	12
Mule Deer	18	29
White-Tailed Deer	16	15
Unclassified Deer	7	0
Bighorn Sheep	18	20
Snowshoe Hare	4	8
Porcupine	4	2
Ground Squirrel	0	8
Raccoon	2	0
Marmot	2	0
Pocket Gopher	0	2
Vole	0	2
Mountain Lion	4	0
Domestic Cat	0	2

Ever wonder why the elk on the game range can be observed resting in large numbers, often 1,000 or more, out on the open prairie grasslands? Elk are less vulnerable to lion predation if they are in large groups and out in the open.

Rocky Mountain Bighorn Sheep

Compared to other studies of food habits of mountain lions in the northwestern United States, bighorn sheep were preyed on extensively in this study. At the time, only one other study in British Columbia noted significant predation by lions on bighorn sheep.

Bighorns were killed by mountain lions almost exclusively during winter and early spring. Most kills were made by a short stalk-ambush near a forest grassland edge. Steep bunchgrass, rocky reefs, and old burns were commonly used by migratory bighorn sheep herds. Based on historical research, Sun River bighorn sheep avoid vulnerable timbered habitats if possible.

Both adult rams and ewes were killed by lions in this study, but ewes dominated the kill sample. Perhaps the traditionally large winter aggregations of female bighorn sheep provide a more dependable food resource for lions. Bighorn sheep were actually a seasonally important prey resource for Sun River mountain lions.

Small Mammals

Small mammals also were preyed on by East Front mountain lions. Most small mammal kills occurred in the summer-fall period and can represent a seasonally important alternative prey resource. Sun River mountain lions killed snowshoe hares, porcupine, and marmots. Small mammals were an important prey item for females with kittens due to increased metabolic demands and perhaps also the need for kitten predatory-play behavior.

Even domestic cats were taken where lion home ranges overlapped recreational cabin sites. I will never forget discovering domestic cat claws in a scat sample back in my lab at MSU. When I identified this lion later, it was found to frequent cabin sites near Gibson Dam.

Wilderness Lions

Another interesting result of our work was that there appeared to be one group of mountain lions that spent their lives solely within the western wilderness interior and another group that inhabited the area where the linear reefs met the open prairie. Although not documented by our work, interchange between these groups, particularly by females, probably occurs.

In almost all other mountain lion research efforts, it has been consistently documented that almost all of the males disperse long distances from their natal home ranges. We did have some male kittens that were born and raised on the southern Front near the Dearborn River disperse to the northern Front near Scoffin Butte and the town of Dupuyer. Dispersal is a life history strategy that ensures the genetic integrity of populations and provides source animals for population sinks.

Mountain Lions and Conflicts

Instead of using the WMA as anticipated, one female lion moved east onto the short-grass prairie, following Barr Creek to Willow Creek. We documented both deer and small mammals that she was able to take down in the willow riparian zone. Unfortunately, we received a call from the MFWP headquarters in Great Falls that a lion was frequenting a school farther out on the prairie in the small town of Augusta.

Using our telemetry receiver, we determined it was our female. After speaking with some teachers and students and learning that she was watching the kids from dense vegetation behind the day care, we decided to euthanize her. Her brief stint with freedom came to an abrupt end.

We released another young lion, which had been raised at the shelter in the Elk Creek area, into a large Douglas fir stand. This cat also immediately moved east out into the prairie and was eventually shot by archery hunters in self-defense a month later in a dense willow stand not far from Augusta.

The time a kitten spends with its mother and learns invaluable survival information cannot be replicated by humans. In addition, the association with humans and human scent and vocalizations in a rearing enclosure habituates these normally secretive cats to people. This level of habitation makes them a potentially dangerous large carnivore, and release into the wild is not recommended. Conflict-related relocations are not advised for mountain lions.

Back in the Bush Plane—All Adventures Eventually End

"Let's get away from this rock wall and back out on the Front," I said as we banked hard left and steered the plane away from the family of lions on Sawtooth Mountain. Almost immediately, we were drifting over foothills and then out over the limber pine forest. In just a brief moment, my receiver picked up another strong beep-beep-beep. "It's an adult male!" I said to Jim Lowe. "He's in the limber pine."

The noise of the plane startled a small band of elk, and they ran over the ridge, away from where we were circling over the male's radio collar signal. "I think we just messed up his ambush," he said over the sound of the plane's motor. "Don't worry, he has lots of choices in this country," I replied. Hopefully, that fact never changes and the area known as Montana's Rocky Mountain Front will always be referred to as Montana's Serengeti and will always be home to mountain lions.

In the end, we discovered that Sun River mountain lions were adaptable predators, as was revealed in both their habitat selection and their seasonal selection of prey species. Overall, mountain lions selected habitats with conifer cover. Wildlife managers in the northern Rocky Mountains should focus their mountain lion detection efforts in areas where seasonal ungulate herd ranges overlap with some form of vegetational cover, particularly with a conifer component.

As I sit here today, twenty years later and writing this chapter, I work in an office as an MFWP wildlife program manager west of the Rocky Mountain Front in Kalispell. After all these years, I have now finally paid off my graduate school loans.

Looking back at my time on the East Front, I realize that being a graduate student at MSU, studying under Dr. Harold Picton, being mentored by the McCarthys, and learning how to stay alive in the mountains with Rocky and Kelly was one of the grandest adventures of my career.

Working in that spectacular intact landscape was a privilege. Heck, if I had known how much I would learn and how much fun it was going to be, I would have paid twice what I did on those student loans.

JIM WILLIAMS earned a bachelor of science degree in marine biology from Florida State University in 1986 and a master of science degree in fish and wildlife management from Montana State University in 1992. Jim has been working for MFWP for twenty years. Jim is currently the wildlife program manager for MFWP in northwestern Montana. Jim studied mountain lion ecology for his master's degree on Montana's Rocky Mountain Front and Bob Marshall Wilderness Complex. As a field biologist for MFWP in central Montana, Jim managed big game populations, initiated wildlife habitat acquisitions, worked with private landowners, conducted aerial surveys of big game populations, and supervised a bighorn sheep and puma interaction doctorate project on Montana's Beartooth Wildlife Management Area. For the past thirteen years, in his role as a wildlife program manager, Jim has supervised a talented group of research and management biologists as well as programs ranging from grizzly bear research and management and big game survey and inventory to habitat conservation and acquisitions. Jim served as the president of the Montana-Patagonia Chapter of the Partners of the Americas. Jim has been traveling to Argentina to work with Patagonia wildlife biologists on puma conservation projects. Jim was also elected to serve as the vice president of the Wild Felid Research and Management Association.

---

1 Shawn J. Riley and D. J. Decker, "Wildlife Stakeholder Acceptance Capacity for Cougars in Montana," *Wildlife Society Bulletin* 28, no. 4 (2000): 931–39.

2 Maurice G. Hornocker and Sharon Negri, eds., *Cougar: Ecology and Conservation* (Chicago: University of Chicago Press, 2010).

3 Harold D. Picton and Terry N. Lonner, *Montana's Wildlife Legacy: Decimation to Restoration* (Bozeman, MT: Media Works, 2008).

4 Kerry M. Murphy, "The Ecology of the Cougar (Puma Concolor) in the Northern Yellowstone Ecosystem: Interactions with Prey, Bears, and Humans" (Ph.D. diss., University of Idaho-Moscow, 1998).

5 Toni K. Ruth, "Patterns of Resource Use among Cougars and Wolves in

Northwestern Montana and Southeastern British Columbia" (Ph.D. diss., University of Idaho-Moscow, 2004).

[6] Hugh S. Robinson and R. M. DeSimone, *The Garnet Range Mountain Lion Study: Characteristics of a Hunted Population in West-Central Montana*, final report (Helena: Montana Department of Fish, Wildlife and Parks, 2011).

[7] Jim Williams, "Ecology of Mountain Lions in the Sun River Area of Northern Montana" (master's thesis, Montana State University-Bozeman, 1992).

[8] Jim S. Williams, J. J. McCarthy, and H. D. Picton, "Cougar Habitat Use and Food Habits on the Montana Rocky Mountain Front," *Intermountain Journal of Science* 1 (1995): 16–28.

[9] R. Robinson et al., "Linking Resource Selection and Morality Modeling for Population Estimation of Mountain Lions in Montana" (manuscript submitted for publication).

[10] Jim Williams, "Ecology of Mountain Lions," 32.

Chapter 13

MOUNTAIN GOATS

Mike Thompson

A few years and several life stages before returning as a graduate student in 1978, the Rocky Mountain Front dawned in the windshield of my Torino GT and it was love at first sight. My sidekick, coincidentally nicknamed "The Goat," cranked up Ry Cooder on the tape deck in celebration. Another kid in a fur coat and a cowboy hat—I have a picture to prove it—rode in the backseat, and the three of us spent the next four days backpacking in the Ahorn Basin country, above Benchmark. An October snowstorm dumped a couple of feet on the old Ford while we were gone, but she plowed gamely, vole-like, through the virgin fluff until her clutch gave out, stranding us for an extra night. Next morning, we wallowed about five miles down to the Cobb Ranch and ventured onto the back porch. I still remember the warm light and the bustle of hospitality in their kitchen, and the long ride in the tow truck. With the deposit of my car at the service station, our economic stimulus to the town of Augusta, Montana, was complete and we hitchhiked, tails between our legs, back to Missoula. That these random events foretold my future was an omen that I missed by a mile, and I did not happen back to the Front before Dr. Harold Picton at Montana State University–Bozeman, awarded me the chance to study mountain goats for my masters.

The Rocky Mountain goat is uniquely suited to its perch atop the spine of the continent. An orphan of taxonomy, *Oreamnos americanus* is the only member of its genus—not even a true goat. From the Pleistocene, it evolved into one of a kind, native to precious little of North America, generally confined to the Coast Range and the Northern Rockies. Laypersons sometimes say "goat" when they mean "sheep," or vice-versa, but there is no comparison. Goats and bighorn sheep may share the high country in summer, but when winter comes, the ewes and curly horned rams retreat to the chinook-warmed bottoms, where families in four-wheel-drives take their pictures. Nobody photographs goats on the Front in winter, with their long, white, yellowing coats billowing defiantly in the gales atop the highest pinnacles. I learned to accept a distance between them and me, while ever scheming to close it.

If I would contribute nothing more to the welfare of mountain goats, it would be entertainment. On one cold day in June, I chased a hot tip up Headquarters Pass. Kicking toeholds into the snow-drifted escarpment seemed not too precarious on the way up, and I was rewarded at the top with what I proclaimed to be goat tracks, earning a line in my field notes. But it seemed a tedious thing to go back down a thousand feet by the same means, so I sat on the sled God gave me and set sail. Digging in with my heels and elbows gave the illusion of control, but my accelerating backpack—still on my back—fought valiantly for the lead. By good fortune did I survive my first life lesson in goat country.

Challenges to Finding Answers

I'm sure that the denizens of Headquarters Pass expected never to see me again, but I kept surviving my narrow escapes and showing up off and on. On one such occasion, I had determined to solve the mystery of their diets, for they are what they eat. Taking cover in the whitebark pine relics overlooking

Our Lake, I observed a dozen of my subjects grazing contentedly in the scree until the wind chill flushed me out. Wisely, I had memorized the precise locations of their bites before running the goats off their dinner, but even on my hands and knees, I found no physical evidence of any plant parts having been bitten. Undaunted, I set about collecting samples of the vegetation. Of course, I knew not one tiny plant from another, so I collected each different-looking one and placed it in its own baggie, carefully labeling each for me to key out later. First lesson on the Front—never set anything down. Soon the baggies took flight, like waxwings in a flock, and I gave chase until my bad knee popped. I let the wind carry off a few choice words with my baggies before regaining my feet, and like a child in the night at the top of the stairs, I caught a lone goat eavesdropping. And with a goat as my witness, I was embarrassed, but I would learn to get used to it.

The process of enumerating all 130 goats between Deep Creek and Birch Creek was—like most exploration—the process of documenting what the locals already knew. Gary Olson, the new Fish and Game biologist in Conrad, heard tell of an old livestock salting ground up the Blackleaf Canyon, where goats were said to lick. We settled on motorbikes for making the sneak. Miraculously, when the exhaust cleared, some twenty-six animals dotted the saddle between Mt. Frazier and Volcano Reef—billies, nannies, and their weeks-old kids. They were bedded in a pastoral arrangement unbefitting mountain goats, like domestics luxuriating in a Swiss meadow of white, purple, and yellow posies. The only things missing were bells around their necks. We were in the heart of it, quite likely the largest aggregation of mountain goats between Glacier National Park and the Dearborn River.

Thereafter commenced a summer-long procession from trailhead to salt lick and back again of contraptions and people hellbent to capture a mountain goat. The daily hikes were notable, though Mother Nature might have spared herself the rockwork scenery just for us, had she known that little Blackleaf Creek would seldom challenge its banks. *Banks* is a misleading term, implying soil, which was not much present. Picture instead the limestone ramparts of a narrow canyon, sculpted incrementally by freeze-and-thaw events in any and every little fissure of the facade, the debris of rock chips—talus—piled and ever piling along its sides and on the canyon floor. Blackleaf Creek simply wetted a ribbon in the bottom of it.

I remember what it sounded like to hike on the trails across the talus. Something close might be shards of window glass crunching underfoot in an old building, but in talus you have the resonate clinking of rock pieces sliding and tumbling back into your footfalls. Pocket change jingling might give you a sense of it, but you wouldn't make wind chimes from pennies. I might try making wind chimes from talus chips someday, but they might not be as musical without an echo chamber the size of the Blackleaf Canyon. And hang them a long way away from the Front, please—someplace where a gentle breeze might tickle the chips appreciatively. You don't see many wind chimes hung along the Front; someone downwind could get hurt.

The Department of Fish and Game supplied me with a pickup truck—an attractive brown Dodge—to support my studies in my first of two summers on the Front. It was a two-wheel-drive model, which to my mind was an implicit message that I should take a running start at high rpm to traverse the few mountain roads that afforded me access. Wear and tear ensued, but the first serious blow to the exterior fit and finish of the little brown Dodge was delivered by the wind—and let this be a lesson. One day a gust of wind tore the door from my grasp while I was carelessly exiting the vehicle and buckled it against the front quarter panel. For a few days it was necessary to tie the driver's side door shut, but over time it would close and latch with a well-delivered slam. Other nicks and scratches, too few to mention, accumulated over the summer, and I was able to drive the biggest piece back to the Fish and Game headquarters at Freezeout Lake Wildlife Management Area before heading back to college. No one was on hand to receive me on the day when I returned the truck, but I was later informed that its condition had disappointed. It was a mountain goat study—did they want me to start hiking from the pavement?

Wind, Wind, and More Wind

The wind along the Rocky Mountain Front is legendary. Sustained blasts of a hundred miles an hour may command for several days at a time; the wind once held me prisoner for eight days inside Henry Ostle's old ranch house—in the year before the Ostle Ranch became the Blackleaf Wildlife Management Area—listening to the windows rattle and watching my grandma's gift of a little Jeep CJ-5 bounce on its springs. I assured myself that an old building still standing on the Front was windproof or else it would not be still standing. Unlike earthquakes, hurricanes, or tornados, the wind on the Front does not allow one the comfort of denial—of assuming that the big one won't strike, this year or next. The wind always blows on the Front. It just blows harder on some days than others.

On the plus side, a good windstorm seemed to compromise the superior senses of North America's most elusive and magnificent wildlife. Does scent smell when traveling at a hundred miles an hour? Surely the roar of the wind overwhelms other sounds that normally would give warning. On the windiest days, I watched grizzly bears feeding out in the open where I never caught them otherwise, and I even saw one cuff the other as if the Teton River was the Mackenzie. The biggest ram I ever saw never saw me, halfway up Cave Mountain, while the wind battered the both of us. Some years later, my wife, Sharon, and I drove up on a mountain lion—caught red handed in the exposed, rubble riverbed of the Dearborn—and watched it pretend we didn't see it for a good five minutes before it escaped in a single bound. I'm not the least bit ashamed that some of my most lasting memories of wildlife were wind aided.

The Blackleaf Canyon delivers wind like a sledgehammer. It's not the strongest or most devastating wind on earth, I would say, though I'm not that well traveled. But the canyons on the Front are the only places where I've been hit with hammers of wind that almost hurt. Hiking upwind with a backpack is like playing football with a ponytail—it's just asking for trouble—and I usually removed the pack when navigating narrow trails on exposed ledges. But wearing a backpack can be fun on the return trip. One time, I dug the heels of my Converse sneakers into the talus, leaned back, and windsurfed across a wide spot in the Blackleaf Canyon, just so I would have this story to tell.

Goat Lick Site

The goats were spared my shenanigans in the lower canyon by the grace of distance, elevation, and obscurement. The Blackleaf salt lick was 6,320 feet above sea level, about 1,300 feet above the canyon floor, on a saddle beyond and behind the north canyon wall. More ominous loomed Mt. Frazier, at 8,315 feet, which overlooked the last mile of the two-mile hike to the lick. Oddly, it seemed that mountain goats had no particular interest in Mt. Frazier until they had a mind to lick. On such occasions, which occurred as often as not from June to September, the day could be lost if I or my compatriots were spied by sentinel goats. So we would abandon the exposed trail to the lick for the sheltered draw that drained from the saddle down into the canyon, the secret passage to our blind—a grove of about a dozen stunted Douglas fir. From thence would our day's vigil begin, punctuated by feeding bouts (ours) consisting mainly of canned tuna, Oreos, and Coke.

The lick itself was an oval of bare ground, measuring roughly twenty by thirty feet, if memory serves. A few random pedestals of soil with sedges on top lent microrelief to the larger hoof-scoured feature. The site had not been refreshed with salt blocks in several years, nor did I bump into any livestock in the area, but this did not deter the goats. They would paw and eat soil in the places where historic salt blocks dissolved, mining potholes up to a foot deep. The smell of goat was pervasive, not a little enhanced by the urine, droppings, and downy tufts of white hair stuck on branches or matted on the earth. Goat scent, as I recall it now, was not as rich and sweet as elk but was thicker than deer.

Eastward from the lick, and separated from it by the little draw that delivered a trickle of water occasionally, rose the backside of Volcano Reef. Its rise was gradual, boulder strewn, and scantily sheltered by the gnarled vestiges of limber pine, the works of a bonsai-or-die imperative in the face of the relentless gales. Its terminus was the sky, and beneath the sky the Great Plains, separated from Volcano Reef by little more than the width of a vertical escarpment. Only after conversing with Keith Aune one night over a hot beef san at the Log Cabin Café in Choteau did it occur to me that grizzly bears were responsible for the rocks flipped over on the backside of Volcano Reef, and that I should be a lot more respectful than ignorance had allowed me. Yet, in all the hours that I stared at Volcano Reef, I never caught a grizzly in the act.

Westward from the lick, and across a deep and wide ravine, arose Mt. Frazier. Unlike the backside of Volcano Reef, a structurally supportive and workmanlike slice of topography, Mt. Frazier was a star in its own right—solitary, independent, and inspiring; a destination worth admiring. One day in November, I climbed it by accident, having set out at first to assail its neighbor to the south, Mt. Werner. As I struck the pass between the two giants, a band of stampeding bighorn startled me. They belonged up on Werner, I knew, but when I spotted two grizzlies coming off its shoulder, I decided to heed the bighorns' advice. From a hastily acquired vantage point partway up Frazier, I watched through binoculars while first one bear, and then the other, would plop its butt on the snowfield and slide. It wasn't much of a ride. From a half mile off, it was hard to judge distance and velocity, but I'd say they were lucky if they broke ten feet and a couple of miles per hour. Pretty pedestrian compared with my butt slide off Headquarters Pass, but a photograph hanging in my office preserves the view of endless mountains, in shades of green-gray and white giving way to a metallic sky.

A shot of adrenaline surged through me whenever I noticed a goat appear on the northeastern face of Mt. Frazier, about a mile away from the lick—first base. Goats are incredibly patient, and it's not like they have a lot else to do. So, invariably, the first goat on Frazier would stare down at the lick for an extended period of time, its gaze seeming to pierce my thin cover. The minutes might turn into an hour before it made its next move down a well-worn trail and through a patch of timber to a high point a couple hundred feet below—second base. Other goats, if any, would fall in line behind. If all was well, they would not linger long before moving to the next point down the mountain—third base, the make-or-break.

Here's where they would dally, tease, and titillate, sometimes bedding down for added effect. If they turned upslope again, they were gone for the day. But, if the lead goat got that devil-may-care look in its eyes and took a first step down, then Katie bar the door, here they came! Sometimes they'd break into a trot and kick up their heels before disappearing into the deep ravine at the bottom.

That mile of distance and 2,000 feet in elevation had shrunk to 100 feet and eye level by the time the goats reappeared on the near side of the ravine. Upon positive identification of the lick, they would saunter the last few yards like a wide receiver scoring a breakaway touchdown. Excessive celebration would take place in the end zone. For all of the care invested in their hour(s)-long stalk down Mt. Frazier, the goats threw caution to the wind when their hooves hit pay dirt, as if the lick was a safety zone and all of their predators knew the rules.

Two goats on the lick were one too many. Mountain goats fiercely defend their personal space, and with nearly two square miles per goat, space was seldom at issue. Except on the lick. When you have as many as thirty-five goats on the lick at one time, you soon discover the pecking order, and it is not unlike that of humans. An adult female (nanny) with her month(s)-old kid at her side is *numero uno*. And the butt of every joke is the teenager—the yearling (ages 13 to 23 months). The purpose of the yearling was to serve as a beach ball on the lick, bouncing from one goat to the next until it invariably crowded a maternal nanny by mistake, which put an end to the hijinks with a vicious swipe of her black, dagger-shaped horns—fair warning 'til next time. The syncopated hoof beats on the percussion of compacted earth accompanied their bovid *River Dance,* and more than once the opening refrain was my first clue that the goats had snuck in under my radar.

Why Salt?

Why does a goat lick salt? My major professor, Dr. Picton, was expert on the subject and made it his project to inform me. In spring and summer, mountain goats seek and consume the most digestible plants and plant parts to fuel the demands of weight gain and, in the case of nannies, milk production. Contained within these succulent greens are elevated levels of potassium, which gives goats the runs, and the runs deplete elements that may be replenished at the lick. Do not think harshly of Dr. Picton if my memory of physiology differs from reality. He taught me well, but it was a long time ago.

A chip off the old block, I conducted an accidental experiment involving urination. Early in my career as a goat scientist, I made an overnight excursion to Teton Pass, on the Great Divide. I spent the first day scouring the top of Washboard Reef for goat sign before retreating down to camp. With nightfall came the stark realization that I was solo, and the easiest meal on the Front. But, I had not come to the mountains without skills and I set about applying them to the situation. A liter of Coke stoked my bladder, which I proceeded to empty in the construction of a scent fence at about a 100-foot radius around my tent. As everyone knows, a scent fence allows a grizzly to investigate your odor at a safe distance, without bothering your sleep.

No sooner had I crawled into my sleeping bag and turned off the flashlight than steps in the night became audible. Big steps. Heavy steps. Crunch, crunch, crunch. My mind raced through a rapid process of elimination and landed on *Ursus arctos horribilus* and I promptly undertook preparations. I sat up in my flimsy nylon tent, facing the door, and quietly fingered its zipper with one hand while I held my open jackknife at the ready in the other—I would exit the door in civilized fashion if the attack came from the rear, or cut my way out the back if it came through the front. And the steps came closer.

Then all turned quiet, the calm before the storm. As the seconds ticked, my heart threw a fit, until the spell was broken by a curious slurping sound, like a housecat drinking water. The longer I listened, the more relieved I became, and I worked up the nerve to shine my light to confirm my suspicion. It was a mule deer licking the salt from my scent fence, doubtless the victim of succulent-forage consumption. Cause for celebration, except I never got used to the crunch, crunch, crunch of footsteps on my scent fence, all night long.

Capture Is Timing

Green came to goat country well after the lawnmowers revved up in Choteau, and goat visits to the Blackleaf lick began shortly afterward. The first goat of spring bloomed white on the lick on June 9 in 1979, according to my notes, and the last addict departed on September 24. Adult males (billies) were the earliest arrivals in spring, perhaps stealing a brief window of social dominance while the nannies were stuck on the cliffs with their newborns. Thereafter, nursing nannies visited most often. In 1979, I saw 102 goats on the lick, including repeated observations of the same goats. Of these, 33 percent were adult nannies, 24 percent were kids, 26 percent were adult billies, 12 percent were two-year-olds, and 5 percent were much maligned yearlings—or perhaps a single yearling seen five times.

Where did these goats live when they weren't on the Blackleaf lick or loitering on Mt. Frazier? I needed to know, and the best way to find out was to catch some and put radio collars on them. I believe it was John McCarthy, the Fish and Game biologist in Augusta, who put me on to the very western technique of *goat roping*. He swore up and down that biologists had captured goats on the Olympic peninsula this way, and it involved setting a loop out on the lick and waiting for a goat to step in it, at which point he or I would yank our end of the rope from the cover of nearby bushes and pray that the roped goat would pull rather than push.

I had to admit that the lick seemed ideally suited for this form of goat roping, with its divots providing depth for the loop to cinch above the hoof. So we selected a suitably proportioned pothole and carefully laid a loop around its rim. Then we ran the rope to a low, scrubby pine close by, where I took a stand and waited. John positioned himself in thicker timber on the opposite side of the lick and served as scout. When the goats arrived, they appeared to me as little more than legs rushing in and out of my view, only a few feet away, from my tightly constrained and exposed vantage point. Unbeknownst to me, Mr. McCarthy, the scout, was gesturing to me as wildly as his cover would conceal, while he watched goat after goat step deep into our loop. "Pull the rope!" he screamed in every silent way he could think of, but to no avail, because I was too exposed to risk lifting my head toward him or toward the goats for a better view. Before long, one of the goats inadvertently kicked the loop off the top of its pothole, igniting waves of indecision and panic throughout my being. Reflexively, I gave the rope a yank, sending the loop skittering a short couple of feet across the dirt, like a cannon ball dropping meekly out the end of the barrel, like Wile E. Coyote waiting for the anvil to fall from the sky.

Unlike the Road Runner, mountain goats making their escape from our trap were not a study in adaptation. Rather, goats stampeding across the flat were embarrassing, their gait resembling that of caterpillars in fast-motion video. That McCarthy and I could not run them down on foot served more to highlight our own maladaptation than to inspire goat envy. The experience caused me to reflect on the power of salt hunger that would attract these fish so far out of water—so far from the cliffs—at greatly elevated risk to their well-being. And I had plenty of time for reflection after the dust settled since my workload did not yet include the tracking of a radio-collared mountain goat.

Perhaps the most exciting tool in Wile E. Coyote's toolbox was the *rocket net,* which was precisely what the term implies. The net was stout and large enough to cover the entire lick. The cannons and rockets (solid iron) made for a heavy, bulky load. How to make it arrive on the lick was a problem that John solved with the contribution of his eighteen-year-old steed, Irving. No small endeavor, John packed the whole shebang in a pliable canvas tarp, called a mantie. Iron and fabric had to be perfectly balanced in the mantie so that Irving could carry it and prevent it from shifting as he swayed seductively from side to side on the narrow trail up the Blackleaf Canyon. One stumble in the wrong spot would launch our apparatus, and perhaps Irving, catastrophically downward into space. John led Irving forward, and I followed behind to document the result.

Surely, the goat telegraph lit up as faraway sentinels relayed their translations of our exploits. Irving contentedly nipped the heads of elk thistle while we unrolled and untangled the net to its full extent atop the lick. Next, John showed me how to draw the net back to one edge of the lick, like stuffing a parachute, so that it would deploy without a hitch when fired. We tied iron projectiles to the leading edge of the net, which was now perched on the top of a tidy bundle, poised for launch. Then we inserted the half dozen projectiles into small cannons welded onto steel tee posts that we had driven at equal intervals along one side of the lick, the bundled net at their feet. Lastly, John loaded explosives into the butt of each cannon and wired them in series to a safe place where we could hide, observe, and fire.

Did I detect a swagger of disrespect the next time a band of goats, fresh off their victory in the goat roping event, danced on the lick? If so, it was soon quieted with the detonation of the powder-charged rockets. We ran through a sulphurous cloud to work our first catch under the net—an adult and a couple of two-year-olds, all billies, on July 14. Over the summer, we discharged the net on four occasions at eleven goats, capturing eight. Irving's toils were not in vain.

Mountain goats in hand were smaller than their coats and demeanor had intimated at a distance. We were not equipped to weigh our catch, but as we handled them they seemed to be more hair than not. The average weight of adults is about 130 pounds, according to the literature. We also learned that mountain goats play dead—at least we prayed that they were playing. It was a convenient trait—kind of like playing dead in a cougar attack—because it just made handling that much easier. In the case of multiple captures, it was possible to leave one goat unattended to work the next, and if the former roused, only a touch was required to subdue it again. When we were ready to release a goat, it was often necessary for us to point it in the right direction and go hide. The untethered animal would lie still for several minutes before raising its head tentatively, in peek-a-boo fashion, and then making a break for it if the coast was clear. I wondered which natural predator is fooled by goats that play dead.

Nomadic Routine

Radioed goats led me away from the cozy confines of the Blackleaf lick to their secret and secluded native haunts. To the south arose Mt. Werner, and—more particular to goat ecology—the head of Jones Creek. These two areas were the center of activity for about half of the sixty different goats that I attributed to the lick. To the north ran the South Fork of Dupuyer Creek, just short of Old Man of the Hills, where the rest of the Blackleaf goats lived between trips to the lick. Nary shall the two mingle, save for those weekly or biweekly rendezvous at the lick. Even then, seldom were both tribes present at the lick at the same time. "Here come the Joneses," one can imagine the Dupuyer bunch muttering as they made their hasty departure.

From the beginning, nomadism has been the way of life on the Front. Native peoples traveled the Old North Trail north and south in the shadow of the Front for thousands of miles for thousands of years. To stand on a relict thread of bare ground sent a shiver up my spine when Gary Olson pointed out the trail to me near the Antelope Butte one day. As the Front guides the traveler north and south like a fence, it passes the elk, the deer, the sheep, and the grizzly bear east and west through its notches and canyons, like gates, in the spring and the fall. Unlike the Midwest, or the East, where the land grows roots deep, the Front is a body in motion—a continent for its backyard.

I lived a largely solitary existence in my days on the Front, journeying to Choteau on Saturdays to buy groceries and use the laundromat, perhaps not unlike a goat to the lick. Gary and John were great about introducing me to people—it's just that people were few and far between. Nights alone on the Ostle Ranch were dark, a perfectly unspoiled palette for the moon and the stars, some incredible displays of lightning, the aurora borealis, and occasional meteor showers. Nights with the Rockies to my back made it seem as though the prairie were still home to the buffalo, and little else, for as far as my eye could see.

My routine was adjusted one night by an invitation to attend the warming of the Preiwerts' new house, down the road a piece. The wind and the grizzly bears usually kept the pilgrims at bay, so new home construction was a happening. The Preiwerts' house raising was the talk of Bynum, the closest burg only twenty miles down the washboard road, and I had the pleasure of monitoring its progress almost every day when I drove by, unless I headed out across the Newman Ranch instead. We all hoped the Preiwerts liked bears because they could hardly have picked a more grizzly-friendly location, hugging the tortured aspen forest in the Blackleaf swamp. Aesthetically, the house met with the highest approval—a two-story, farmhouse style, with an old, weathered appearance—and I was curious to visit. Yet, I would be the goat out of my element that night, and I was nervous when I closed my front door behind me and stepped outdoors.

I drew in a deep breath of the night air and cast about my surroundings between the rickety front porch and the far horizon. How many times had I done the same thing, but this would be the time I would always remember. From every corner, near and far, like spokes to the hub, headlights flickered on old country roads—from the houses hidden at the ends of dirt driveways where I never trespassed in my travels; from the places homesteaded by the hospitable people of this land who knew it like nobody else. On this one occasion there they were, and the sight of them humbled me every bit as much as the glimpse of hardpan called the Old North Trail—this migration more than the little goat migration that I studied—for I would be the yearling at the lick that night, even though no one treated me that way. It's just the way that respect comes out in a young person—awkwardly. To drive a set of headlights into that place and time was a milestone I still visit deep inside me.

Where Goats Sojourn

The Blackleaf lick was a window into the social lives of goats, but radios on goats opened their private lives for study in places where trails don't lead and people don't travel. The most efficient way to track radioed goats was by aircraft, and flying the Front is an incomparable experience. Goats bedded unconcerned on the side of Rocky Mountain, watching grizzlies dig a hundred yards away. Bighorn in flight across the top of Walling Reef, their hooves barely clipping a rock here and there. Dawn painted crimson on the Sawtooth Ridge. A sea of mountains for as far as the eye can see, in waves of limestone beaching on the Great Plains. On the rare calm day, when the air is solid, you can drive it like a highway to the very doorstep of a goat that you collared far away, and see in its eyes that you are bwana.

Generally, the longest rock reefs or the tallest individual peaks were not the places where goats made a living. Oh, the reefs were steep enough and rocky, but straight lines of rock grow a fairly limited variety of plants, and even if the reef runs straight for five miles or more, it's just more of the same limited variety. And with a few notable exceptions, the tallest peaks tend to be isolated from other goat rocks by deep valleys and forests, and goats on these habitat islands are sort of stuck. So goats chose the broad, concave headwalls of the drainages that cleave the reefs, where the plants on the south face vary from the plants on the east face and the north. Where there is always shade or always sun, a goat would shuffle a few steps from one side to the other. Where reefs connect in either direction to the next headwall, there was safe travel. The best goat habitat on the Front does not attract the eye of the human beholder—it is not named Ear Mountain or Old Man of the Hills or Castle Reef. Goat habitat is the head of Jones Creek or the head of the South Fork of Dupuyer Creek—places lacking the romantic monikers of man.

North beyond the influence of the Blackleaf lick lived another group of a dozen or so goats on Walling Reef. If ever you've stood on the back deck of the Wildlife Conservation Center on the Theodore Roosevelt Memorial Ranch, then you have admired Walling Reef, close-up. Walling Reef is an example of what might have happened had Mother Nature employed a wildlife biologist on her staff. To the casual observer, it looks like every other rock wall sprouting vertically from the plains. But near the top and out of sight, she carved a wet bench, perhaps a couple hundred yards wide and a mile or more long, where alpine meadows grow in rips and tears upon the rock, and from its back sprouts the rest of the reef upward. The bench drained gradually northward, allowing reasonably pedestrian trail access from Swift Dam and Birch Creek, albeit a long hike. At its southern terminus, the bench tumbled all at once into the North Fork of Dupuyer Creek. The bench made all the difference to the goats.

I chose the north access for my maiden voyage to Walling Reef and established a spike camp at the near end of the bench. On one occasion—when the wind didn't blow and when a cold rain descended in the heat of the summer—dense fog enveloped the Front like an iceberg. I guess I wouldn't know that it's silly to soak in a nylon tent for most of three days and try to spot goats in the fog if I hadn't tried it. And Walling Reef continued to pose a challenge, unmet.

Three days in search of a dozen goats was hard to justify in my time budget, especially when factoring in failure. Thus, I sought a more direct route to that little piece of goat paradise on Walling Reef. It appeared to present itself on the south end of the reef.

The International Harvester flatbed with which Fish and Game equipped me as punishment for the Dodge rested in a service station in Choteau off and on for most of the summer. So I forded the North Fork in my Jeep. At the road's end, I parked and hiked the lightly traveled trail up the creek to a likely looking departure point for ascending the rock fall. It was one step forward and two steps back in the talus until I began to recognize solid foot falls at frequent enough intervals to gain ground.

Bighorn scattered as I neared the top. Walling Reef was one of the only places in my study area where bighorn sheep and mountain goats closely intermingled. To my mind, this was another indication of its productivity—diverse habitat efficiently distributed. In fact the bench—perched high upon the east face of Walling Reef—seemed like something from another planet. The weathered skull of a billy with thirteen rings on its horns was a grim reminder that this might not be a place where a man would want to break a leg and wait for help. The bench was moist, supplied with a trickle of running water and a small pool or two, but rocky nonetheless. I have memory of its back wall weeping from time to time and of snow patches sheltered from the sun. Generally, it seemed a chilly place on a summer day. My mission was to watch goats eat, classify them by sex and age, and sample the vegetation on their feeding sites. But Walling Reef was a tough place to observe goats undisturbed from a distance. I kept bumping into them at close range, which kept bringing me back. Dark to dark on Walling Reef was a day once a month to look forward to.

The hike off the reef was the cherry on my sundae. While slipping downward in the rock debris was a disadvantage when climbing, it was a great enhancement in descent. A running motion at the top of the talus created a slow-paced talus avalanche, and I learned to ride its wave for the several hundred feet from bench to bottom. Talus surfing afforded the added benefit of creating quite a ruckus, which I hoped had flushed the bears from the thickets along the North Fork before I ran the dimly lit and darkening gauntlet to my Jeep.

I was away at college in the winter and spring, but I tried to stay in touch. I'm not saying that I invented the technique of counting goats in the winter, but mountain goats are white and snow is white. My pilot, Doug Getz, was inclined to mention that. But we discovered that goats leave tracks in the snow, and in the Bell helicopter we found a goat standing at the end of every trail. On a sunny day in March 1980, we searched every nook and cranny in the mountains from the North Fork of the Teton to Walling Reef and found fifty-four tracks with goats in them. Since then, some of us have come to believe that snow is a distinct advantage for counting goats from the air.

However, the goats were not entirely cooperative. If there was a notch in the rock, or a scrubby pine on the ledge, the animal would retreat backward from the hovering whirlybird until little more than a nose stuck out to be counted. They worked a snowdrift like DaVinci, sweeping their butts like the head of a bison bull. The snow would fly from side to side and over the top until they made an igloo to peek out of. If you wanted a look at the horns, to guess at billy or nanny, you had to look fast because Nature's snowblower did not tarry.

Golden eagles prey on mountain goats, and we fancied that we might look like an accessorized eagle to the goats. I could understand how backing into a crevice or under a tree would stifle an eagle attack, but it was harder to imagine how a soft snow igloo would repel their talons. Maybe eagles need high-definition images of their prey to prompt their stoops and strikes.

The Numbers

After tallying the numbers and multiplying by the ratios, I determined that it takes a lot of mountain goats to produce one single, surviving replacement. To be precise, the combined efforts of fifty-four goats were required to add a single two-year-old female to the breeding population in 1979. This left precious little room for a fatal misstep or senescence among the older nannies if the population were to be maintained. The good fortune of this insight has since served me well in my career as a wildlife biologist and manager. Hunters ask no more than to hunt where a harvestable surplus exists, and they trust Montana Fish, Wildlife and Parks to prevent them from hunting where their harvest might harm the population. In my career, we have borne in mind the need to account for at least fifty goats before we hunt them. Coincidentally, wildlife scientists in Canada have more rigorously arrived at a similar conclusion. In retrospect, my conscience can bear the sacrifice of one little brown Dodge.

I was working my way off a mountain one afternoon when the warm sun intoxicated me and I plopped down on the ground to drink more of it up. A black bear foraged by the creek far below, and the prairie spread before me for untold miles toward the Mississippi. I wondered if the summation of hours like these would produce a thesis, a degree, a career. I was older and more experienced at that moment than ever before, yet never had life been more a mystery to me. Such is adolescence. But sitting on that slope that day, the sun on my face, I spoke out loud that no matter whether I got a degree, no matter what next, no one could take this away from me—this time in my life.

Thirty-three years after, when I think back, and when I consider what the Front is to me in my life today, I realize that there are darned few of us, really—darned few, who know the Front like we do, who see what we see when they drive by on the way to Glacier Park. The Sun River Game Range is a storied place to me; the people who made their lives on the Front, my heroes. But our circle seems smaller than it did when I was young. It's a funny thing. I don't know that I would live there again, and I struggle with that when I visit these days.

I don't know what that means—it is almost as if forsaking a love, a loyalty. From a distance it seems that the Front still teaches me about life, about myself. How perfect the place that draws you in then lets you go. Like Mom and Dad, I guess.

And in this most elemental way, the Front forever hanged me.

My Gratitude

An old green-covered publication dated 1950 sits beside me on my cluttered desktop. My predecessors in goat science—Robert Casebeer, Merle Rognrud, and Stewart Brandborg—are its authors,[1] and my rambles and scrambles over the rocks in an eight-by-thirty-mile slice of the Front pale in comparison to their inspection of several times the area. In my thesis I wrote: "Their population estimate of 174 goats [in my study area] may be viewed with skepticism since it is based on a single survey by horseback."[2] I suppose. More likely their work is a benchmark of biological and cultural importance, and surely the effort and the people I have met—Merle and Stewart—are to be admired. After me came Gayle Joslin, whose work dwarfed mine as well.[3]

Right now we are cramped for office space and charged with emptying more boxes of old reports and files, and it frightens me to think that someday this historic trail from heritage to future might grow in and be forgotten.

MIKE THOMPSON came to Montana from upstate New York in 1974, prospecting for a career in wildlife management. He earned a bachelor of science degree in wildlife biology from the University of Montana-Missoula in 1976, and a master of science degree in fish and wildlife management from Montana State University-Bozeman in 1981. The mountain goats of the Rocky Mountain Front were the subjects of his master's thesis. He married Sharon Rose in October 1981, and they have shared careers with Montana Fish, Wildlife and Parks ever since. They are presently at home in Missoula.

---

[1] Robert L. Casebeer, Merle J. Rognrud, and Stewart Brandborg, The *Rocky Mountain Goat in Montana* (Helena: Montana Fish and Game Commission, 1950).

[2] Michael J. Thompson, "Mountain Goat Distribution, Population Characteristics and Habitat Use in the Sawtooth Range, Montana" (master's thesis, Montana State University-Bozeman, 1981), 60.

[3] Gayle Joslin, *Montana Mountain Goat Investigations, Rocky Mountain Front*, final report (Helena: Montana Department of Fish, Wildlife and Parks, August 1986).

Chapter 14

CONSERVATION ETHIC AND HUNTING

Jim Posewitz

When Stone Age hunters found their way into North America and dispersed across the continent, wildlife of the Rocky Mountain Front sustained them and drew them southward. Some paleontologists suggest that mammoths might have been as abundant as the buffalo, providing the fuel, the incentive, and the challenge for early North American hunters. Then, as now, rhythms of life cycled with the seasons. Periods of drought and times of plenty visited the people. Changes that played across their landscape were gradual, perhaps perceptible only in the tales storytellers told of distant generations. The constant was the thawing landscape's capacity to sustain the early hunters, with bits of evidence suggesting that the hunters, too, were among the instruments of change. In time, the Pleistocene extinctions would claim the mammoths, musk ox, and saber tooth. Still later, the Late Pleistocene pedestrians would in time yield to eighteenth-century pony-mounted buffalo hunters.

Evidence suggests that the Sun River and the canyon through which it enters the Great Plains have been a center of attention as the saga of the Rocky Mountain Front ran its course through history. An abundance of medicine wheels, tipi rings, petroglyphs, and other artifacts suggests that the more recent Native American hunters found sustenance where their predecessors may have dined on the wooly mammoth.

The European perception of what America was, and what it was to become, was not quite three decades old when Thomas Jefferson cut a deal with Napoleon and consummated the Louisiana Purchase from France in 1803. At the time, the acquisition doubled the land mass of our nation. The price included cancellation of debt and cash that totaled about $15 million. Thus, the Rocky Mountain Front, and a lot of other real estate, was added to our nation for about three cents an acre. Had the deal been made in 2011, it would have amounted to a bit less than forty-two cents an acre. The wildlife and the people being sustained by the hunt on that landscape were not consulted and took little immediate notice. Two years later, Captains Lewis and Clark passed to the east of the Rocky Mountain Front on their epic Voyage of Discovery. They were to report on what Jefferson had purchased.

Aboriginal Abundance

Upon entering what would become the state of Montana, Lewis and Clark noted in their journals the abundance of wildlife. On May 9, 1805, they had just passed the mouth of the Milk River as they moved up the Missouri River when they wrote: "The game is now in great quantities, particularly the elk and buffalo, which last is so gentle that the men are obliged to drive them out of the way with sticks and stones."[1]

On June 17, 1805, considerably closer to the Rocky Mountain Front, they addressed the Great Falls of the Missouri, noting:

> There are vast quantities of buffaloe feeding on the plains or watering in the river, which is also strewed

> with the floating carcasses and limbs of these animals. They go in large herds to water about the falls, and as all the passages to the river near that place are narrow and steep, the foremost are pressed into the river by the impatience of those behind. In this way we have seen ten or a dozen disappear over the falls in a few minutes. They afford excellent food for the wolves, bears, and birds of prey; and this circumstance may account for the reluctance of the bears to yield their dominion over the neighborhood.[2]

After wintering at Fort Clatsop at the mouth of the Columbia River, the journal notes:

> Many reasons had determined us to remain at fort Clatsop till the first of April . . . About the middle of March however, we become seriously alarmed for the want of food: The elk, our chief dependence, had . . . deserted their usual haunts in our neighborhood . . . were too poor to purchase other food from the Indians . . .[3]

As the explorers reentered Montana on their return trip, their journals continued to reflect the struggle they were having with keeping fed. On the 25th of June in 1806, they reunited with two hunters who had gone ahead and "who had killed nothing." Two days later, as they traveled from Hungry Creek toward Traveler's Rest in the Bitterroot, they noted: "As for ourselves, the whole stock of meat being gone, we distributed to each mess a pint of bear's oil, which, with boiled roots, made an agreeable dish."[4]

When the eastward-bound Captain Lewis crossed the Continental Divide and came down on the Rocky Mountain Front, he noted that they "now felt, by the luxury of our food, that we were approaching once more the plains of the Missouri, so rich in game" (July 8, 1806).[5]

A few days later, on July 11, 1806, their journals tell us:

> The buffalo are in such numbers, that on a moderate computation, there could not have been fewer than ten thousand within a circuit of two miles. At this season, they are bellowing in every direction, so as to form an almost continued roar, which at first alarmed our horses, who being from west of the mountains, are unused to the noise and appearance of these animals.[6]

The wildlife resource of the Rocky Mountain Front and the northern Great Plains was indeed awesome in its proportion. The animals took only casual notice of the Voyage of Discovery; however, an epic change was at hand. As recently as the mid-nineteenth century, the native people challenged one another over access to the abundance. In the 1850s, an estimated 5,000 Blackfeet battled a similar number of Crow warriors in the Sun River Valley, a contest in which the Blackfeet Nation prevailed. Time, however, was running out for the aboriginal hunters of the Rocky Mountain Front and the wild resources that had sustained them for thousands of years. As early as the 1870s, there were sizable elk populations reported in the Sun River drainage that were beginning to attract the attention of the buffalo shooters already looking for alternative hide sources.[7]

The Collapse

While the Blackfeet and Crow battled for hunting ground on a piece of what would soon be Montana Territory, the collapse of wildlife was well under way, particularly on the southern and central Great Plains. In his book *Last Stand*, author Michael Punke gives us a dramatic glimpse into the mind of one of the shooters engaged in the commercial slaughter of buffalo. He quotes Charles "Buffalo" Jones, who left of this dramatic image:

> Often while hunting these animals as a business, I fully realized the cruelty of slaying the poor creatures. Many times did I "swear off," and fully determine I would break my gun over a wagon-wheel when I arrived at camp . . . The next morning I would hear the guns of other hunters booming in all directions and

> would make up my mind that even if I did not kill any more, the buffalo would soon all be slain just the same.[8]

Through the rest of the nineteenth century, Montana wildlife endured hard times. The *continual* roar of the buffalo herd that greeted Captain Lewis in July 1806 was rapidly fading into silence—it would be an absolute silence. Seventy years after Lewis and Clark, the commercial slaughter of buffalo was unrestrained, and in 1876, 80,000 buffalo hides were shipped down the Missouri out of Fort Benton, Montana—it was the peak year. In eight years, the number would fall to zero.[9] Montana pioneer and statesman Granville Stuart left the following account of what was going on east of the Missouri River in the Judith Basin of central Montana during that same time period:

> It would be impossible to make persons not present on the Montana cattle ranges realize the rapid change that took place on those ranges in two years. In 1880 the country was practically uninhabited. One could travel for miles without seeing so much as a trapper's bivouac. Thousands of buffalo darkened the rolling plains. There were deer, antelope, elk, wolves, and coyotes on every hill and in every ravine and thicket. In the whole territory of Montana there were but two hundred and fifty thousand head of cattle, including dairy cattle and work oxen.
>
> In the fall of 1883 there was not one buffalo remaining on the range and the antelope, elk and deer were indeed scarce. In 1880 no one had heard tell of a cowboy in "this niche of the woods" and Charlie Russell had made no pictures of them; but in the fall of 1883 there were six hundred thousand head of cattle on the range. The cowboy, with leather chaps, wide hats, and gay handkerchiefs, clanking silver spurs, and skin fitting high heeled boots was no longer a novelty but had become an institution.[10]

The reason artist Charlie Russell had made no pictures of a cowboy yet was that he had just got off the train and was pretty busy being one of the cowboys. Russell found his way to Montana in 1880 as a sixteen-year-old lad in search of adventure and life in the West. Fate and fortune put this exceptional and talented lad in the Judith Basin during the exact time frame Granville Stuart used to describe the obliteration of that area's wildlife. The young, impressionable Russell witnessed the last stages of the wildlife slaughter, the open-range cattle industry that sought to replace it, and the collapse of the notion of easy exploitation that followed during the hard winter of 1886 to 1887. The young artistic genius lived through and within this dramatic transition right in the heart of Montana. Then he wrote: "The West is dead! You may lose a sweetheart, But you won't forget her."[11]

Across the western landscape, there are numerous stories of *the last buffalo* killed in a particular area during this dark period in American wildlife history. We were a nation absent a conservation ethic. Two such stories will be told—one, for the message it carries, and the other, for the transition in our relationship with wildlife that it represents.

The first story comes from Montana's Tongue River area and was part of a record of those times kept by Nannie Alderson:

> The summer after I came out Mr. Alderson killed the last buffalo ever seen in our part of Montana. A man staying with us was out fishing when he saw this lonesome old bull . . . above our house—the first live buffalo seen in many months. He came home and reported it, saying: "Walt, why don't you go get him?" And next morning Mr. Alderson did go get him.
>
> That afternoon he suggested that we take the spring wagon and go up to where the old bull had fallen. There he lay . . . —the last of many millions—with the bushes propping him up so that he looked quite lifelike. I had brought my scissors, and I snipped a sackfull of the coarse, curly hair from his mane to stuff a pillow with.

> I am afraid that the conservation of buffalo, or of any other wild game, simply never occurred to the westerner of those days.[12]

The ranchers and farmers who settled the West in the immediate wake of the commercial wildlife killers were pretty much as just described. There were, however, others who showed up on the western landscape with the simple hope of being able to sample the American West before this "sweetheart" of Charlie Russell's was laid to rest. One of them was a twenty-four-year-old New York state legislator.

In the summer of 1883, North Dakota had one of its last commercial slaughters of buffalo. About a month later, a young Theodore Roosevelt stepped off the train in Little Missouri, North Dakota, borrowed a rifle big enough to kill a buffalo, and engaged local resident Joe Ferris to help him find one. On the ninth day of hunting, having just crossed into Montana Territory, they prevailed. The young Roosevelt wrote to his wife, Alice, the following:

> On the ninth [day] it culminated . . . I crawled up to the edge, not thirty yards from the great, grim looking beast, and sent a shot from the heavy rifle into him just behind the shoulder, the ball going clean through his body. He dropped dead before going a hundred yards . . . With a thousand kisses for you, my own heart's darling I am ever your loving, Thee.[13]

The story of the same hunt as told by another author, Herman Hagedorn, does a better job of capturing the expectation and excitement that the idea of being a sport hunter on the American frontier generated in the young Mr. Roosevelt:

> Roosevelt, with all his intellectual maturity, was a good deal of a boy, and the Indian war-dance he executed around the prostrate buffalo left nothing in the way of delight unexpressed. Joe [Ferris] watched the performance open-mouthed . . . "I never saw any one so

> enthused in my life," he said in after days . . . Roosevelt, out of the gladness of his heart, then and there presented him with a hundred dollars; so there was another reason for Joe to be happy.[14]

The Montana landscape was screaming through an incredible transition in the early 1880s, and the Rocky Mountain Front, as well as the wild landscapes to the west, were all being swept along by the temper of those times. The transition from a wild natural landscape to one of domestic livestock and farming was the new reality. As it happened, the genius of Charley Russell's art and his photographic memory were recording three themes to remind us what the *sweetheart* he valued was like when he first met her. Those themes were the lifestyle of the Native American hunters, the life of the open-range cowboy, and the aboriginal abundance of wildlife. The lifestyles of the native hunters and open-range cowboys have in all likelihood passed beyond retrieval. For wildlife, however, there emerged another kind of story. At that time, almost all the species captured in Russell's art stared into the black abyss of oblivion; however, they were then rescued by a conservation ethic embraced by a handful of North American sportsmen—the recreational hunters.

The Wildlife Conservation Epiphany

It is hard to imagine Montana in the 1880s as the commercial slaughter of wildlife ran its fateful course. The record hide shipments down the Missouri from Fort Benton that peaked in 1876 were fading fast. The newly constructed railroads began hauling hides eastward. The straggling remnants of buffalo were falling to recreational hunters desperate to participate, while pioneer ranchers shot them just because they were there. The Rocky Mountain Front was not immune, and the constant roar of the buffalo mentioned by Captain Lewis fell hopelessly silent while other wildlife of the compromised wildland was in serious decline.

The spring of 1887 followed the worst winter on record to hammer the Great Plains. Roosevelt returned to assess his investment in livestock made during his Dakota years. He called it a "perfect smashup," and in assessing his losses he rode for three days without seeing a live steer.[15] Roosevelt's North Dakota years were coming to an end. It was time he had spent both ranching on the Little Missouri and probing the mountains of Wyoming, Montana, Idaho, and parts of Canada to pursue his passion as a hunter on a fading frontier. In addition to his livestock venture, Roosevelt spent considerable time writing articles about his hunting adventures. In that process, he clearly saw the need to stop the unrestrained killing and—perhaps more important—made the acquaintance of George Bird Grinnell. Editor-in-chief of the early sporting journal *Forest and Stream*, Grinnell was a vigorous advocate for the sporting code, a conservation ethic, and wildlife restoration.

The association of Theodore Roosevelt and George Bird Grinnell simply contained way too much vision and energy for something not to happen. One contemporary conservation writer summed it up as "a warm friendship and one of the most powerful coalitions in conservation history."[16] In December 1887, these two men hosted a dinner for a group of prominent patrician sportsmen in New York. The dinner turned out to be the first meeting of the Boone and Crockett Club, which became America's first national wildlife conservation organization.[17] Among the young organizational and education goals of the club were ending the commercial killing, promoting the sporting code, and protecting wild places. To this day, Grinnell is also recognized as a prominent figure in the establishment of Glacier National Park, the Rocky Mountain Front's northern ecological anchor. Conservation was beginning to take root in our nation. Hunters were bringing the ethic, and its impact on the Rocky Mountain Front wildlife would be profound.

Embedding the Conservation Ethic

One project of the early Boone and Crockett Club was to lobby through Congress an additional section in "An Act to Repeal Timber Culture Laws and other Purposes ..."[18] The 1891 act included a section giving presidents authority to designate unclaimed public land as national forest reserves to protect wildlife, timber supplies, and watersheds. At the time, the immediate threat was commercial development in and around Yellowstone National Park that included proposed railroads, resorts, and "cutting timber and 'improving' the attractions by defacing rock formations and killing off [remnant] buffalo" and other wildlife.[19] The law became known as the Creative Act and contained the following language:

> The President of the United States may . . . set apart and reserve, in any State or Territory having lands bearing forests, in any part of the public lands wholly or in part covered with timber or undergrowth, whether of commercial value or not, as public reservations.[20]

The act was quickly utilized by President Benjamin Harrison to protect more than a million acres around the south and east boundaries of Yellowstone Park. It was still a dark period in Montana history, and nineteenth-century market hunters were purging the wildlife resource to near extinction. The forest reserves were intended to both protect the forests and provide core habitat to facilitate wildlife recovery. On February 22, 1897, President Grover Cleveland designated the Lewis and Clark and Flathead Forest Reserves, giving Montana wildlands and, eventually, wildlife of the Rocky Mountain Front a reason to hope. When Theodore Roosevelt ascended to the presidency, the Creative Act wound up in the hands of two of its creators: Roosevelt and America's forester Gifford Pinchot. In their custody, the forest reserves were consolidated into the national forest system and expanded from about 40 million acres to over 190 million acres.[21]

The Long Road Back

The restoration of wildlife took time, but the compass now had a heading. When the U.S. Forest Service was new, ranger Elers Koch left the following account of wildlife populations on the forest lands that included the Sun River, portions of the Rocky Mountain Front, and the wildlands to the west:

> It is probable that the period through the nineties and early nineteen hundreds witnessed the lowest level in game numbers through most of Montana . . . at that time game was so scarce that the sight of a single deer, elk, or sheep was most unusual. I often traveled for weeks . . . through the high mountain country without seeing any big game. The South Fork of the Flathead and the Sun River country is today considered excellent game country. Deer, elk, and goats are relatively abundant, yet in the fall of 1905 and again in 1906 I rode for a month . . . through the wildest part of that country with a rifle on my saddle, and with the exception of one goat never saw or got a shot at a single big game animal . . .[22]

Since Koch's observations, we have experienced more than a century of public and private commitment to land stewardship and wildlife restoration on the Rocky Mountain Front. In the desperate times of early wildlife conservation, creating wildlife refuges was often the most direct and straightforward approach. In 1913, seven years after Koch's ride, the Montana state legislature created the Sun River Game Range to advance the wildlife recovery. In all probability, the action was intended to afford some immediate sanctuary for elk, deer, and bighorn sheep. However, it also extended protection to the Montana grizzly bear sixty years before the Endangered Species Act of 1973. In 1931, Montana made the grizzly a game animal so that it might be protected and managed. The Endangered Species Act was still forty-two years off.

In 1940, the U.S. Forest Service designated a portion of the Lewis and Clark National Forest as the Bob Marshall Wilderness, thus offering this unique wild place as much protection as they could within their regulatory authority. It would be another twenty-four years before the U. S. Congress would pass the Wilderness Act.

Early in the twentieth century, the wildlife recovery debate was sharply focused on the competition between wildlife and domestic livestock along the Rocky Mountain Front. Petitions to remove livestock from critical areas were advanced as were counterpetitions favoring livestock production.

Since the Office of the State Game Warden was considered unstable and the state still lacked professional wildlife managers, the U.S. Forest Service was the target of the dueling parties.[23] Early estimates of the number of elk remaining in the Sun River portion of the Rocky Mountain Front were highly variable, with the minimum estimate as low as 300 animals around 1910. Wildlife, however, was responding to the protection offered, and by 1917, the estimates for elk in the Sun River ranged from 1,708 to 5,000.

As the tough times in American history remembered as the *Dirty Thirties* approached, the competition between domestic livestock and wildlife grew more intense. The result was severe overgrazing, a declining wildlife reproductive rate, and a growing number of elk seeking forage on private lands. In addition, bighorn sheep and mule deer were likewise recovering, although the stressed forage base was believed to have triggered bighorn sheep die-offs in the 1930s.[24]

In Tom Messelt's book *A Layman and Wildlife,* the following passage describes the circumstance as the Rocky Mountain Front entered the 1940s:

> In the Sun River . . . Hard winters, lack of winter range drove the elk onto the ranches to invade haystacks and livestock winter range . . . not every winter . . . but the ranchers had accepted it as one of the hazards of ranching in a big game area.
>
> However, there was one rancher new to raising livestock who had visited Montana on vacation and finally decided to go into ranching there. He resisted the elk damage to his range and haystacks to the point of advertising in New York papers for machine gunners to clear the ranch of elk.[25]

In the classic American conservation tradition, a Great Falls, Montana, businessman and hunter, Tom Messelt, stepped forward as a volunteer to become the first secretary of the Montana Wildlife Federation. It was a position he held for eighteen years. In 1943, the Montana Department of Fish and Game and the U.S. Forest Service asked Tom to organize a sportsmen and rancher group, the Sun River Conservation

Council, to seek a solution. As it turned out, the basis for a solution was found on a cattle train going from Great Falls to the stockyards of Chicago.

The matchmaker turned out to be a freight traffic manager for the Great Northern Railway who noticed that one of the ranchers could not go, thus opening up a space on the train. He also noted that some of the stockmen who would be on the train had been enduring considerable elk use on their private places. At the traffic manager's suggestion, Tom hopped the open space, and by the time they all got back to Montana, he had convinced Augusta rancher Charles Willard that a cooperative solution could be found. Willard agreed to help find it. When the Sun River Conservation Council was formalized, Choteau area rancher Carl Malone became the group's chairman and Tom Messelt the secretary. The group's conclusion would be to find and buy the elk a range they could call their winter home.

The big break came in 1947 when an elderly rancher with a fondness for elk offered his place for sale. There was, however, a catch. Tom Messelt tells the story best:

> There was a catch—it was then eleven o'clock on Saturday, the banks closed at twelve and he had to have a certified check for ten percent down payment that day. Another buyer had his check there in case the Department (Montana Fish and Game) failed to take it.[26]

There was no way the state could move fast enough to hold the acquisition with the necessary 10 percent down payment in one hour. In this moment of crisis, rancher Malone and hunter Messelt put up their own personal funds, thus combining a land ethic and a hunter's wildlife conservation ethic to acquire the critical winter range absolutely essential for Rocky Mountain Front wildlife. The Sun River Wildlife Management Area became a reality, and a conservation pattern was set.

As the years passed, other critical habitats were acquired along the Rocky Mountain Front. Using funds that taxed hunters through an excise tax on firearms and ammunition, the state acquired the Ear Mountain and Blackleaf Wildlife Management Areas. The Nature Conservancy joined the effort through the acquisition of the Pine Butte Swamp Preserve, and together these places meant critical winter ranges for elk, deer, and bighorn sheep, as well as wetlands that were soon favored by grizzly bears.

This conservation response to the wildlife needs—as restoration evolved along the Rocky Mountain Front—all basically started when President Grover Cleveland used his executive power to designate the Lewis and Clark and Flathead Forest Reserves. His authority to do that was derived from legislation lobbied through Congress by the ethic held by recreational hunters of the Boone and Crockett Club in 1891. The club itself was formed in 1887 to curb the commercial killing, introduce a sporting code, and begin wildlife restoration. As the Boone and Crockett Club approached its 100th anniversary, it invited various states to propose a conservation challenge that the club might respond to in observance of its centennial year. The challenge the club responded to was submitted by the State of Montana. It was a proposal that directed the club's attention to the wildlife restoration in progress along the Rocky Mountain Front and the potential still held by this exceptional place.

In 1987, the Boone and Crockett Club honored the spirit of its founders and made a commitment to the future with the acquisition of the 6,000-acre Theodore Roosevelt Memorial Ranch. The property is located north of the Blackleaf Wildlife Management Area, south of the Blackfeet Indian Reservation, and west of the town of Dupuyer, Montana. The ranch quickly became home to virtually all of the species of wildlife that had occurred there in presettlement years, except the buffalo. The path of the grizzly is still seasonally occupied. The current wild residents include black bear, cougar, elk, mountain goat, bighorn sheep, mule and white-tailed deer, wolf, a rich avian community of hawks, eagles, and owls, and a broad, diverse community of less obvious but equally important species.

It is also quite important to appreciate that the ranch and its research programs are dedicated to finding solutions to the often competitive relationship between wildlife and livestock.

This focus brings us back full circle to that ride on the stock train headed from Great Falls to Chicago. It was the journey in which hunter Tom Messelt and rancher Charley Willard determined that collaboration was preferable to confrontation—for the good of both wildlife and livestock along the Rocky Mountain Front. It was a philosophy given life and meaning when Tom the hunter and forward-thinking rancher Carl Malone stepped up to secure the Sun River Wildlife Management Area in 1947. It was a commitment sustained forty years later when the Boone and Crockett Club dedicated its investment and program to the same vision.

The list of the times Montana hunters carried a wildlife conservation ethic—and rallied on behalf of the Front—would fill volumes. Some of those tales have already been forgotten by the passing human parade. The record of each contribution, however, is measured by the land and the wildness it sustains. Since Elers Koch's 1905–06 observation of a wildlife-barren landscape, we have experienced a century of public and private commitment to land stewardship and wildlife conservation on the Rocky Mountain Front. In 2011, a *Helena Independent Record* opinion article described the result in a single sentence. The lead sentence read: "When Montana hunters or anglers wonder what awaits them in heaven, it's hard to imagine a place better than the Rocky Mountain Front."[27]

JIM POSEWITZ spent thirty-two years with the Montana Department of Fish, Wildlife and Parks, leading the agency's ecological program for fifteen years of that span. He then founded Orion–the Hunter's Institute, a nonprofit organization dedicated to the preservation of ethical hunting and wild resources essential to that purpose. Jim has published four books: *Beyond Fair Chase*; *Inherit the Hunt*; *Rifle in Hand: How Wild America Was Saved*; and, his latest, *Taking a Bullet for Conservation: The Bull Moose Party, a Centennial Reflection 1912–2012*. Jim also served as executive director of the Cinnabar Foundation since its inception in 1983 until May 2010. Cinnabar awards environmental protection and wildlife conservation grants in Montana and the Greater Yellowstone Ecosystem. Jim is an adjunct professor of history and philosophy at Montana State University. He earned a bachelor's degree and a master's degree in fish and wildlife management from Montana State University–Bozeman.

---

[1] Meriwether Lewis, *The Lewis and Clark Expedition*, ed. Archibald Hanna (Philadelphia: Lippincott, 1961), 1:184.

[2] Lewis, *Lewis and Clark*, 1:237.

[3] Lewis, *Lewis and Clark*, 3:591–92.

[4] Lewis, *Lewis and Clark*, 3:703.

[5] Lewis, *Lewis and Clark*, 3:714.

[6] Lewis, *Lewis and Clark*, 3:716.

[7] Harold Picton and Irene E. Picton, *Saga of the Sun: A History of the Sun River Elk Herd* (Helena: Game Management Division, Montana Department of Fish and Game, 1975).

[8] Michael Punke, *Last Stand: George Bird Grinnell, the Battle to Save the Buffalo, and the Birth of the New West* (New York: Smithsonian Books/ Collins, 2007), 71; Charles Jesse Jones and Henry Inman, *Buffalo Jones' Forty Years of Adventure* (Topeka, KS: Crane & Company, 1899), 235.

[9] Picton and Picton, *Saga of the Sun.*

[10] Granville Stuart, *Pioneering in Montana: The Making of a State, 1864–1887*, ed. Paul C. Phillips (Lincoln: University of Nebraska Press, 1925), 187–88.

[11] Charles M. Russell, *Good Medicine: Memories of the Real West* (New York: Garden City, 1929), vii.

[12] William Kittredge and Annick Smith, eds., *The Last Best Place: A Montana Anthology* (Helena: Montana Historical Society Press, 1988), 364–65; Nannie T. Alderson and Helena Huntington Smith, *A Bride Goes West* (Lincoln: University of Nebraska Press, 1942), 16–17.

[13] Nathan Miller, *Theodore Roosevelt: A Life* (New York: William Morrow, 1992), 151–52.

[14] Herman Hagedorn, *Roosevelt in the Bad Lands*, a publication of the Roosevelt Memorial Association (Boston: Houghton Mifflin, 1921), 45.

[15] David G. McCulloch, *Mornings on Horseback* (New York: Simon and Schuster, 1981), 354.

[16] Shane Mahoney, "The North American Conservation Model: Triumph for Man and Nature," *Bugle*, January/February 2005, 90.

[17] George Reiger, "A Shared Journey," *Field and Stream*, August 1995.

[18] John F. Reiger, *American Sportsmen and the Origins of Conservation* (Norman: University of Oklahoma Press, 1986).

[19] Miller, *Theodore Roosevelt*, 196.

[20] James B. Trefethen, *An American Crusade for Wildlife* (New York: Winchester, 1975), 123–24.

[21] U.S. Forest Service, *Establishment and Modification of National Forest Boundaries and National Grasslands*, USDA FS 612, November 1997.

[22] Elers Koch, "Big Game in Montana from Early Historical Records," *Journal of Wildlife Management* 5, no. 4 (1941): 368.

[23] Picton and Picton, *Saga of the Sun*.

[24] Picton and Picton, *Saga of the Sun*.

[25] Tom Messelt, *A Layman and Wildlife, and a Layman and Wilderness* (Great Falls: Montana Stationery Company, 1971), 62.

[26] Messelt, *Layman and Wildlife*, 69.

[27] Jack Chambers, "An Economic Engine That Keeps on Ticking," *Helena Independent Record*, August 9, 2011.

Chapter 15

RAMPING UP THE FRONT: A CONSERVATION SUCCESS STORY

Bob Kiesling

Montana's Rocky Mountain Front, like so many national parks, is eye candy from the standpoint of topography and geology. The Front makes your eyes get big, your jaw drop, and your hands grab a camera. It is one of those earthly places that constantly produce what were known before the advent of digital photography as *Kodak moments*. Its compelling landscapes and light shows, its remarkable wildlife, and its sturdy ranching and community culture combine to make it a place worth preserving.

From a biological perspective, the Front has evolved phenomenally over a 200-year period. Once abundant with a diversity of life-forms reflecting its diversity of elevations, habitat types, and watersheds, the Front nearly lost its biological assets in the 150-year period following Lewis and Clark's Voyage of Discovery. Its current state of healthy diversity is traceable by following the confluences of sometimes serendipitous, often deliberate ebbs and flows of conservation action over the past century.

To glimpse any permanent conservation sanctuaries along the Rocky Mountain Front in the 1970s, you'd have had to stand on the shoulders of a few visionary citizens and squint to see a small number of protected areas. Some farsighted conservation advocates pushed for establishment of the Sun River Game Preserve, in 1913, and three other wildlife management areas (WMAs): Sun River WMA, in 1947, and the Ear Mountain WMA and Blackleaf WMA in the 1970s. Together, they provided sanctuaries for wildlife and secured public access and use. All of these areas are owned by the State of Montana and managed by the Montana Fish, Wildlife and Parks agency.

Major wildland designations flowed in the wake of the 1964 Wilderness Act. This act statutorily defined the Bob Marshall Wilderness, a tract of federal wildlands that had been managed as a primitive area by the U.S. Forest Service since 1929. In 1973, the Scapegoat Wilderness was added to the wilderness system, and in 1978 the Great Bear Wilderness was designated; both were escorted through the congressional approval gauntlet by passionate citizen advocates over the objections of the Forest Service. These wilderness areas, however, protected mountainous terrain west of the Front. None of them included the stunning limestone ramparts and creek and river cuts, nor the more subtle foothills and limber pine savannahs, that we know as the Front, stretching some 150 miles north from Highway 200 all the way to the U.S.-Canada border.

Need for Permanent Conservation

The confluence of numerous events later in the 1970s created new momentum toward permanent conservation of the Front as a large, *restored,* mostly intact landscape. The restored condition of the Front had to do with gradual recovery through time of lands that had been savaged of wildlife. Once-vast herds of bison were massacred to the brink of extinction. Commercial meat hunters came close to wiping out the deer, moose, elk, and bear.

Fuelwood mongers, railroad tie hackers, and saw loggers reduced the forested lands of the Front from timber to toothpicks over just a few decades. These natural resource commodities were harvested to supply the growth needs of Great Falls, the burgeoning metro center to the east of the Front. It was a restored Front from which the trickle of conservation in the 1970s gathered into a stream during the 1980s and 1990s, then a cascade of conservation, rapidly bouncing and bobbing to the present.

Prior to the conservation initiatives of the 1970s, as the Front was recovering from the ravages of resource stripping, its best friends were climate and weather. The Front was always known to be a land of extremes. Here it was possible to slip on the ice, fall in the mud, get up, and dust yourself off. Such conditions delayed homesteading and community settlement. Blessedly, they also slowed habitat fragmentation from rural subdivision pressures and more road building.

During the 1970s, there had been substantial growth in public use of the Land and Water Conservation Fund (LWCF), a congressionally established source of dollars for habitat, outdoor recreation, and open space conservation. Funded by lease revenues from energy-rich, federally controlled property, this public kitty was allocated for use by federal land agencies and apportioned to all fifty states as well.

Anticipating more access to this fund, the U.S. Fish and Wildlife Service solicited ideas from hundreds of different knowledgeable sources about which areas of the country were important enough to merit formal conservation. The project was known as the Unique Wildlife Systems Inventory. The Rocky Mountain Front in general and the wetlands around Pine Butte (west of Choteau) in particular were often cited as conservation worthy.

In roughly the same time frame, an increase in oil and gas exploration fueled speculation that the Front was destined for an inevitable energy development boom with the attendant explosion of roads, influx of workers, power lines, pipelines, banks, bars, and brothels.

The 1970s also witnessed a significant expansion of environmental consciousness. In part, it was this heightened awareness that led to a decade-long interagency (federal and state) project to inventory and map the wildlife resources of the Front. The idea was to gather this information so that decisions regarding access and extractive land uses could be more proactive and collaborative than ever before. Such cooperation among state and federal agencies was also more cost-effective than individual agency efforts alone could be. It was forward-looking in terms of timing, budgeting, and allocation of agencies' limited dollars and personnel. Moreover, the collaboration would yield a set of best management practices for energy exploration and development along the Front—a list of practices informed by the invited participation of the energy industry and conservation organizations.

In this same time period, advancing age became a factor among key private landowners along the Front. For example, Kenny and Alice Gleason, who founded the Circle Eight Guest Ranch west of Choteau from tent-camp beginnings in the 1930s, had no heirs interested in assuming the operation of the ranch.

Responding to the information that Pine Butte and the surrounding wetlands ranked as one of the unique wildlife areas of the United States, The Nature Conservancy (TNC), a private nonprofit conservation organization, began exploring the potential for protecting the premier biological attributes of the neighborhood. With the visionary leadership of northwest regional director Spencer Beebe, TNC assumed that key conservation land acquisitions, assembled first by the Conservancy, might later be converted into a U.S. Fish and Wildlife Refuge.

But things did not turn out that way. The capital for such an outcome dried up with a change in national political administration. In hindsight, the zenith of spending on public land projects was reached in the latter years of the Carter administration during a fiscal year when more than $800 billion of congressional funding was allocated to the Land and Water Conservation Fund nationwide. By 1980, the newly elected Reagan administration, however, backed by a legion of western state Sagebrush Rebels, made it clear that selling off and privatizing federal land trumped any public policy agenda for acquiring more public domain.

As public capital resources slowed to a trickle on all levels, the need for private land conservation programs increased. But at the national level, TNC's interest in committing capital to the Front abated synchronously with the decline of public resources.

There was another quandary. Over the years, TNC had become more smartly science-based in its conservation activities. Its institutional intelligence was increasingly driven by adherence to identifying and conserving the rarest of *biological elements.* Most typically, this meant rare, threatened, or endangered plant species. Usually, it was easier to identify, catalog, and protect a population of blue-fringed hoary flaxworts than red-toed mousey swamp twaddlers. Mobile, wide-ranging animal species, often using habitats only seasonally, presented especially difficult conservation challenges. When it came to grizzly bears, the keystone species of Rocky Mountain Front conservation, The Nature Conservancy questioned whether a private land trust could take actions crucial to the great bears' survival.

An aside on the biology: It is useful to note that it wasn't until the middle of the twentieth century that a few individual charismatic species drew attention for conservation. In the 1970s, the Endangered Species Act was passed, the emphasis of which was also the preservation of individually rare species.

It was sometime later that the ideas of island biogeography, wildlife corridors, large-landscape conservation, and other seminal notions emerged. These ideas began morphing and reshaping the science-based intelligence of preserve selection and design, not to mention the practical, political, and economic issues facing land conservation.

Yet, it wasn't until 1985 that the Society for Conservation Biology was founded, and it was sometime thereafter that large-scale conservation started to supplant individual species protection as the guiding paradigm for conservation. The evolution of behavior often lags behind the evolution of ideas.

In any event, having purchased the Circle Eight Ranch and several other private land holdings around Pine Butte (which became known as TNC's *Pine Butte Swamp Preserve*), TNC had one oar in and another oar out of making further commitments to the Front.

By the time the 1970s receded, TNC had launched a field office in Montana. With considerable time and resources already tied up in the Pine Butte Swamp Preserve, the conservation of the area became the tail that wagged the new field office dog. Much of the wag came from trying to dig out of the debt created by these early sanctuary acquisitions while simultaneously fetching additional biologically important acres for the Pine Butte Swamp Preserve.

Another condition became glaringly evident. The task of conserving the Front was simply too big for one, two, or even a handful of players to carry out by working solo.

Collaborators Abound

The Montana Fish, Wildlife, and Parks department felt politically constrained from conducting significant additional land acquisition because it already had established three wildlife management areas along the Front. Adding more would risk criticism that the department was expending too many resources in a geographically unbalanced way, when its mission was to serve the entire state of Montana.

TNC was constrained both by debt and by national office wariness toward undertaking additional Front projects beyond the Pine Butte Swamp Preserve.

The federal agencies (U.S. Forest Service, Bureau of Land Management [BLM], U.S. Fish and Wildlife Service [USFWS]) were hamstrung by Reagan administration dictates to *cease and desist* any efforts to pursue land conservation. The USFWS, for example, had to boot half of its realty division nationwide. In Montana, that meant the number of full-time people working on wildlife real estate projects shrank from five to just one. In other words, there were precious few private or public resources to tap for the Front.

So, just a little slower than fruit flies do in lab experiments, TNC began adapting to these conditions. Raising capital for conservation is difficult even in the best of times. It is yet harder to do so in rural states with small populations, a paucity of philanthropic institutions, very low per capita income, and a vocal sector of the population opposed to allocating any more land to the tree huggers or government agencies of any stripe. Yet, as the old saw goes, necessity is the mother of invention. Occasionally, inventive mothers can attract attention.

After visiting the fledgling Pine Butte Swamp Preserve, getting saddle sore from a horseback trip into the Bob Marshall Wilderness, and feasting over campfire accounts of grizzly bear research from the legendary John Craighead, trustees of the Richard King Mellon Foundation made a large contribution to TNC's national Land Preservation Fund. They wanted a portion of the grant to be *borrowable* for use in assembling the Pine Butte Swamp Preserve. They also made a founding grant so that John Craighead could launch the Wildlife-Wildlands Institute in Missoula, Montana.

Not too long thereafter, the McKnight Foundation of Minneapolis made a substantial (but good for one year only) challenge grant to further the effort. A wonderful, publicity-shy, longtime donor to TNC stepped up to help meet the McKnight Foundation's challenge, and she threw in over $1 million. The Murdock Foundation of Vancouver, Washington, topped off this fund-raising drive with a just-in-the-nick-of-time gift earmarked for Pine Butte Swamp Preserve stewardship.

Then serendipity once again jumped into the stream. In the mid-1980s, the Boone and Crockett Club, founded by Theodore Roosevelt in 1887, was hunting for a showcase habitat conservation project to celebrate its upcoming 100th anniversary. The club shotgunned out a letter to all western states' fish and game agencies soliciting ideas for top-notch big game habitat sites deserving of permanent conservation.

Montana Fish, Wildlife and Parks quickly contacted TNC, and together they devised an appeal to attract the Boone and Crockett Club to the Rocky Mountain Front. Most other states had ideas for elk, bighorn sheep, mountain lion, or deer habitat. But Montana's was truly a trophy proposal because the Front boasted *all* those species *plus* moose, black bears and grizzly bears, pronghorn antelope, and Rocky Mountain goats.

Few places in North America harbored such widespread and abundant large mammals. Fortuitously, that interagency, multiyear study of the Front's wildlife resources looked *very* prescient indeed.[1]

After several years of concentrated focus on the Front, the Boone and Crockett Club secured a 6,000-acre, strategically located property west of Dupuyer now known as the Theodore Roosevelt Memorial Ranch. The club "conducts habitat research and demonstrates innovative land management practices, as well as conservation education programs. These activities are linked to a program of graduate scholarships directed by Paul R. Krausman, Boone and Crockett Professor of Wildlife Conservation at the University of Montana."[2]

With the addition of the Theodore Roosevelt Memorial Ranch, the formally protected areas began to resemble pearls threaded on a conservation necklace stretched along the base of the Rocky Mountain Front from the Blackfeet Indian Reservation on the north to Highway 200 at the south; and now you didn't have to squint to see them—they were luminous.

The Montana Nature Conservancy—TNC Montana—continued to adapt to conditions. Recognizing the limits of national office enthusiasm for grand dreams of extensive and holistic conservation of the Front, the Montana office went rogue. Collaborating with longtime land wizard Bruce Bugbee of Missoula, it created a case statement for large-landscape conservation of the Front. Replete with graphically displayed wildlife and plant data and newly available satellite imagery, and accompanied by a compelling slide show, the case statement was trolled quietly past the Conservation Fund, a nimble, creative national nonprofit organization. Intrigued by the scale of needs and opportunities, the Conservation Fund in turn began trolling the vision past funders smitten by the idea of bold-stroke conservation. Interest in the Front grew significantly.

Land Exchange Pooling

Even the slumbering federal agencies emerged from states of torpor and started paying attention. The BLM designated a number of areas under its management and abutting national forest boundary as Outstanding Natural Areas. During the 1980s decade of scant public funding, the BLM expressed interest in swapping out low-public-value lands from its inventory of scattered acres in order to acquire high-public-value lands along riparian corridors, in key wildlife areas, and certainly on the Front.

Bruce Bugbee and TNC Montana collaborated in the design of a systematic way to facilitate public land swaps that became known as *land exchange pooling*. Once again, necessity spurred invention; concepts spawned practical methods. The ideas were presented to the Conservation Fund. It became the champion of this new method inside the beltway of Washington, D.C., urging the U.S. Department of the Interior to authorize some experiments. In times of fiscal austerity, land exchange pooling arose as an alternative to seeking traditional cash funding for more federal agency land acquisition.

Institutional capabilities for conservation began to grow as opportunities increased. The Lewis and Clark National Forest, ably supervised by Gloria Flora, elevated conservation to much higher status among its multiple-use imperatives than ever before. The agency withstood intense political pressure—from proponents of commodity development to advocates of increased motorized access—in order to assign greater weight to wildlife conservation in its once-a-decade forest planning cycles.

Era of Conservation Easements

In the private lands arena, TNC recognized that few landowners could afford to donate their property, and in many cases they were not interested in selling their land outright. This led to increased use of conservation easements as an appropriate method for conserving land, particularly for land-rich, cash-poor ranchers who preferred to keep family lands in family hands.

As a pioneer in the use of conservation easements, TNC understood their importance as a means to advance conservation. In the early 1980s, Montana Fish, Wildlife and Parks had no in-house capacity to create and deploy conservation easements on behalf of habitat conservation. So it was that TNC secured a contract with the state agency to develop the capability—along with a system for objectively ranking prospective projects—both statewide and within Montana Fish, Wildlife and Parks administrative regions.

At the same time, Montana's extensive, experienced, and capable citizen advocates—such as the Montana Wildlife Federation, Montana Audubon, Ducks Unlimited, and sportsmen clubs—joined in promoting legislation to secure more wildlife habitat. In the face of this vigorous clamor, the Montana legislature passed the Habitat Montana bill in 1987. This act—coupled with another, House Bill 720, passed in 1989—expressed preference for conserving habitat using conservation easements over outright fee simple acquisition. Land could remain privately owned, kept on the tax rolls and in productive agricultural use, yet still be protected from habitat fragmentation and loss. In most cases, it could also be opened to public hunting use. House Bill 720 stipulated that in addition to environmental analyses, socioeconomic assessments would have to be done for all Habitat Montana projects.

Strength through Inclusion and Communication

When the 1990s arrived, the federal agency universe began to change for the better. The George H. W. Bush administration took a more accommodating view of public land conservation than had the fire-breathing, ideologically unbending Reaganauts of the 1980s. Clinton administration policies further invited and promoted well-justified, high-public-value conservation initiatives, particularly public-private cooperative efforts. For example, projects that included other partners willing to make financial commitments were often viewed with greater favor than those in which the federal government alone picked up the land conservation tab.

In the 1990s, the importance of large landscapes and ecosystem integrity began to seep into the conservation mainstream. West of the Continental Divide, the Blackfoot Challenge program (1990 to 1991) coalesced around the idea that conservation should be conducted throughout the entire watershed basin of the Blackfoot River and that it should be informed by the active involvement of private landowners, public agencies, nonprofit conservation groups, recreationists, sportsmen organizations, industrial landowners, and others. This kind of inclusivity presented organizational and action challenges to be sure, but it also spawned political strength and lobbying power through consensus building among the stakeholders.

The Nature Conservancy continued to adapt. In its early efforts assembling the Pine Butte Swamp Preserve, TNC went about its business in its usual workmanlike manner—quietly and without investing much time or resources on public outreach and education. A few years into the effort, TNC found itself the subject of ill-informed but angry attacks from various residents and interest groups along the Front. There was a period during which TNC felt about as welcome as a pole dancer at an evangelical tent revival. Lessons were learned.

TNC launched numerous efforts to better communicate its mission, implemented public education projects, and put on task a full-time field director, Dave Carr, to coordinate TNC activities along the Rocky Mountain Front. Carr quickly grasped the need to engage neighbors, landowners, local citizens, and other conservation entities in a larger effort to conserve the integrity of the Front while simultaneously respecting the traditions and aspirations of the ranching families whose lands were key to long-term conservation. TNC worked hard to persuade federal and state agencies of the wisdom of cooperative, large-landscape conservation. So it was that in the mid-1990s the Rocky Mountain Front Advisory Council was established.

A Jewel in the Crown

Late in the 1980s, a few conservation visionaries (among them Gil Lusk, Superintendent of Glacier National Park) conceived of the Crown of the Continent, a bold idea positing *ecosystem conservation* as a framework for protecting key lands of the Northern Continental Divide Ecosystem. The Rocky Mountain Front was an integral part of this larger ecosystem.

By the mid-1990s, many of these grand ideas began to merge and provide rationale for on-the-ground actions.

Once again, thoughtful ideas preceded behaviors; rivulets became streams.

In 1995 to 1996, the U.S. Fish and Wildlife Service began to look at the Rocky Mountain Front holistically as including five watersheds. By 1997 to 1998, the USFWS had protected nearly 40,000 acres of the Front using Migratory Bird program dollars for qualified wetlands.

The Front had long been a compelling place, inspiring awe physically and by sheer animal magnetism. Now it was attracting fans that saw both its grandeur and its role as a crown jewel on the edge of a larger ecosystem. Others joined the parade of support for its protection. For example, the Montana Land Reliance, a statewide land trust, gratefully accepted donated conservation easements from private landowners along the Front. The Vital Ground Foundation helped save key habitats for grizzlies and wolves. The R. K. Mellon Foundation renewed its interest in the Front and was joined by the Wyss Foundation in supporting the push for large-landscape conservation.

The William & Mary Greve Foundation, longtime supporters of the Montana Nature Conservancy operations in general and the Front in particular, purchased a ranch along the Front and then donated it to TNC. With this donation came the idea that TNC use the land for *grass banking* to help provide local ranchers with additional range forage, and to encourage them to put their ranches into conservation easement status, thus leveraging more protection of the Front's working landscapes.

Even children got involved. Kids from all over the country contributed their pennies, nickels, dimes, and dollars to become members of the Kratt Brothers Creature Hero Society. At the instigation of these rabble-rousers for wildlife, especially grizzly bears and wolves, the Creature Hero Society bought 1,200 acres of prime Front habitat as its very first *Creaturefuge.*

Thinking Outside the Box

Conservation on an ecosystem scale required paradigm shifts in thinking—structural, policy, and behavioral changes in institutions. Historically, the USFWS had protected land by buying it then designating it a national wildlife refuge. Opportunities along the Front, however, demanded a different model. The Montana Nature Conservancy urged the USFWS to think outside the box.

Keenly aware of the social and political milieu of the Rocky Mountain Front, the USFWS prepared an environmental assessment suitable for the place and the times. Led by Realty Division state coordinator Gary Sullivan, the USFWS created a new category of land protection that fit the Front. Protection would come in the form of purchased conservation easements, not land purchased for outright federal ownership. Instead of fitting the traditional mold of national wildlife refuges, these protected lands would be called *conservation areas*. This was new nomenclature for the first decade of the new millennium. In other words, the Rocky Mountain Front became the *first* conservation area in America to alter the entrenched formal processes of the nation's foremost wildlife conservation agency. The importance of this creative change within the USFWS cannot be emphasized enough.

Now, into and beyond the first decade of a new century, the collected rivulets, feeder streams, and creeks of past protection efforts have formed a powerful river force of conservation for the future. Now, the steady and strong voices of longtime citizen advocates like Gene Sentz, Bill Cunningham, Dusty Crary, Jennifer Ferenstein, Stoney Burk, Roy Jacobs, Karl Rappold, and so many others have been joined by a growing chorus of citizens, giving voice to formally protecting the Front. Now, a community-based organization, the Coalition to Protect the Rocky Mountain Front, exists.

Elouise Cobell, for one, led the establishment of the Blackfeet Land Trust to further protection projects within the Blackfeet Indian Reservation.

Politicians, once deaf to the case, have helped marshal public funding for worthy conservation projects. More recently, they have promoted public policies to abet formal conservation of key public lands while discouraging the most antithetical commodity extraction activities. Their efforts are less the result of leadership *by* example than they are leadership *responding* to the good example of citizen-initiated support built step-by-step in the past. Still, they are part and parcel of cooperative initiatives that merit applause.

A Conservation Success Story

If all this reads like a conservation success story, it is meant to. It is a story of accretion over time, of gathering conservation forces creating an aggregation of sanctuaries in an area once perilously stripped of its biological integrity.

Flowing from these conservation success stories come lessons for the future of the Rocky Mountain Front. Aldo Leopold wisely observed that, "A thing is right when it tends to preserve the integrity, stability, and beauty of the biotic community. It is wrong when it tends otherwise."[3] Because the current of conservation is now running stronger than ever on the Front, and many *right things* are being accomplished, a few moments of relaxed delight are deserved.

Currents, however, are dynamic, not static. Ongoing efforts to fill out the conservation of the Front must occur. Creative invention of new tools, new funding sources, and, especially, new generations of advocates is de rigueur. Ironically, in the wake of preserving the integrity, stability, and beauty of the Rocky Mountain Front will float a host of people who want to be near this grandeur, who want homes, utilities, access roads, watchable wildlife, and community services. Then, too, the hydro-carbonators never *really* go away. Fights over water will increase over time.

Breathe easy for an exquisite moment, but stay vigilant.

BOB KIESLING is a longtime card-carrying environmentalist who went through the University of Montana's graduate program in environmental sciences in its fledgling years (early 1970s). He was executive director of the Montana Environmental Information Center for a few years before leaving to join The Nature Conservancy (TNC) in 1979 as a roving northwestern regional field agent. Kiesling then founded the Big Sky field office of TNC, serving as its first executive director, and trying with mixed success to handle the biological conservation priorities of both Montana and Wyoming. In this capacity, his top priority in Montana was the ongoing research and development of the Pine Butte Swamp Preserve and, by extension, helping to shape the future of habitat conservation along the Rocky Mountain Front.

---

[1] U.S. Bureau of Land Management, *Interagency Rocky Mountain Front Wildlife Monitoring/Evaluation Program: Management Guidelines for Selected Species, Rocky Mountain Front Studies* (Billings, MT: U.S. Bureau of Land Management, September 1987).

[2] "Boone and Crocket Club," accessed August 6, 2013, http://www.boone-crockett.org/conservation/conservation_trmr.asp?area=conservation.

[3] Aldo Leopold, *A Sand County Almanac: And Sketches Here and There* (London: Oxford University Press, 1949), 224–25.

Chapter 16

BACKING THE FRONT

Gloria Flora

Squinting out over the chatting hikers, I stared in amazement at our stunning backdrop, Montana's Rocky Mountain Front. We were going to explore one of its ridges today under the guidance of Lou Bruno from the Montana Wilderness Association. I had just arrived in Montana a few days earlier to literally get my feet on the ground before starting my new job as forest supervisor of the Lewis and Clark National Forest. Taking advantage of one of the Association's Wilderness Walks would connect me with a part of my new forest and some citizens who cared about it. My first footsteps in 1995 into those mountains became my first footsteps into decades of working to protect an incredible landscape.

The Rocky Mountain Front in Montana, or as it's known locally, the Front, runs from the Canadian border almost to Helena, about 150 miles south. This is the overthrust belt, the eastern edge of the Rocky Mountains, which have literally smashed into the Great Plains, forcing thick strata of limestone 4,000 feet in the air above the rolling grassy plains. Row after row of these reefs jut east, backed by the Bob Marshall, Scapegoat, and Great Bear Wildernesses. These formations have created diverse and biologically rich ecosystems that teem with wildlife, fish, and precious water. Every species that Lewis and Clark encountered on their Voyage of Discovery still thrives here, with the unfortunate exception of free-roaming bison. Only superlatives can describe the Front, home to the second-largest elk herd in the United States, the largest wintering herd of mule deer, and every charismatic carnivore you find in the West. Threatened and endangered species abound and are rebounding: grizzly bears here are becoming Plains animals again, as they were two hundred years ago.

Over 365,000 acres of this intriguing landscape are sandwiched in between the wilderness and the sparsely populated private ranch country. It's public land managed by the U.S. Forest Service, with some Bureau of Land Management (BLM) lands scattered along its edge. Despite over 100 years of management, the Forest Service is a latecomer after the Blackfeet, who call this country *Miistakis*, the "Backbone of the World" where they were created. Then came the explorers, trappers, miners, and ranchers carving their existence from this beautiful but unforgiving landscape. After the Forest Service came the outfitters, the loggers, and the oil companies. Others showed up as well, in the guise of *normal folks*, people from all walks of life who were drawn like a magnet to this landscape, or were born here and just couldn't bring themselves to leave. And they started forming a quiet line of resistance against the unraveling of the Front.

Gas or Gassed

An eighteen-year Forest Service veteran, I took the helm at Lewis and Clark National Forest—which includes much of the Rocky Mountain Front—just shy of my fortieth birthday. I soon learned that much of the Front had been leased to oil and gas companies fantasizing about the possibility of large pockets of gas trapped beneath its formidable surface—and not without reason, as Canada's Rocky Mountain Front in Alberta is heavily veined with roads, pipelines, well pads, and all the appurtenances of gas depletion. (The common euphemistic use of the term *gas production* rankles me. We're not *producing* fossil fuels; we're depleting something produced millions of years ago.) A few exploratory wells from decades past gave some excitement but nothing commercially viable on the Montana side. Many geologists believe the layers that hold the gas on the Canadian Front become progressively thinner—down to as little as a few feet—this far south. Some spectacularly deep holes drilled in recent years have come up dry.

My staff was in the throes of an oil and gas leasing analysis when I arrived. Just five years before, a new law shifted responsibility for the surface management in oil and gas development, calling for the Forest Service to take a closer look at which lands might be leased—and if they were, under what stipulations. The assessment was forestwide, but all eyes were on the Front.

Diving into this multiyear assessment, I spoke with hundreds of citizens, industry representatives, politicians, and Native Americans. A surprising number of people were advocating for no leasing. Despite agency norms, it was abundantly clear to me that leasing more lands for speculative energy development wasn't the highest and best use of this land. Thousands of acres were being leased for energy, but there was only one Rocky Mountain Front, and there was no replacing it. Public land managers have the honor, privilege, and responsibility of giving voice to the land, speaking for trees, wildlife, and water as well as for the unborn of all species. After all, our mandate is to ensure that future generations can enjoy the same kinds of goods, services, and experiences from public land as the current population. Who else would, could, or should speak for them?

So here was the Front, an awesome set of ecosystems largely and luckily intact. It was a landscape that many swore to me was their spiritual beacon, an irreplaceable treasure that would continue as a source of endless enriching experiences if it were to remain intact. Looking at the triple bottom line—that is, weighing the economic, environmental, and social costs and benefits on a level playing field—made it clear that lacing the land with roads, pipelines, and flaring gas wells replete with truck traffic, noise, and pollution just didn't add up for the Front. Culturally and ecologically, the Front held values simply too important to lose. Even from a business perspective, it was crazy to try to develop wildcat wells on this rugged landscape. Why not focus on lands with fewer physical obstacles, a supporting infrastructure, transportation linkages, a willing community, and a reliable resource? The Front offered none of these, which in a way made it very alluring to risk takers in the gas business.

The Tribe in Green Isn't Necessarily Green

Despite the imprudence of drilling on the Front, the Forest Service culture is one of compromise. If an entity wants something from public lands, the Forest Service typically will at least give them half of what they want. A decade later, another half is traded off, and the next decade, and so forth. It isn't hard to see how, piece by piece, America is losing its unroaded wildlands. To decide to not give in was to risk my career and fraternal acceptance in the Forest Service tribe. But one evening, sitting on the banks of the Smith River as it glided past my home en route to the mighty Missouri, I realized the absurdity of my thinking. How could my career trajectory be a concern when the future of one of the most significant landscapes in the United States was at stake?

I made my decision: no leasing on the Front. I explained it to my supervisors all the way through the chain of command to the undersecretaries of the U.S. Department of Agriculture and the U.S. Department of the Interior. There were some ashen faces, muttered expletives, and comments like, "Well, you have to give them something!" But no one could come up with a solid, cogent argument for why drilling holes in the Front was wiser than protecting and conserving this landscape for generations. They all thought I was walking the plank, falling on my sword and in for my comeuppance. Some said they were backing me, but most were so far behind me they were nowhere to be seen.

As I signed the official Record of Decision, putting the Rocky Mountain Front off-limits to oil and gas leasing for the next ten to fifteen years (the extent of my authority), I realized it was the twentieth anniversary of my joining the Forest Service. Even if I got shipped off to Timbuktu, it was worth twenty years.

Of course, while the decision was mine to make, I didn't make it alone. Quite a few persistent, farsighted people had already been pressing for protection for the Front for years before I showed up. Their steadfast defense of the land and its inhabitants, including the winged, finned, and four-leggeds, was truly remarkable. They proved to me again and again that it's not the commodities that come from public lands that make the difference in the quality of our lives; it's the experiences and memories, the sum of our relationship with the lands we love, that make us better human beings. Our legacy of wild landscapes is worth far more than money can buy.

The Decision

I held a press conference to announce the long-awaited decision. There were undercover agents in the crowd in case anyone got overly upset. I quietly explained the conclusions reached from the extensive scientific and cultural information in the environmental impact statement (EIS). Ecologically and culturally, the Front was too important to develop. People's sense of place, their attachment to this land and the values of its wildness, was worth more than energy development.

The response still moves me. I received over 400 letters and phone calls from around the country thanking me. I got notes from Forest Service employees I didn't know saying, "Today I was proud to put on my uniform." People sent me flowers and even pictures of their grandchildren saying, "Here's who you made that decision for."

A surprisingly small segment of the upset fossil fuel industry took the decision to court. In an attempt to soften public opinion, they tried a variety of tacks. Perhaps, as a woman, she was too soft-hearted to the pleas of citizens, or maybe she was premenopausal and not thinking clearly? Maybe she made this whole sense-of-place thing up? One industry rep summed up the problem (and I swear to God she actually said it), "She listened too much to the public." By this time, my agency, seeing the flood of positive support, boldly stepped forward taking bows.

The judges at the District and the Ninth Circuit Court couldn't find a single point in the industry's arguments that bore support, and the case held completely in favor of the Forest Service. The plaintiffs didn't stop until the Supreme Court refused to hear the case.

All victories are but steps along the way. In 1998, I went off to the Humboldt-Toiyabe National Forest in Nevada, where I ended up resigning from the Forest Service to call attention to the antifederal government forces who were behaving in abysmal and life-threatening ways to the land and to my employees. They were egged on by a few right-wing members of Congress with a mission to emasculate the Forest Service and its regulations. But that is a story for another day.

The Coalition Is Forged

Now free to choose where to live and what to do, I returned to Montana, to the Front. I started Sustainable Obtainable Solutions (SOS), a nonprofit organization dedicated to ensuring the sustainability of public lands and of the plant, animal, and human communities that depend on them. It's the Forest Service mandate in my words.

I circled back to the Front like a hummingbird homing in on a bedazzling red flower. There, of course, had been no new leases, but interest was stirring to drill on leases just south of Glacier National Park bordering the Blackfeet Indian Reservation—in an area steeped in rich tradition and history—known as the Badger–Two Medicine and in the Blindhorse area just north of the Teton River.

It felt like a David-and-Goliath matchup now with George W. Bush and Dick Cheney in the White House, a scion of oil and a former oil company CEO. What were the odds we could keep their pals at bay, even on the Front? The individual efforts of concerned citizens and regional organizations seemed no match for the fossil fuel industry juggernaut.

A call from Gene Sentz, Choteau schoolteacher, part-time guide, and full-time engaged citizen, shifted gears for all of us. Gene had started Friends of the Rocky Mountain Front in the 1980s to bring together locals who didn't want to see the Bob Marshall Wilderness carved up with seismic lines or drill pads sprinkling the Front like toxic confetti or mines. (They deserve a round of applause, along with Congressman Pat Williams, for stopping the wilderness seismic work with the *Don't Bomb the Bob* campaign.)

Gene suggested that his and other groups join up, combining our resources and brains to bird-dog issues on the Front. Four organizations joined with the Friends and became the core of the Coalition to Protect the Rocky Mountain Front: Montana Wildlife Federation, The Wilderness Society/Northern Region, Montana Wilderness Association, and my group, Sustainable Obtainable Solutions. *United we stand . . .* proved very fruitful. We purposefully opted not to become an official nonprofit. Members were simply those who said they were members. No hierarchy, no designated leader, no bylaws—then or now. We had the power of a single purpose: *"To protect and defend the biodiversity, beauty, integrity and stability of the Montana Rocky Mountain Front as it has flourished through the ages."* It bound us more solidly than any business model. We applied for grants jointly, designating one of the core bona fide nonprofits to share and manage the grant.

A plethora of organizations, citizens, and businesses joined in our meetings and conference calls. We added detail to the mission with a shared set of principles. Then we set to work with a defined strategy, timelines, and responsibilities. Each member's skills were assessed and roles assigned. SOS became the tribal/public lands liaison and national media coordinator. Our weekly organizers' calls began—and continue now, a decade later.

Inroads for No Roads

In 2001, the Lewis and Clark National Forest was struggling to update its *travel plan* (the plan that determines which roads and trails will be open, and when, to motorized or nonmotorized travel for the next fifteen to twenty years). This access planning is arguably one of the most contentious National Forest processes, given the high stakes people place on the freedom to recreate how and where they want. Under the old travel plan in sensitive areas, like the Badger–Two Medicine, all-terrain-vehicles (ATVs) and motorbikes had carved deep eroding channels across steep slopes. And dirt bikes were now scaring the bejesus out of horses sharing the trail.

The Forest tried to shortcut the planning process by developing a disastrous in-house revision that greatly expanded motorized use. In short order, 2,000 letters of protest, generated by the Coalition, forced the Forest Service back to the drawing board.

In the meantime, energy leasing and development were running amok on public lands throughout the West, with corporations taking advantage of the leniency, encouragement, and perverse incentives of the Bush administration. Agencies like the BLM were directed to streamline permit processes, setting up entire field offices devoted to rubber-stamping energy permits with performance rated on the number of permits completed. On the ground, inspection and enforcement were light to nonexistent, with reprimands for those who discovered too many problems or slowed the process.

In 2001, Startech/Thunder Energy, a Canadian company, proposed exploratory drilling for deep-well natural gas in the BLM's Blindhorse Outstanding Natural Area (ONA) on the Front. Yes, you read that correctly. BLM rules allowed for oil and gas drilling just about anywhere, including their own, officially designated outstanding natural areas. Perched high on a verdant plateau overlooking the plains, the proposed drill site would be accessed by a road requiring four switchbacks across the mountain face. Over 100 hundred semitruck loads of materials would be hauled up to drill four horizontal wells in the unyielding rock toward targets as small as a few feet, testing the limits in distance and accuracy of the nascent technology.

Concurrently, the Arctic National Wildlife Refuge (ANWR) was also in the crosshairs of the oil industry and the Bush administration. Both the Front and ANWR exemplified the finest gems in our national treasure chest of public lands. We knew if the Bush administration could break the back of the public and the environmental movement by drilling and roading these two places, then no place was too precious to drill.

The Coalition developed a comprehensive strategy to expose this ill-conceived desecration of the Front for what it was—destruction of the beauty and ecological integrity of the land, stripping future generations of irreplaceable values. This wasn't just about saving the Front anymore; this was about defending the American legacy of wildlands. We were determined to show, using the Front as the exemplar, that when the people lead, we can make the leaders follow.

Seeing Is Believing

Armed with clear, compelling information and photographs, we stayed on message and we kept delivering it. The Coalition was completely clear that our intent was to stop this proposed development, and our reasons were sound. The proposed drilling and what it could lead to in a full-field development scenario would destroy irreplaceable values. Wildlife, including threatened and endangered species such as grizzly bear, wolves, and cutthroat trout, as well as the abundant deer, elk, mountain goat, and bighorn sheep populations, would be severely impacted. Cultural values such as the traces of the Old North Trail, over 10,000 years old, were threatened. Water, the lifeblood of the communities, ranches and farms, would be affected. Historical and traditional uses and values would be laid to waste. All this for what geologists estimated was a 2 to 3 percent chance of finding an economically viable gas field.

Following the adage "seeing is believing," we partnered with Bruce Gordon of EcoFlight, an organization specializing in providing an aerial perspective on threats to the environment. Over the past decade, through EcoFlight, the Coalition has arranged air tours of the Front for reporters, photographers, opinion leaders, and public officials. With a local Coalition member as guide, the flights cruise up the Front, with its jaw-dropping beauty and untrammeled sweeps of land worthy of national park designation. The fact that this incredible land lacks any particular designation or protection starts to sink in.

How did this land escape notice? And how has it remained undeveloped for so long?

We explain the 100-plus years of conservation history of the Front: a grassroots-driven—but not particularly coordinated—saving of one piece at a time.

Over the Blindhorse ONA, the site of the proposed drilling, we circle. "You've got to be kidding," is frequently heard at this point.

We glide north past Glacier and Waterton National Parks into the gas fields of Alberta. Here, the land—or what's left of it—speaks for itself. Overlain on the same once-stunning landscape as the Front are the trappings and appurtenances of full-on energy development. It's heartbreaking. Every drainage has a road up the bottom, each with multiple drill pads. Clouds of dust rise from the heavy truck traffic, blending with the pyre-like fires of flaring gas. (On the ground, the deep whooshing sound of combustion is only overridden by deafening compressors.) Pipelines spread through forest and farms. Taking advantage of the openings, erosion from ATV tracks follows the pipelines, just as the timber companies have followed the roads. Clear-cuts dangle down steep mountainsides above the drill pads. I recall Montana governor Brian Schweitzer, a candidate at that time, shaking his head disbelievingly as he uttered, "They said the footprint would be small."

And then there's the sweetening plant. There's no need to say more, so we just turn around here over the sprawling industrial plant taking up over 100 acres with its trailing network of railroads and roads. The sour gas in this area is laden with sulfur dioxide, a poisonous gas that needs to be removed. The by-product is sulfur—a lot of it. The neat geometric piles of bright yellow sulfur look big enough from the air, but on the ground they dwarf you. Multiple football fields in size, they tower three stories in the air, with pale yellow clouds of dust wafting off them. Local ranchers complain of the high rate of cattle mortality here. The gas is sour in Montana too.

The Coalition's first billboard juxtaposed two photographs: one of the Front in all its glory and the other of the Alberta sweetening plant. Above them, respectively, "A long-term love affair?" and "Or a one-night stand?" It got your attention.

Momentum continued to build in our favor, but every step was hard-won. Veteran county commissioners, who never saw a development they didn't love, stumped hard for industry. Attempts were made to undermine the Coalition, claiming we were national groups trying to manipulate local opinion. But by this time, local citizen members were deeply engaged with the Coalition and were calling the shots as often as the original coordinating organizations. The public, becoming better informed, started to ask hard questions and express strong opinions against drilling.

A quiet parallel effort outside the Coalition began gathering names of people who would be willing to physically protest, putting themselves between the bulldozers and the Front if it came to that. The list quickly swelled to over 400 names before we stopped counting. This was our public land and our grandchildren's public land, and we weren't going to sell out.

The Armor Cracks

The Front and its spokespeople appeared in documentaries and major media from the *Los Angeles Times* to the *New York Times*, from *Time* magazine to the *Economist*. Editorials urged protection, and reports chronicled how far the Bush administration was willing to go to feed the hungry maw of energy companies. PBS's Bill Moyers sent David Brancaccio out to cover the story. David and producer Brian Myers were spellbound by the landscape and its stories and by the fate that could befall it. The fifteen-minute piece they produced for *NOW with Bill Moyers* tracked my history with the Front and its current peril.

The day before the show's airing in October 2004, the producer got a call from the Department of the Interior's Press Office. "We know you are going to excoriate us. We want to inform you we are terminating the EIS," meaning they were canceling the project. "You need to pull the piece or announce our intention," the agency demanded. When Brian Myers relayed that to me, I said, "They're lying. Ask them . . ." and I proceeded with a list of questions and requests. The call came back; they had answered all the questions. I still didn't believe them and sent back another set of questions, which they answered satisfactorily. The piece aired with the closing note that the EIS had just been withdrawn. It was the first and only time an oil and gas EIS had been terminated midstream.

The Department of the Interior formally announced not only that the BLM was terminating the EIS on the proposed drilling but also that they were advising current leaseholders to consider selling their leases back to the government and were instituting programs to protect up to 170,000 acres of private land by buying conservation easements from willing sellers. You could have knocked me over with a feather.

I'd love to give the Coalition full credit for this, but we were just luckily in the right place on the timeline of history, one month before elections and Bush's reelection bid. He had announced to conservative sporting groups, after decimating wetlands protections, that indeed there were places too special to drill (although he failed to identify any). It is likely his administration was flailing around for a place to make good on his statement, and here was the Coalition making an unending ruckus in the media about the Front, scoring points by describing what Bush's ruthless energy policy looked like on the ground. And, Thunder Energy was a Canadian company that obviously had not contributed directly to Bush's campaign. Since ANWR wasn't negotiable, suddenly the Front looked like just the right bone to throw. Call me cynical. Maybe it was just divine intervention.

It turns out that BLM's Montana director, Marty Ott, had informed his supervisors of the unyielding opposition and the growing costs of the proposed drilling project. The BLM had already spent over $1 million and was just getting started. Ott had also described to the proponents the real timeline—under the best circumstances, they could be looking at a decade before a bit might bite the Front's soil. The Coalition had many tools and overwhelming public opinion in our court, and he knew we were more than ready for engagement in an actual court.

Jubilant from our victory of stopping the proposed drilling, we turned our attention back to gaining more permanent protection, as my original 1997 moratorium was running out. Sending Coalition members to Washington, D.C., to meet with our representatives and agency heads proved very effective. And it was pure West: cowboys and American Indians, with the right boots and hats—and many of them Republicans. Senator Conrad Burns (R-MT) despite having declared publically that I was an idiot who never made one right decision, in October 2006 introduced legislation to make my moratorium permanent and also ban hard rock mining. He didn't survive reelection, so Senator Max Baucus (D-MT) picked it up and helped it pass into law by January 2007.

We had a big public party for that one!

We're on a Roll

The Forest Service released its new draft travel plan in 2005. The Coalition helped generate 37,000 comments, the vast majority supporting quiet recreation and wildlife protection. The final travel plan released in 2007 was reasonable, rational, and ground-truthed. With few exceptions, it fit traditional patterns and showed true regard for the wildlife and fish of the Front. In the Badger–Two Medicine, thanks to Keith Tatsey and other leaders in the Blackfeet Nation, the Forest Service honored the no-motorized-traffic alternative supported by the Blackfeet. Score again!

Now we were ready to move forward with the *Big Idea:* a citizen-driven collaborative effort to design a bill that would indeed permanently protect the Front and keep it like it is. This was shaky ground for us organization types accustomed to being campaign leaders and the designers of bills. Our plan was straightforward: we'd work in concentric circles of stakeholders. We'd kick off the first meeting, but then the inner circle, the Coalition members, had to hammer out a vision and strategy, form a steering committee, and hone the tactics. We aimed for consensus, even if it was grudgingly given.

The next circle included more of the community, especially those with a vested interest in keeping the Front the way it is, including people we assumed would be opposed. The proposal was certainly going to add wilderness, include grazing leases, and put the fear of uncontrolled wildfire into people's hearts. Those are all *fightin' words* in the West.

It was pretty brutal at times. Negotiations were hard won, and the lines on the map moved regularly. Feelings were hurt, and some people walked out (they usually came back). But we pressed on. For four years, we held planning meetings, personal visits, surveys, interviews, barbeques, public meetings, agency meetings, tribal meetings, events, and traveling lectures, and we published press releases, articles, op-eds, editorial board visits, economic studies, and even a visitor's map in partnership with the Chamber of Commerce that rivals a national park brochure. Coalition members went to scores of organization meetings to explain what we were building and ask for input.

We worked closely with state and federal agency people and politicians. We gathered supporting organizations (numbering sixty-five and rising), opinion leaders, and elected officials. Three former chiefs of the Forest Service and five former forest supervisors of the Lewis and Clark National Forest signed on.

The weekly conference calls continued. Jennifer Ferenstein of the Wilderness Society in Montana rode herd and kept us organizers on point with remarkable aplomb and effectiveness. The organizers' faces have changed over time, but the intent and commitment have never wavered. I have deep respect for every Coalition organizer and member of the steering committee, each driven by a selfless passion for the Front. They have given me and the American public a gift beyond measure.

From the chaos emerged the Rocky Mountain Front Heritage Act, a fine citizen-crafted, highly supported act that does three things: adds lands that are already managed as de facto wilderness to the actual wilderness system, designates the rest of the lands as a conservation management area, and raises the priority of fighting noxious weeds on public and private lands. After answering some hard questions and satisfying his concerns, Senator Baucus agreed to sponsor the bill. In March 2011, the bill was heard in the Energy and Natural Resources Committee. As I write, we're hoping the Rocky Mountain Front Heritage Act comes before Congress in the next few months.

But dark clouds are on the horizon. The latest threat is increased oil and gas leasing and exploration on private and state lands along the Front. Some believe the Front may be the new Bakken Formation, which has fueled an energy boom in North Dakota. Using new technological developments like horizontal drilling and fracking, energy companies believe they can finally make a killing on the Front. Just in the past year, hundreds of thousands of acres have been leased by oil companies along the Front, and exploratory drilling is now occurring. The worry of some is that if the Heritage Act isn't passed soon, the momentum for energy development and perhaps even a reversal on the drill ban for the federal lands will make the public lands of the Front vulnerable once again.

The Coalition continues to work in support of the Heritage Act, in large part debunking myths and misconceptions. Despite eight public meetings, hundreds of personal meetings, and dozens of articles over the past four years, opponents claim the Heritage Act is a government takeover (it's all federal lands already), vanquishes grazing privileges (just the opposite), and was created in secret under the national direction of out-of-touch organizations back East. Some anti-environment attitudes never change regardless of the subject.

But that's our intent regarding the Front. It should never change, at least not at the hands of humans who are looking for a one-night stand with its resources. The dream holds steady: sustain the Front as it is by living in harmony and respect with its wild inhabitants, holding this place and space for future generations of all species. Dreams can come true.

GLORIA FLORA works for public land sustainability through her organization Sustainable Obtainable Solutions, focusing on large landscape conservation, state-based climate change solutions, and promoting the production and use of biochar. She's a fellow of the Post Carbon Institute and the Center for Natural Resources and Environmental Policy. In her twenty-three years with the U.S. Forest Service, she served as the forest supervisor on two national forests. She has won multiple awards for her leadership, courage, and environmental stewardship.

Chapter 17

LOOK TO THE FUTURE: THE ROCKY MOUNTAIN FRONT HERITAGE ACT

Stoney Burk

The Rocky Mountain Front Heritage Act (hereafter "RMF-HA" or "the Act") is the child of a large number of citizens, some closely involved in the actual structure and ensuing public process and many who have given personal and emotional support to the process. Love of this land is the rallying focus. After years of thoughtful effort, consultation, and community involvement, the Coalition to Protect the Rocky Mountain Front crafted a unique grassroots plan that, in legislative terms, is formally known as the Rocky Mountain Front Heritage Act. The legislation was originally introduced to a congressional committee on November 1, 2011, as Senate Bill 1774 and reintroduced on February 15, 2013, as Senate Bill 364.

At the time of this writing, the Act is now waiting for Congress to enact protective legislation that will basically *preserve, largely as it now exists, the federal public lands along the east slope of the Rocky Mountains in north-central Montana.*

The Front means different things to many people. The Rocky Mountain Front is a magnificent tract of public lands located on the east side of the Continental Divide, east of and abutting the Bob Marshall Wilderness and Scapegoat Wilderness in north-central Montana. The Act includes only federal public lands (lands managed by the U.S. Forest Service [USFS] and the Bureau of Land Management [BLM]) along the Front and does not include the Badger–Two Medicine, except that the stipulation regarding weed treatment does apply to the Badger–Two Medicine.

Details of the Act

Details of the Rocky Mountain Front Heritage Act, a *Montana-made* proposal, comprises three basic components: (1) establishment of a conservation management area, (2) creating wilderness additions, and (3) providing for noxious weedcontrol.

Conservation management area (CMA). The first component of the Act is a new concept of land management designation that encompasses 208,112 acres of USFS and BLM lands along the Front. The CMA provision directs that land management decisions be made favoring conservation. In the case of the Front, this means little to no change to current management. This CMA maintains current USFS travel plan rules for all forms of access and use. The following uses will continue where and as authorized by the travel plan: chainsaw use, mountain biking, outfitting, hunting and fishing, hiking and camping, horseback travel, livestock grazing, motorized recreation, timber thinning, post and pole cutting, firewood gathering, road building (temporary roads within one-quarter mile of most existing roads), hunting and game cart use, and wildland firefighting.

Wilderness additions. The second component of the RMFHA designates 67,160 acres of wilderness in the lands west of Choteau and northwest of Augusta in the West Fork of the Teton River and Deep Creek areas. It would add 50,449 acres to the Bob Marshall Wilderness and 16,711 acres to the Scapegoat Wilderness. Note that in designated wilderness, all activities

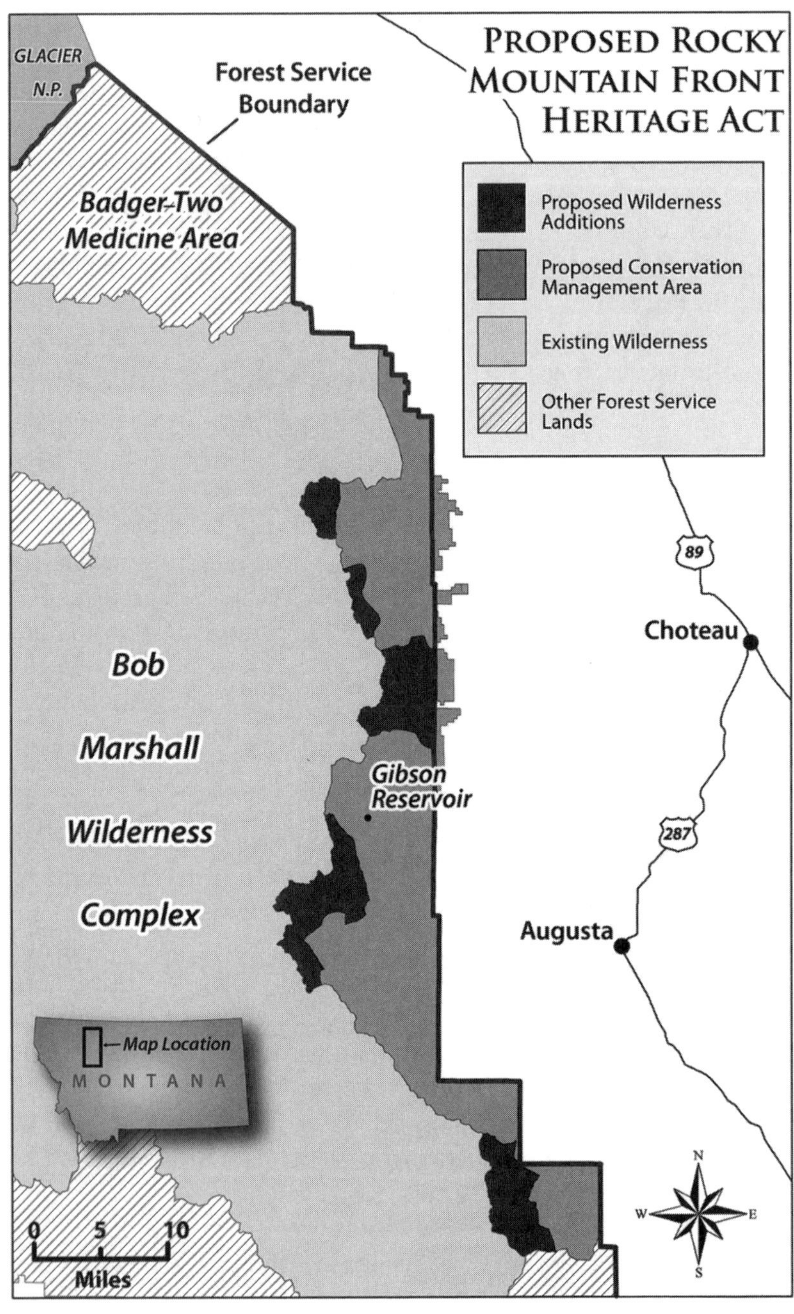
Proposed Rocky Mountain Front Heritage Act
Proposed Wilderness Additions
Proposed Conservation Management Area
Existing Wilderness
Other Forest Service Lands
GLACIER N.P.
Forest Service Boundary
Badger-Two Medicine Area
Bob Marshall Wilderness Complex
Gibson Reservoir
89
Choteau
287
Augusta
Map Location
MONTANA
0 5 10
Miles
N
W
E
S

will be governed by the 1964 Wilderness Act and that nothing in the RMFHA will change that. These lands have been managed by the USFS as wilderness for decades since they were identified as having extremely high potential for wilderness, through both the Roadless Area Review and Evaluation process and subsequent forest planning processes.

A critical and sometimes hotly contested part of the wilderness designation provides for recognition of grazing permits by existing leaseholders. Several of the permit holders expressed great concern about how the designation of wilderness might affect their current cattle grazing permits. The Act will provide certainty. However, just as these permits are conditional to Forest Service management, they will continue to be under the new designation. The Wilderness Act, as amended, sets out specific guidance regarding grazing; that is, wilderness designation is not to be a consideration in the permitting and administration of grazing permits except as to motorized use.

The Act has no effect on current grazing leases or a rancher's ability to pass the leases on to future generations. Also, in addition to confirming the continuation of the grazing leases, the Act verifies preservation of the Benchmark small-plane landing strip about thirty-five miles west of Augusta.

Noxious weed control. The third component provides for noxious weed prevention, control, and eradication. This is a unique and creative component initiated by the Coalition to Protect the Rocky Mountain Front to recognize and, ideally, establish a mechanism for funding by Congress. This component is largely supported by agricultural interests, including some who do not support the CMA or wilderness designations in the Act. The Act would require the USFS and BLM to prioritize the management of noxious weeds on the public lands covered in the Act and in the Badger–Two Medicine.

Nothing in the Act restricts mineral leasing, exploration, and development on private lands or lands along the Front outside of those included in the Act. The lands within the Act were already withdrawn from mineral leasing in 1997. State and federal lands outside of the Act's boundaries are subject to the regulations governing those lands.

The specific areas included in the Act are public lands from the east boundary of the Bob Marshall Wilderness starting on its north end at Swift Reservoir (approximately fifteen miles west of Dupuyer, Montana) traversing south along public lands of the east slope of the overthrust belt to a point where the area abuts Highway 200 as it climbs over Rogers Pass (see the map earlier in this chapter).

The area known as the Badger-Two Medicine was purposely left out of the proposal in deference to the complicated and often contentious history of issues affecting the Blackfeet Tribe as an area of special religious significance to the tribe.

Details of the Act, outreach, news releases, legislative updates, maps, and contact information can be found at the Coalition's website: http://www.savethefront.org.

A Coalition Is Born

Responding to the mounting need for action—and knowing that Congress and our government agencies were not going to take action—a small group of mostly local citizens created the *Coalition to Protect the Rocky Mountain Front.* The Coalition acted upon the urgency of threats, initially from oil and gas exploration, and later when the U.S. Forest Service *travel plan* process was applied to this special place. The impending threats gave impetus for citizen-based solutions. The Coalition took the initiative. That small group of local citizens, namely Gene Sentz, retired schoolteacher and backcountry packer; Roy Jacobs, taxidermist; Karl Rappold, rancher; Dusty Crary, rancher; Stoney Burk, attorney; Bill Cunningham, outdoor businessman; and Tony Porcarelli, contractor, were the original local members of what is now known as the Coalition.

Major considerations for the Coalition were to involve as many people as possible, consider all views, and present a workable legislative bill for presentation to Congress. Citizen input was—and continues to be—a primary focal point of the Coalition's plan.

Integral parts for the planning and creation of details for the Act came from substantial contacts, inputs, and recommendations from government agencies and individuals, such as Lewis and Clark National Forest former forest supervisor

Spike Thompson; district ranger Mike Munoz and staff of the Rocky Mountain Ranger District; Montana Fish, Wildlife and Parks officials; and other federal land managers. All provided substantial information and detail about regulations, maps, cattle lease grazing permits, boundaries, and management areas. The local Weed Board and other related groups helped greatly.

The contacts and information gleaned from multiple meetings with agency personal formed a solid foundation for intermeshing of the various planning and management rules for the Act. In the end, the planning and coordination resulted in solid support from active managers and former managers at all levels.

Economic and Other Benefits

Major selling points for preserving these special places include the economic benefits derived from sustainable and exponentially growing economic activity. Tourism is the number-one *growth* industry in Montana.

A 2013 peer-reviewed analysis for the National Park Service conducted by Michigan State University reports that in the year 2011, 1.85 million Glacier National Park visitors spent about $98 million in the Park and in nearby communities.[1] The report states 1,386 jobs were supported in the local area.

The park highlighted the report in a news release that further notes: "'Glacier National Park has historically been an economic driver in the state and region,' said Glacier National Park Acting Superintendent Kym Hall. 'This report shows the positive economic impact that Glacier and other National Park Service Sites have on our local and national economy.'"[2]

Like Glacier National Park, its neighbor—the Rocky Mountain Front—also draws thousands of visitors every year.

People often overlook the ever-increasing value of this financial benefit for our state and local communities. Opponents to formal designation of additional wildland and scenic areas often cite short-term benefits of resource exploitation while ignoring the long-term loss of future incomes, aesthetic values, and immeasurable future values encompassed in these special areas like the Rocky Mountain Front.

People do not travel every year to view oil fields or coal mines, which often leave us with multimillion-dollar cleanup and sometimes severely damaged other annually renewable resources. One attractive motivation for protecting the Front is that it does draw a multitude of visitors who have a wide spectrum of uses that grow in value every year.

A Sense of Urgency

To set the stage for the logic behind the urgency of protection of this landscape, one need only look at personal experience and listen to the voices of those who preceded us with warnings about failure to plan and failure to protect our ever-diminishing special places. The Front is a unique blend of majestic views, extraordinary populations of wildlife and plant species, and a treasure of history and spiritual resources. Because these wonderful resources cannot speak for themselves, we must speak for them.

Conservationist Aldo Leopold reminds us: "We abuse land because we regard it as a commodity belonging to us. When we see land as a community to which we belong, we may begin to use it with love and respect."[3] The great author continues: "A land ethic changes the role of *Homo sapiens* from conqueror of the land-community to plain member and citizen of it. It implies respect for his fellow-members, and also respect for the community as such."[4]

Concerns about the future of these majestic lands and associated wildlife did not start with one specific threat. All of the initial members of the Coalition had been fighting for decades for protection of this special place. The seeds for the Act started in the 1990s with the battle over oil and gas exploration along this fragile ecosystem. That battle resulted in the courageous decision of Lewis and Clark National Forest supervisor Gloria Flora in 1997 to withdraw most of these areas from oil and gas exploitation.

The hard-fought battle over the Birch Creek South Forest Service Travel Plan (2007) resulted in a plan consistent with the balance of past uses and included reasonable protections for wildlife and watersheds. But, such travel plans come up for review and more challenges every fifteen years.

When considering the existence of oil and gas leases in fragile areas (which were eventually bought out or voluntarily retired), the ever-increasing threats from off-road vehicles (and other motorized travel), the expansion of oil and gas exploration, and the ever-increasing impacts on the wildlife and habitat, the Coalition concluded that if something was not done to minimize these impacts, the nation would lose an extremely important and irreplaceable part of its national heritage.

Jennifer Ferenstein of The Wilderness Society, who is an irreplaceable asset to the Coalition, commented on the work of the Coalition:

> What history has shown is that when people who love a place deeply and honestly get together and work towards protecting special places, they get so much more out of it. I firmly believe that if not for the Coalition to Protect the Rocky Mountain Front, that other conservation measures would not have had as much chance of getting traction. The people, who came together, put aside petty differences and rolled up their sleeves to fight, cuss and finally come to agreement showed the world that anything can be accomplished. This wasn't top down, Washington edict. The Rocky Mountain Front has been saved for future generations not only by the Coalition, but by the local advocates and their friends outside the Front, working together to make good things happen. The process that the Coalition embarked upon should be followed and studied.
>
> In ten years of working on conservation, never have livestock producers, outfitters, hikers, hunters, anglers, small business owners and even the detractors had such a seat at the negotiating table.

A Sense of Home

Many are not aware that this is the home of the Old North Trail, where Indian tribes, conquistadors, trappers, and historians have traveled and sojourned for centuries. It is the home of the late A. B. Guthrie Jr., fiction writer and Pulitzer Prize winner for his novel *The Way West*. The Front has historic, aesthetic, and emotional meaning to thousands and perhaps millions of citizens. It belongs to all of us. There is no other place like it.

The Front is home to the largest population of bighorn sheep in Montana, the second largest migratory elk herd in the United States, the largest population of grizzly bears outside of a national park, and myriad other wildlife, including white-tailed deer, mule deer, wolves, bobcat, lynx, mountain goats, antelope, eagles, and literally hundreds of species of plants and smaller animals. The geology is unique and a source for study by students from several universities as well as scientists. Many outfitters, dude ranchers, writers, photographers, and other business owners thrive in the area. Small businesses are an annually growing resource.

Opposition, Outreach, Collaboration

In 2006, the Coalition agreed that a temporary fix was not going to solve the problem of continual threats of development along the Front south of the Badger–Two Medicine. A small group of locals, supported by many other concerned citizens, decided to start this citizen-based *made in Montana* movement.

Make no mistake, there are still some who reject and object to any effort to add a layer of protection to these federal lands. However, all indications from public meetings and polls taken through the years show tremendous public support for this Act. Most of the objections stem from personal financial or industry motives or from lack of trust in government management. The impacts of fire on adjoining private lands and restrictions on development or off-road vehicle users seem to be the major complaints. Some reject any action on principle if it contains any wilderness or wilderness study designations. Based on comments made in the press and at public meetings, opponents frequently have no idea of what the Act actually proposes. Conversely, some wilderness advocates are adamantly opposed to the Act because of the small acreage of proposed wilderness. Some ranchers holding subsidized grazing leases along the Front are opposed because of fears that the Act and attendant scrutiny might jeopardize their existing leases. The Coalition has always asked citizens to look at what kind of interest a person or business may have.

In 2008, the Coalition expanded efforts to include other ranchers, grazing permit holders, local businesses, county commissioners, and any and all citizens interested in working toward protection of the Front. Although some never joined the battle, the Coalition rapidly expanded to a point where support comes from throughout the nation. Many observers of and objectors to the Act overlook the hundreds of hours, endless negotiations, and great detail that went into the formulation of the Act, maps, and bill language, including numerous open public meetings beginning in 2009.

In 2009 and 2010, the Coalition hosted multiple meetings in various towns and locations along the Front, including Helena, Augusta, Choteau, and Great Falls. The Coalition invited Montana's congressmen, regional political leaders, and citizens from all immediate counties. U.S. senator Max Baucus (Democrat) and staff attended several meetings and suggested several revisions that were incorporated into the Act.

Specific attention has been given to the control of noxious weeds and to the preservation of grazing leases on BLM and Forest Service lands. Included in the outreach for support of the legislation came letters of support in 2010 from three former chiefs of the Forest Service and from three retired Montana Fish, Wildlife and Parks directors. In 2011, Senator Baucus decided the time was right to protect these valuable public lands by sponsoring the Rocky Mountain Front Heritage Act.

Support from All Directions

Several other significant contributors to the formation and direction of the group include Gloria Flora, former supervisor of the Lewis and Clark National Forest and founder and current executive director of Sustainable, Obtainable Solutions; Peter Aengst and Jennifer Ferenstein of The Wilderness Society, Gerry Jennings of the Montana Wilderness Association; and, later, Ben Lamb of the Montana Wildlife Federation. EcoFlight of Colorado has provided a very special service to all by flying numerous tours for a large variety of legislators, politicians, and interested parties. An aerial view of the Front gives special insight into the unique character and beauty of the proposed area within the Act. Few people are aware of the herculean efforts of Jennifer Ferenstein and a few others to organize meetings, work with the media, and raise public awareness. Her contribution to keeping the group organized and the Act ready for Congress is immeasurable.

One would be remiss to not mention the valuable contribution of thoughts, encouragement, and inspiration from our friends on the Blackfeet Indian Reservation and from the Glacier–Two Medicine Alliance. Of course, the contributions of spouses and significant others at all levels was and is of immeasurable value. Some of the members of the Blackfeet Nation and some residents in the Browning to East Glacier Park area include Keith Tatsey, Lou Bruno, Donna Caruso-Hirst, and Kendall Flint, to mention just a few.

Tony Bynum, a terrific photographer from East Glacier, has significantly helped the public experience the Front through his photos depicting the beauty and richness of wildlife and landscapes. Jeff Van Tyne, Dave Wedum, and many other excellent photographers too numerous to mention have displayed the splendor of this majestic place.

Others active and avid supporters of the Act have included Chuck and Sharon Blixrud, owners of the Seven Lazy P Guest Ranch west of Choteau; Joe Perry, a farmer from Brady; members of the Montana Wilderness Association (Gerry Jennings and Mark Good of Great Falls, Brad Borst and John Gatchel of Helena, Gabe Furshong of Missoula, and Holly Baker of Choteau); Jared White of The Wilderness Society; Merlyn Huso, former president of Back Country Horsemen; Mike Aderhold, retired regional supervisor of Region 4 of Montana Fish, Wildlife and Parks; and Jim Posewitz, retired from Montana Fish, Wildlife and Parks and current president of Orion–The Hunter's Institute of Helena. Many others too numerous to list, such as Tim Baker, Montana Wilderness Association of Helena; Hal Herring, a terrific writer from Augusta; and Corlene Martin of Choteau, have doggedly, and with great fervor, worked to preserve this special place.

Rick and Susie Graetz, writers and photographers, have produced fabulous photos and books throughout many years that have presented the unparalleled beauty of the Front. Twenty-eight years ago, Rick Graetz, founder and former publisher of *Montana Magazine,* wrote in his popular book *Montana's Bob Marshall Country:*

> I've covered the Rocky Mountain Front in more detail than the other geographic regions of the Bob Marshall country for several reasons. First, it is my favorite place of all the wild country I've ever been privileged to see. The combination of beautiful rolling prairie, sheer mountain majesty, awesome canyons and such a wide expanse is unsurpassed. The roads that venture into the canyons give those who aren't able to, or choose not to, ride horseback or walk, the opportunity to see all that the wilderness traveler observes. It gives these people a touch of wildness on a grand scale. If formal wilderness designation comes to the wild lands near and beyond these roads, the roads will remain open, and what the visitor sees will be further enhanced.
>
> The only way we can improve on what we see now from the roads and trails is to designate the areas deserving of it, wilderness status. Some of the ranchers in the area would like to see the country remain as is without wilderness protection. That would be perfectly desirable except that administrations in Washington and the Forest Service change and we can't be assured of protection forever. It must be emphasized that any gas potential or timber value is miniscule compared to the value that wildness gives to the country, both in real economic terms and multiple-use values of recreation, watershed protection, wildlife habitat and grazing.[5]

The list of supporters for the RMFHA is so long it is impossible to name them all. Among political supporters are Derek Brown, former Lewis and Clark County commissioner; Jane Weber, commissioner from Cascade County; mayor

Larry Bonderud of Shelby; and Randy Gray, former mayor of Great Falls. Randy has a long history of fighting for the Front. Mary Sexton, former head of Montana's Department of Natural Resources and Conservation, and her husband, Rich Clough, have worked hard for the preservation of the Front for decades.

And . . . Nonsupport

Many of the opponents express the concern about more government, more wilderness, and more possible impacts on their family ranching operations and the federal grazing leases they have held, sometimes for generations. Conversely, other fourth- and fifth-generation ranchers support the bill because they want the Front to remain as it is. A recurrent objection from a number of locals is the effects of fire management resulting from more wilderness.

Throughout the many years and multiple public hearings, the objections range from personal financial concerns relating to the use of public lands for grazing to distaste for wilderness and fear of fire threats. Some just plain do not like the government and believe that less government involvement in managing these resources is best.

Many area newspapers—the *Choteau Acantha* in particular—have highlighted the various public meetings and have provided excellent reporting on the pros and cons that surface from those meetings. Additionally, the newspapers have pointed out statements and positions of various supporters and nonsupporters of the RMFHA.

Republican congressman Denny Rehberg came to the table much later in the process and never did express support for the Act. Teton County commissioners Joe Dellwo, Arnie Gettel, and Jim Hodgskiss expressed opposition to the bill with concerns about fires, ineffective federal government, taxes, and unforeseen future impacts. Republican state senator Rick Ripley, a retired school administrator and rancher from Augusta, opposed the Act because of concerns about effects it may have on ranching, grazing leases, and fires. Mark Salmond, a local rancher from a long line of family ranchers along the Front, opposes the Act, as does his cousin, Christy Clark, a Republican state representative and rancher.

Newly elected Republican congressman Steve Daines held a hearing in Choteau in April 2013 to get citizen input to determine his position. The Coalition and general public are grateful for his interest. The Coalition is hoping he will support the RMFHA legislation.

Educating the Values of RMFHA

One difficulty we all face in dealing with issues of such significance is educating interested and uninterested parties. The Coalition has spent hundreds of hours and a great deal of personal sacrifice to get the bill before Congress. The number of objectors is relatively small in viewing the total. However, the Coalition has taken the objectors' concerns very seriously and has attempted—in numerous public and private meetings—to address those concerns. The Coalition, which has many, many supporters in the agricultural community, believes that the protections offered by the Act will give greater assurance to agricultural interests in the long run than if the Act were not passed. For example, the protection of water sources, support of federal grazing leases, landscape protection, wildlife, and myriad other benefits consistent with their way of life will be enhanced by passage of the Act.

The Coalition took extra effort to reach out and receive input from concerned parties. Former Republican state senator John Cobb of Augusta, a multigenerational rancher from Augusta, was extremely helpful in reviewing and recommending language in the Act that will ensure continuity of federal grazing leases.

There exists an interesting contradiction that is present in the grazing lease issue. What ranching interests may not realize is that there are many, many wilderness advocates who are staunchly opposed to cattle grazing on public lands, period—the irony being that many traditional wilderness supporters are not in support of an Act that adds more wilderness, simply because of the grazing issue.

Everyone cannot have everything each wants. If we are to maintain this national treasure, we must compromise for the benefit of the resource and of future generations. Few people now argue against Glacier or Yellowstone National Parks, although there was strong local opposition when they were being proposed. Most people are very thankful that those areas were preserved for us and for future generations.

Many opponents decline to recognize that this land belongs to 350 million existing Americans and to multimillions of future citizens. History shows that these special places yield tremendous, continuing benefits for those living near the special areas and are a great spiritual and economic resource for current and future generations.

Congressional, National, and Local Backing

Of course, the proposal would go nowhere without a congressman to champion the bill. That is where Senator Baucus and his staff have been so instrumental. Senator Baucus has been a champion of the Front for decades. His staff worked tirelessly to get a balanced Act that would stand the rigors of Washington and the keen eye of Montanans. A fifth-generation Montanan, Paul Wilkins, helped the Coalition understand the torturous legislative process early on.

Another hard-working Baucus staffer was David Cobb, who came to Montana and met with members of the Coalition and the public when Senator Baucus held hearings on the RMFHA proposal. He was followed by Spencer Gray, another Baucus staff member, and another great help in getting public involvement and information to all about meetings, hearings, and the legislative processes. The RMFHA would go nowhere without a channel for presentation to Congress. Senator Baucus and his staff have been invaluable to the process.

At a more local level, Karl Rappold is a rancher from the Dupuyer area and member of the Coalition. Karl and his wife, Teri, who ranch several thousand acres along the Front, are strong supporters of the Act and have dedicated their lives to preserving their way of life and the majesty of the area in which they live. Rappold proudly asserts, "My family has been ranching here for 128 years and the Act will help protect The Front's wild lands and working landscapes for generations to come."

Similarly, Dusty Crary, another founding member of the Coalition, is a local rancher who, with his wife, Danelle, ranches west of Choteau. Dusty's family has ranched on the Front since the early 1900s. Crary testified in support of the Rocky Mountain Front Heritage Act before the Senate Subcommittee on Public Lands and Forests in March 2012. His statement follows:

> Some people don't think there is a need for additional legislation on the Front. Others feel it is only part of a larger conspiracy of control. But the plain and simple truth is this: When asked, people overwhelmingly respond that they like the Front just the way it is. The RMFHA is a document that promises to keep it that way, or to paraphrase Ronald Reagan, "Trust, but verify." That was our single purpose from the get go and after a considerable amount of effort I think we nailed it.

Roy Jacobs, taxidermist from Dupuyer and original member of the Coalition, has, along with Gene Sentz, been instrumental in educating many about the history of the Front. He has been to Washington, along with Dusty Crary, to meet with congressional staffers and politicians. Jacobs has helped educate politicians and the public, including news media, on the various EcoFlights along the Front. His knowledge of the wildlife, habitat, and history of the Front is amazing.

The Coalition has grown over the years to include local ranchers, outfitters, hunters, business owners, conservationists, farmers, former and current land managers, tribal members, and a substantial list of various interest groups. Other supporting citizens and citizen groups—too numerous to list here—have contributed greatly to the advancement and introduction of the Act. Sportsmen's and outdoor groups, such as Backcountry Horsemen, Montana Wildlife Federation, Wild Sheep Foundation, Backcountry Hunters & Anglers, and Orion–The Hunter's Institute, representing thousands of supporters, have been instrumental in broadening support for the legislation.

The Coalition made extensive efforts to invite congressional members, commissioners, and politicians of every surrounding town to participate in the process. In fact, the Coalition held eight public meetings, making seven prior attempts to get Congressman Rehberg to attend before he held a meeting in Choteau in April 2012. Senator Baucus held seven public meetings. Congressman Rehberg held one. Newly elected Congressman Daines has held one.

From the beginning, the Coalition recognized the need to build citizen-initiated agreement for solutions to the stagnant and seemingly ineffective land management planning for our national forests. The Coalition pushed the arduous and sometimes contentious task of drafting the proposed Act, involving the public, educating opponents and proponents, and ultimately creating the currently proposed Act to be introduced for congressional consideration. The experience of the group in 2001 while dealing with the retirement of existing oil and gas leases and the battle over the travel plan—as well as the push by industry to road and drill for gas and oil—led to consensus by the Coalition to create a more focused and effective group to fight for permanent protection.

Gloria Flora, a significant Coalition member, former forest supervisor of Lewis and Clark National Forest, and author of the crucial 1997 decision to halt further leasing of oil and gas on the public lands now included in the Act, talks of the formation of the RMFHA and the Coalition:

> We have always intended to get to the point where we could have strong, effective, community-supported legislation. It took many steps to create not only the regulatory and political seedbed—including public outreach, media, etc.—but also to create the *brand* of the Rocky Mountain Front in the eyes of the public. Many years of work has led to the incredible public support and the immutable understanding that the Front is too special to develop or destroy in any way. The Rocky Mountain Front Heritage Act is the result of something far more strategic

> than just a group of concerned citizens getting together to write a bill. It is based on foresight, incredible commitment, and an amazing dedication to bringing a vision into reality.

The courageous and thoughtful decision in 1997 by Gloria Flora ultimately became law. The bill was sponsored by former U.S. senator Conrad Burns (R-MT). Senator Burns' legislation withdrew leasing of federal oil and gas on public lands within a six-mile buffer from the eastern boundary of public lands along the Front. It is important to note that, contrary to misinformation by detractors, that withdrawal did not affect oil and gas leasing on private lands along the Front.

A Decade of Work . . . Then Disappointment

In 2006, the Coalition began the task of talking with landowners, private and public land managers, ranchers, hunters, anglers, elected officials, and interested citizens to solicit ideas on protecting the public lands along the Front.

In 2008 and 2009, the group opened more discussions with grazing permittees, the Bureau of Land Management, Forest Service officials, and commissioners from Teton, Glacier, Pondera, and Lewis and Clark Counties. Members of the Coalition met with many supporters and nonsupporters in the area.

In the fall of 2009, the Coalition held four well-publicized meetings in Helena, Augusta, Choteau, and Great Falls. It disbursed extensive Internet communications, made announcements in newspaper publications, and conducted numerous presentations to various groups. These efforts provided outreach across the state of Montana.

The Coalition held numerous follow-up meetings through the summer and early fall of 2011. This outreach resulted in numerous changes to the original draft of the Act to incorporate some of the input. One of the glitches along the way surfaced in 2011 following objections from a group of local citizens in the Lincoln, Montana, area. This culminated in dropping some of the proposed acreage northeast of Lincoln.

The concept and actual creation of this proposal has spanned nearly a decade. Literally, hundreds of hours, and multiple tens of meetings—some of which included some extremely heated arguments—resulted in the reworking of proposals, maps, and draft legislation and dealing with special claims or interests of individuals and groups. Some of the wilderness advocates were—and still are—extremely unhappy about the limited acres proposed for wilderness. Yet, others wanted no wilderness at all. Other special interest groups, including mountain bikers, off-road vehicle (ORV) users, some cattle grazing permit holders, and anti-environmentalists presented heated arguments against the proposal. However, as more hearings, editorials, letters to the editors, and public meetings have taken place, the majority agree that this Act is a good, broad-based, citizen-backed proposal. There will always be some who will be against the bill.

Strong commendation needs to be offered for Mike Munoz and staff at the U.S. Forest Service, Rocky Mountain Ranger District, office in Choteau for their professional and diligent responses for information requests.

On October 28, 2011, more than ten years after the initial formation of the Coalition, Montana senator Max Baucus initially introduced the Rocky Mountain Front Heritage Act to Congress.[6] The bill failed to get out of committee. The fate of the bill is still in the hands of Congress. Senator Baucus has been a longtime supporter of the Front, having hiked the area and gone on pack trips into the Bob Marshall Wilderness. His staff has been and continues to be instrumental in working with the Coalition and the public by holding multiple public hearings and assisting in the drafting of the bill, in all forms of dialogue, public involvement, communication, and ultimately introduction of the Act. One can only hope that our leaders will recognize just how important this Act is for now and generations to come.

On February 21, 2013, Senator Baucus, who reintroduced the bill along with cosponsor Senator Jon Tester (D-MT), remarked: "We owe it to our kids and grandkids to protect unique treasures like the Front that make Montana the greatest place on earth. On top of that, protecting the Front is good for business and good for Montana jobs, with more than $10 million spent each year in the Front during hunting season alone."[7]

Quotes from Those Who Know

Gene Sentz, a retired schoolteacher, backcountry guide and packer, and grandfather of the Coalition, has been quoted many times in newspapers, magazines, and brochures. The *Choteau Acantha* quoted Sentz as saying, "This land defines what we are. It represents the soul of Montana. This is the best of the best."[8]

Sentz believes there are lots of reasons for saving the Front, but he explains that one of the best reasons came from a crusty old Montana native who told his congressman, "There are certain places on Earth which should be left alone, even if solid gold were beneath it . . . the Rocky Mountain Front is such a place."[9]

A good illustration for recognizing consensus building and support of this Act is represented by the comments of Larry Bonderud, mayor of Shelby, Montana:

> For the past several years, I have always believed that Montana has had enough areas designated as wilderness. I observed with extreme interest as many of my close friends expressed strong support for Sen. Max Baucus' recently introduced Heritage Act. I decided to give the proposal a very close review. My analysis has led me to supporting the act for the following reasons:
>
> 1. The Heritage Act development brought together many people with many different perspectives and created something that would not have been accomplished alone with limited participants.
>
> 2. The act would serve to diversify the economy of northern Montana. Diversity in economic development is something I have supported and worked on for many years.
>
> 3. The Heritage Act as proposed by Baucus is about balance. It is about maintaining our healthy

> communities, diversifying our economic development opportunities and insuring that we will continue to have abundant wildlife and clean water for our kids and grandkids.
>
> It is this analysis that led me to my support of the Heritage Act. I would ask that all Montanans support Baucus' Heritage Act. It is the right thing to do.[10]

Chuck Blixrud and his wife, Sharon, have operated the Seven Lazy P Guest Ranch west of Choteau for over five decades. The guest ranch is a significant local employer. The Blixruds have written several editorials and testified numerous times in favor of the Act. The couple have been very active supporters of all efforts to save the Rocky Mountain Front and have been an integral help to the Coalition and related efforts through the years. From their beautiful and relaxed guest ranch setting, Sharon reflects, "It's just a very special place, and it gets more special because the world gets crazier."[11] A lifelong resident of the Front, Chuck expresses the depth of his attachment to the land when he says, "I was born on a ranch outside the Front. I got into the mountains as soon as I could. I wanted to work with people, horses and in the mountains. Nothing grabs me like this country."[12]

Gerry Jennings, former president of the Montana Wilderness Association, a significant member of the Coalition, and a pivotal fighter for preservation of this spectacular part of our nation, speaks of the lure of the Front:

> The Rocky Mountain Front loomed large in luring us 38 years ago to settle in Montana. It reminds us daily of the need to protect this unique landscape, so those who follow us can have the same incredible adventures and spiritual re-birth that we've experienced.
>
> These awe-inspiring landscapes, abundant wildlife and sparkling streams exude the essence of The Great Spirit, the land of The Vision Quest, The Big Sky. Brilliant colors, orange, alizarin crimson, yellow ochre, bright yellow, all the shades of blue, green, red, yellow, and combinations thereof inspire painters, photographers,

> hikers, backpackers, campers and multiple other visitors. An annually renewable, never ending, exponentially valuable resource is here for the saving. Thank God for Teddy Roosevelt, John Muir, Bob Marshall, Gifford Pinchot and others who thought beyond the demands of current exploiters, who loved the intangible and tangible character of these last remaining, unique wild lands.[13]

Tony Porcarelli, a contractor, avid hunter, and Coalition member from Fairfield, Montana, along with his wife, Deb, has worked hard for protection of this resource. Tony says, "The Front keeps bringing me back. The Heritage Act would ensure future generations the freedom of a traditional fair-chase hunt in these wildlife-rich mountains."[14]

In a Missoula, Montana, newspaper guest column, former federal land resource leaders collectively voiced their support for the RMFHA. Lewis and Clark National Forest supervisors Spike Thompson (2004–2011), Rick Prausa (1999–2003), and Gloria Flora (1995–1998) wrote an opinion. They were joined by former supervisors Dale Gorman (1980–1995) and the late George N. Engler (1967–1976). Their solidarity illustrates strong support from former high-level agency heads. They state:

> Joining the three chiefs of the Forest Service and three former Montana Bureau of Land Management directors are five former Lewis and Clark National Forest supervisors. Together these land managers had 38 years of line officer experience spanning nine different administrations dating back to President Lyndon Johnson.
>
> We support the Heritage Act because, based upon our experience, the best way to protect the wildlife, clean water, outstanding natural scenery, and cultural heritage of the Front is to develop a balanced plan. The Heritage Act meets these criteria by providing the Forest Service with the management flexibility to fight fire, harvest trees and provide for motorized and nonmotorized recreation while defining a clear mandate to

protect native habitat and opportunities for traditional backcountry experiences on foot and horseback.

Citizen-based collaborative problem-solving is a relatively new phenomenon for management of our national forests. Thankfully, the Heritage Act was developed using an exemplary collaboration that encouraged broad and meaningful public participation.

The Heritage Act, a sensible and balanced proposal put forth by the Coalition to Protect the Rocky Mountain Front, was developed by ranchers, conservationists and others who live in and around the Front. Hunters support the Heritage Act because it assures access to their favorite game areas and protects habitat for thriving wildlife populations. Motorized recreation users support it because it doesn't close a single mile of roads or trails currently open for their use. Conservationists back it because it is a comprehensive plan that includes wilderness. Ranchers back it because it maintains their grazing privileges while helping to fight noxious weeds across all ownerships.

For these reasons, we wholeheartedly support this bill and urge the delegation to work to secure its speedy passage. We join our former forest chiefs and agree this is the right prescription for the right place at the right time.

By enacting the Rocky Mountain Heritage Act, Congress will be laying down a solid framework for the careful conservation of the multiple resources and values of this extraordinary landscape. We endorse both the hard work that's gone into crafting the Heritage Act and the final product itself. [15]

Ivan Doig, an eloquent writer and childhood resident of the Rocky Mountain Front, describes the Front west of Dupuyer in his book *This House of Sky:*

Here was a thought. Dad and I had lived our lifetimes beneath weather-making mountains, none of which tusked up into storm clouds as mightily as this Sawtooth Range of the Rockies would. In front of us now

> loomed the reefline of the entire continent, where the surf of weather broke and came flooding across, and both of us knew what could be ahead when full winter poured down off the north peaks. Yet for this instant, to have come upon grandness anywhere near this spavined ranch, neither of us had the heart to care.[16]

A. B. "Bud" Guthrie Jr. lived and wrote his spellbinding novels *The Big Sky. The Way West,* and *Fair Land, Fair Land* under the spell of Ear Mountain west of Choteau. Guthrie Jr. was inspired by the glory of the jutting cliffs, rolling pine hills, and sweeping plains on the east slope of the crown of the continent. To this day, *The Big Sky* is synonymous with this special place. From his home near Choteau, Guthrie wrote, "I look to the north and the south, where foothills rise, east to the great roll of the high plains and west to the mountains and my vision site of Ear Mountain, and good medicine lies all around."[17]

Status as of Mid-2013

Currently, the Act is anticipated for further hearing before the Natural Resources Committee sometime before the end of 2013. With Senator Baucus recently announcing that he will not seek a seventh term in the Senate, no one is exactly sure of the path the Heritage Act will take to passage. Senator Baucus has stated repeatedly that the RMFHA is one of his top legislative priorities and that he will do everything in his power to enact the bill before his retirement. Unfortunately, Congress appears to be unable to focus on doing what is good for our country; rather, they prefer to focus on what they perceive as being politically beneficial to each respective party. We hope that Senator Baucus can convince his compatriots to pass this extremely important legislation. Preserving such a magnificent place should not depend on political persuasion. This is a national treasure and does not belong to a few local or special interests or any particular political party. The benefit is for our people, for this grand place, and, most importantly, to preserve this heritage for future generations.

The battle for protection of the Front is ongoing. At present, the Rocky Mountain Front Heritage Act is awaiting congressional action. The fate of this national treasure is in the hands of mostly strangers to its beauty.

An innocent, beautiful child, waiting to be adopted.

Concluding Thoughts

There is little dispute among most who have visited the Rocky Mountain Front that this place is something very special. This majestic piece of our American heritage stirs emotions of indescribable depths. The history of the great Old North Trail, stories of conquistadores and of warring tribes, the great Blackfeet Nation, mountain men, buffalo hunters, trappers, traders, early settlers, and ultimate development of this spectacular area is embedded in our conscious and subconscious being. Those who want to mar this beautiful landscape and taint the historical significance for short-term gain often try to minimize the exponentially increasing value of this special place. Artists, writers, farmers, ranchers, teachers, hunters, fishermen, backpackers, hikers, outfitters, historians, local residents, tourists, and myriad other users see this place as a wellspring of spiritual and aesthetic inspiration. To lose this heritage to commercial exploitation for short-term gain would be a tragedy.

STONEY BURK is an attorney and lives in Choteau, Montana, where he has a law practice. An avid outdoorsman, he has hunted and hiked for many years and many miles of the Rocky Mountain Front.

---

[1] Yue Cui, Ed Mahoney, and Teresa Herbowicz, *Economic Benefits to Local Communities from National Park Visitation,* 2011, Natural Resource Report NPS/NRSS/ARD/NRR—2013/632 (Fort Collins, CO: National Park Service, February 2013).

[2] Denise Germann, "New Report Shows Visitor Spending in Area Creates," *Glacier National Park Service* (news release), February 26, 2013, http://www.nps.gov/glac/parknews/new-report-shows-visitor-spending-in-area-creates.htm.

[3] Aldo Leopold, *A Sand County Almanac: And Sketches Here and There* (London: Oxford University Press, 1949), viii.

[4] Leopold, *A Sand County Almanac*, 204.

[5] Rick Graetz, *Montana's Bob Marshall Country: The Bob Marshall, Scapegoat, Great Bear Wildness Areas and Surrounding Wildlands* (Helena: *Montana Magazine*, 1985), 32.

[6] Melody Martinsen, "Baucus to Carry Legislation for RMF Heritage Act," *Choteau Acantha*, November 9, 2011.

[7] Karl Puckett, "Baucus Reintroduces Heritage Bill: Act Aims to Protect Public Land on the Front," *Great Falls Tribune*, February 21, 3013.

[8] Melody Martinsen, "Rehberg Hears Pros, Cons on RMF Heritage Act Proposal," *Choteau Acantha*, April 25, 2012.

[9] Rick Graetz, "This is Montana: Rocky Mountain Front Wildlife," *Helena Independent Record*, November 23, 2000.

[10] Larry J. Bonderud, "Supporting Baucus' Heritage Act Is Right Thing to Do," *Billings Gazette*, January 12, 2012.

[11] Jeff Welsch, "Protecting the Backbone of the World," *Montana Quarterly*, Fall 2011.

[12] Nancy Thornton, "Roadless Plan Could Restrict Ski-Area Development," *Choteau Acantha*, November 29, 2000.

[13] Gerry Jennings, personal communication to author, 2013.

[14] Tony Porcararelli, personal communication to author, 2013.

[15] Spike Thompson, Rick Prausa, and Gloria Flora, "Support Legislation to Protect the Front," *Missoulian*, January 20, 2012.

[16] Ivan Doig, *This House of Sky: Landscapes of a Western Mind* (Orlando: Harvest, 1978), 181.

[17] A. B. Guthrie Jr., "The Rocky Mountain Front: One Man's Religion," *Montana Magazine*, September/October 1987.

BIBLIOGRAPHY

Editor's Note: Bibliographic documents provided by individual chapter authors contain first name and last name initials in braces { }. All other documents are provided by the editor.

Alderson, Nannie T., and Helena Huntington Smith. *A Bride Goes West.* Lincoln, NE: University of Nebraska Press, 1942. {JP}

Alt, David D., and Donald W. Hyndman. *Roadside Geology of Montana*, Missoula, MT: Mountain Press Publishing Co., 1986. {KP}

Alwin, John A. Pelts, Provisions & Perceptions: The Hudson's Bay Company Mandan Indian Trade, 1795-1812. *Montana: The Magazine of Western History*, Summer 1979.

Andryk, Timothy Alan. "Ecology of Bighorn Sheep in Relation to Oil and Gas Development Along the East Slope of the Rocky Mountains, Northcentral Montana." Master's thesis, Montana State University - Bozeman, 1983.

Applegate, Brock. Blackleaf Canyon: Target of Destruction. *Journal of the Rocky Mountain Front*, Spring 1991.

Arno, Stephen F., Lars Ostlund, and Robert E. Keane. Living Artifacts: The Ancient Ponderosa Pines of the West. *Montana: The Magazine of Western History,* Spring 2008.

Arthur, George. *Pictographs in Central Montana, Part III, Comments*. Anthropology and Sociology Papers, No. 21. Missoula: MT: Montana State University, 1960.

Ashby, Christopher S. "The Blackfeet Agreement of 1895 and Glacier National Park: A Case History." Master's thesis, University of Montana - Missoula, 1985.

Auchly, Bruce. Devil Bear. *Montana Outdoors*, September/October, 1995.

———. On the Front Lines: As the Grizzly Population Expands, More Montanans are Coming Face to Face with the Emboldened Bears. *Montana Outdoors*, November/December 2002.

Auchly, Bruce, and Joe Moll. *Grizzly Bears of Montana: A Resource Guide for Educators*. Missoula, MT: Boone and Crockett Club, 2001.

Aune, Keith. "Comparative Ecology of Black and Grizzly Bears on the Rocky Mountain Front, Montana." *Bears: Their Biology and Management* 9, part 1 (1995): 365-374. Ninth International Conference on Bear Research and Management. {KA}

———. "Impacts of Winter Recreationists on Wildlife in a Portion of Yellowstone National Park, Wyoming." Master's thesis, Montana State University - Bozeman, 1981.

———. *Rocky Mountain Front Grizzly Bear Monitoring and Investigation*. Helena, MT: Montana Department of Fish, Wildlife,and Parks, 1985.

Aune, Keith, and Bob Brannon. *East Front Grizzly Studies*. Helena, MT: Montana Dept. of Fish, Wildlife, and Parks, March 1987.

Aune, Keith, Mike Madel, and Carrie Hunt. *Rocky Mountain Front Grizzly Bear Monitoring and Investigation*. Helena,MT: Montana Department of Fish, Wildlife, and Parks, May 1986.

Aune, Keith, and T. Stivers. *Ecological Studies of the Grizzly Bear in the Pine Butte Preserve.* Helena, MT: Montana Department of Fish, Wildlife, and Parks, 1985.

———. *Rocky Mountain Front Grizzly Bear Monitoring and Investigation*. Helena, MT: Montana Department of Fish, Wildlife, and Parks, 1981.

———. *Rocky Mountain Front Grizzly Bear Monitoring and Investigation*. Helena, MT: Montana Department of Fish, Wildlife, and Parks, 1982.

———. *Rocky Mountain Front Grizzly Bear Monitoring and Investigation.* Helena, MT: Montana Department of Fish, Wildlife, and Parks, 1983.

Aune, Keith, T. Stivers, and M. Madel. *Rocky Mountain Grizzly Bear Monitoring and Investigation*. Helena, MT: Montana Department of Fish, Wildlife, and Parks, 1984.

Aune, Keith. E., and W. F. Kasworm. *Final Report: East Front Grizzly Studies*. Helena, MT: Montana Dept. of Fish, Wildlife, and Parks, April 1989. {KA}

Aune, Keith E., Richard D. Mace, and Daniel W. Carney. "The Reproductive Biology of Female Grizzly Bears in the Northern Continental Divide Ecosystem with Supplemental Data from the Yellowstone Ecosystem." *Bears: Their Biology and Management* 9, part 1 (1995): 451-458. Ninth International Conference on Bear Research and Management, {KA}

Axline, John. The Last of Its Kind: The Dearborn River High Bridge. Montana: *The Magazine of Western History*, Winter 2002.

Ayers, H. B. *The Lewis and Clark Forest Reserve, Montana*. Extract from 21st Annual Report of U.S. Geological Survey, 1899-1900. Washington, D.C.: Government Printing Office, 1900. {KA}

Bader, Michael G., and Robert J. Yetter. *Appeal of the Record of Decision for the Fina Oil and Chemical Company Oil/Gas Well, Federal South Glacier No. 1-26 and Environmental Impact Statement for Proposed Oil and Gas Drilling Near Badger Creek and Hall Creek in the Badger-Two Medicine Area of the Lewis and Clark National Forest in Montana*. Missoula, MT: Alliance for the Wild Rockies and Badger Chapter, April 15, 1991.

Ball, Stephen D., Jr. "Wilderness vs. Development Case Study: The Badger-Two Medicine." Bachelor's thesis, University of California - Santa Barbara, 1991.

Barrett, Stephen. Indians & Fire: Fire Management May Be Older Than the Forest Service. *Western Wildlands*, Spring 1980.

———. "Indian-Scarred Trees." *American Forests*, 91, no. 1 (1985): 39.

Barrett, Stephen W. "Fire Regimes in the Northern Rockies." *Fire Management Today* 64, no. 2 (2004): 32-38.

Barrett, Stephen W., Thomas W. Swetnam, and William L. Baker. "Indian Fire Use: Deflating the Legend," *Fire Management Today* 65, no. 3 (2005): 31-33.

Bauer, Erwin A. *Erwin Bauer's Bear in Their World*. New York: NY: Outdoor Life Books, 1990.

Baumeister, Dayna A. "Effects of *Pinus Flexilis* on the Dynamics and Structure of Plant Communities on the Northern Rocky Mountain Front, and, Training Biologists for Emerging Niches in Non-traditional Jobs." PhD diss., University of Montana - Missoula, 2002.

Baumeister, Thomas R. "Field-testing the Accuracy and Generality of Selected Wildlife-habitat Models." PhD diss., University of Montana - Missoula, 1999.

Beattie, Judith H. "Indian Maps in the Hudson's Bay Company Archives: A Comparison of Five Area Maps Recorded by Peter Fidler, 1801-1802." *Archivaria* 21 (Winter 1985-86): 166-175.

Beyond ... The Shadows of the Rockies: History of the Augusta Area. Augusta Area Historical Society, [Augusta, Mont.]: Anderson Publication, 2007.

Binnema, Theodore. *Common and Contested Ground: A Human and Environmental History of the Northwestern Plains.* Norman, OK: University of Oklahoma Press, 2001.

———. "Old Swan, Big Man, and the Siksika Bands, 1794-1815." *Canadian Historical Review* 77, no. 1 (1996): 1-32.

Bisnett, Bud. "Discussion Concerning the Old North Trail." Interview with David Louter, September 20, 1986. Oral History 167-2. Archives and Special Collections, Mansfield Library, University of Montana - Missoula, MT.

Blackfeet Fish and Wildlife Department. *Bear Management Plan and Guidelines for Bear Management on the Blackfeet Indian Reservation*. Draft Guidelines. Browning, MT: Blackfeet Fish and Wildlife Department, December 1998.

Blackfeet Tribal Business Council. *Blackfeet Cultural Preservation Act: Blackfeet Tribal Ordinance #100*. Browning, MT: Blackfeet Tribal Business Council, April 2004.

Bob Marshall Alliance v. Hodel. 852 F.2d 1223 (9th Cir. 1988). http://www.leagle.com/decision/19882075852F2d1223_11873

Books, Dave. A Century of Conservation. *Montana Outdoors*, November/December, 2000.

Boulanger, John, Katherine C. Kendall, Jeffrey B. Stetz, David A. Roon, Lisette P. Waits, and David Paetkau. "Multiple Data Sources Improve DNA-Based Mark–Recapture Population Estimates of Grizzly Bears." *Ecological Applications* 18, no. 3 (2008): 577–589.

Bradley, Trina Jo, ed. *Turning Back the Pages: A Pictoral History of Valier and Dupuyer*. Valier, MT: *The Valierian*, 2005.

Brannon, Robert. Managing the Grizzly Bear. *Montana Outdoors*, May/June 1986.

Brannon, Robert D., Richard D. Mace, and Arnold R. Dood. "Grizzly Bear Mortality in the Northern Continental Divide Ecosystem, Montana." *Wildlife Society Bulletin*. 16, no. 3 (1988): 262-269.

Breuninger, Ray. A *Geologic Historian Looks at the Rocky Mountain Front*. Last Chance Audubon Society's 1999 Natural History Lecture Series. Helena, MT, March 24, 1999. Videocassette (VHS), 60 min.

Brown, Mark H. Yellowstone Tourists and the Nez Perce. *Montana: The Magazine of Western History,* Summer 1966.

Brownell, Joan Louise. "The Genesis of Wildlife Conservation in Montana." Master's thesis. Montana State University - Bozeman, 1987.

Bullchild, Percy. *The Sun Came Down*. San Francisco, CA: Harper & Row, 1985. {MS}

Busch, Robert. *The Grizzly Almanac*. New York, NY: Lyons Press, 2000.

Butler, David R. "The Impact of Climate Change on Patterns of Zoogeomorphological Influence: Examples from the Rocky Mountains of the Western U.S.A." *Geomorphology* 157-158 (2012): 183-191.

Bynum Centennial Committee. *Bynum–a Roundup of Memories: The Story of Bynum, Montana, and its People*. Bynum, MT: The Committee, 1986.

Byron, Eve. Seven Feet Under. *Life in the Helena Area*. Fall/Winter 2010.

———. The Keeper of the Cave. *Life in the Helena Area*. Fall/Winter 2011.

Caesar, Gene. The Bear That Killed Ken Scott. *Sports Afield*, January 1958.

Cahalane, V. H. *A Preliminary Study of Distribution and Numbers of Cougar, Grizzly and Wolf in North America*. Bronx, NY: New York Zoological Society, 1964. {KA}

Calloway, Colin G. *One Vast Winter Count: The Native American West Before Lewis and Clark*. Lincoln, NE: University of Nebraska Press, 2003.

Campanella, Joseph, Terry Lonner, Tom Manning, and Jack Stonnell. Back From the Brink: *Montana's Wildlife Legacy*. Bozeman, MT: Media Works, 2005. DVD, 120 min.

Campbell, Newell P. *Caves of Montana*. Butte, MT: Montana College of Mineral Science and Technology, 1978.

Cannon, Kenneth P. "'They Went as High as They Choose:' What an Isolated Skull Can Tell Us about the Biogeography of High-Altitude Bison Arctic." *Antarctic and Alpine Research* 39, no. 1 (2007): 44–56.

Carlsen, Tom, and Glenn Erickson. *Montana Bighorn Sheep Conservation Strategy*. Helena, MT: Montana Department of Fish, Wildlife, and Parks, January 2010. {HP}

Casebeer, Robert L., Merle J. Rognrud, and Stewart Brandborg. *The Rocky Mountain Goat in Montana*. Helena, MT: Montana Fish and Game Commission, 1950. {MT}

Cattet, Marc, Gordon Stenhouse, and Trent Bollinger. "Exertional Myopathy in a Grizzly Bear (Ursus arctos) Captured by Leghold Snare." *Journal of Wildlife Diseases* 44, no. 4 (2008): 973-978.

Cattet, Marc, John Boulanger, Gordon Stenhouse, Roger A. Powell, and Melissa J. Reynolds-Hogland. "An Evaluation of Long-Term Capture Effects in Ursids: Implications for Wildlife Welfare and Research." *Journal of Mammalogy* 89, no. 4 (2008): 973-990.

Chalmers, Ann Leslie. "Quaternary Glacial Geology and Geomorphology of the Teton Drainage Area, Teton County, Montana." Master's thesis. Montana State University - Bozeman, 1968.

Chevron USA Production Company. *Proposal to Helena National Forest: Oil and Gas Leasing Analysis, Final Environmental Impact Statement and Record of Decision*. Alice Creek FHRAA. Houston, TX: Chevron U.S.A. Production Co., October 1996.

Clarkson, Peter, and Linda Sutterlin. *Bear Essentials: A Source Book and Guide to Planning Bear Education Programs.* Missoula, MT: University of Montana, 1984.

Clifford, Frank. *The Backbone of the World: A Portrait of a Vanishing West Along the Continental Divide*. New York: Broadway Books, 2002.

Cole, Glen F. "Grizzly Bear-Elk Relationships in Yellowstone National Park." *Journal of Wildlife Management* 36, no. 2 (1972): 556-561.

Colson, Amy. *There's a Freedom Here: Choices and Change on Montana's Rocky Mountain Front*. Bozeman, MT: Peak Recording & Sound, 2006. DVD, 57 min.

Confluence of Cultures Symposium. *A Confluence of Cultures: Symposium Proceedings*. Missoula, MT: University of Montana Printing & Graphic Services, 2003.

Cooney, Bob. Paul Hazel: 60 Years in the Wilderness. *Montana Magazine*, September/October 1979.

Cooney, Robert F. "Elk Problems in Montana." *Journal of Range Management* 5, no. 1 (1952): 3-7.

———. The Grizzly Bear: An Endangered Species, November 14, 1955. In *Grizzly - General 1955 - 1972*, Pg. 1, 1955. Microfiche. Available at Montana State Fish, Wildlife, and Parks, Helena, MT.

———. *Grizzly Bear Study.* Quarterly Report. Helena, MT: Montana Fish and Game Department, 1941. {KA}

———. Wildlife survey field notebooks. 1940. Montana Department of Fish, Wildlife and Parks, Kalispell. {HP}

Copenhaver, Howard. *They Left Their Tracks: Recollection of 60 Years as a Bob Marshall Wilderness Outfitter*. Stevensville, MT: Stoneydale Press Publishing Co., 1990.

Coues, Elliot, ed. *The History of the Lewis and Clark Expedition*. Vol. II. New York, NY: Dover, 1997.

Couey, Faye Morrison. *Sun River Elk Damage Investigation: Flathead - Willow Creek*. Helena, MT: Wildlife Restoration Division, Montana Fish & Game Department, 1947.

Cowdrey, Mike, Ned Martin, Jody Martin, Nakia Williamson, Paul M. Raczka, and Winfield Coleman. *Bridles of the Americas. Vol. 2, Horses & Bridles of the North American Indians*. Nicasio, CA: Hawk Hill Press, 2012.

Craighead, John J., J. S. Sumner, and G. B. Scaggs. *A Definitive System for Analysis of Grizzly Bear Habitat and Other Wilderness Resources*. Wildlife-Wildlands Institute Mongograph 1. Missoula, MT: University of Montana, 1982. {KA}

Craighead, John J., Jay S. Sumner, and John A. Mitchell. *The Grizzly Bears of Yellowstone: Their Ecology in the Yellowstone Ecosystem, 1959-1992*. Washington, D.C: Island Press, 1995.

Craighead, John W. *An Archaeological Reconnaissance of the Pine Butte Area, Teton County, Montana*. Nature Conservancy Contract. Missoula, MT: Wildlife /Wildlands Institute, 1979.

Crenshaw, J. *A Faunistic Survey of Pine Butte Swamp*. Final Report. [Helena, MT]: The Nature Conservancy, 1979.

Cui, Yue, Ed Mahoney, and Teresa Herbowicz. *Economic Benefits to Local Communities from National Park Visitation, 2011*. Natural Resource Report NPS/NRSS/ARD/NRR—2013/632. Fort Collins, CO: National Park Service, February 2013. {SB}

Cunniff, Jeffrey L. A Tale of Two Towns. *Montana: The Magazine of Western History*, Spring 1976.

Cunningham, Bill. The Badger-Two Medicine: Blackfeet Holy Land. *Montana Magazine*, November/December 1989. {BC}

———. Bob Marshall Wilderness: East Side. *Montana Magazine*, September/October 1985.

———. Chief Challenge. *Montana Magazine*, July/August 2010.

———. Choteau Mountain-Teton Peaks. *Montana Magazine*, August 1992. {BC}

———. Deep Creek: Heart of the Rocky Mountain Front. *Montana Magazine*, July/August 1990. {BC}

———. The Front of the Front: Where the Trees Lean East and the People Lean West. *Montana Magazine*, June 1994.

———. *Montana Wildlands: From Northwest Peaks to Deadhorse Badlands*. Montana Geographic Series 16. Helena, MT: American Geographic Publishing, 1990. {BC}

———. Pack it In, Pack it Out. *Montana Magazine*, September/October 2012.

———. Pilgrimage to a Holy Land: The Threatened Badger-Two Medicine. *Montana Magazine*, November/December 1991.

———. Wild Country: Atop the Front: Winter Day Trips. *Montana Magazine*, January/February 2000. {BC}

———. Wild Country: Atop the Front: Winter Day Trips (Part II). *Montana Magazine*, March/April 2001. {BC}

———. Wild Country: Blind Horse Outstanding Natural Area. *Montana Magazine*, March/April 2004. {BC}

———. Wild Country: Front Range Evolving: A Look at the Southern Ramparts. *Montana Magazine*, June 1991. {BC}

———. Wild Country: The Renshaw Region: Central Highlands of the Rocky Mountain Front. *Montana Magazine*, October 1991. {BC}

———. Wild Country: Sawtooth Ridge: Ragged, Roaring Rampart. *Montana Magazine*, September/October 2002. {BC}

———. *Wild Montana: A Guide to 55 Roadless Recreation Areas.* Helena, MT: Falcon Press, 1995. {BC}

———. Wildly Accessible: Weekend Adventures Abound on Montana's Rocky Mountain Front. *Montana Magazine*, January/February 2008. {BC}

Cunningham, William P. *Montana's Continental Divide*. Montana Geographic Series 12. Helena, MT: *Montana Magazine*, 1986. {BC}

Curtis, Sam. Cream of the Crop. *Montana Outdoors*, September/October 2007.

Cushman, Dan. *The Great North Trail: America's Route of the Ages*. New York, NY: McGraw-Hill, 1966.

Dale, Adolph. "The Old North Trail." Interview with David Louter, November 4, 1986. Oral History 167-1. Archives and Special Collections, Mansfield Library, University of Montana - Missoula,MT.

Davis, Les. In Search of Early Elephants. *Montana Outdoors*, November/December 1986.

———. Quarries of Stone. *Montana Outdoors*, July/August 1987.

———. A Thousand Winters Ago. *Montana Outdoors*, March/April 1986.

———. Tipi Rings: Circle of Stones. *Montana Outdoors*, May/June 1985.

———, ed. "Panel Discussion: Symposium on Bison Procurement and Utilization." *Plains Anthropologist* 23, no. 82, part 2 (1978): 287-311.

Davis, Leslie. *The Paleoindian Occupation of the Rocky Mountain Front in Montana, 11,500 to 7,500 Years Ago: Landscapes, Resources, and Adaptations by First Peoples*. Last Chance Audubon Society's 1999 Natural History Lecture Series. Helena, MT, March 10, 1999. Videocassette (VHS), 60 min.

Day, Gary, Charles Jonkel, and Terry Werner. *Relocations of Grizzlies in the Border Grizzly Area*. Special Report No. 14, Border Grizzly Project. Missoula, MT: University of Montana, March 1978.

Dearborn Homemakers. *Dearborn Country: A History of the Dearborn, Wolf Creek and Craig Areas*. Fairfield, MT: Fairfield Times, 1976.

Deaver, Sherri. *Blackfeet Use of the Badger-Two Medicine*. Prepared for Lewis and Clark National Forest. Billings, MT: Ethnoscience, June 1998.

———. *Ethnographic Overview of Selected Portions of the Lewis and Clark National Forest and Adjacent Bureau of Land Management Lands*. (Vols. 1 & 2). Prepared for Lewis and Clark National Forest. Billings, MT: Ethnoscience, August 1995.

Dempsey, Hugh *A. Indian Tribes of Alberta*. Calgary, AB: Glenbow-Alberta Institute, 1979.

Dempsey, Hugh Aylmer. *Big Bear: The End of Freedom*. Lincoln, NE: University of Nebraska Press, 1984.

Denig, Edwin Thompson, and J. N. B. Hewitt. *The Assiniboine*. Norman, OK: University of Oklahoma Press, 2000.

Denig, Edwin Thompson, and John C. Ewers. *Five Indian Tribes of the Upper Missouri: Sioux, Arickaras, Assiniboines, Crees, Crows*. Norman, OK: University of Oklahoma Press, 1961.

DeSanto, Jerry. *Bitterroot*. Babb, MT: Lere Press, 1993.

De Smet, Pierre-Jean. *Life, Letters, and Travels*. New York, NY: Francis P. Harper, 1905.

———. *Western Missions and Missionaries: A Series of Letters*. New York, 1859.

Devine, Heather. *People Who Own Themselves: Aboriginal Ethnogenesis in a Canadian Family, 1660-1900*. Calgary, AB: University of Calgary Press, 2004. {MS}

Diamond, Seth J., and Pat Finnegan. *Harlequin Duck Ecology on Montana's Rocky Mountain Front*. Choteau, MT: Lewis and Clark National Forest, Rocky Mountain District, June 1992.

———. *Wolf Recolonization Along Montana's Rocky Mountain Front*. Great Falls, MT: Lewis and Clark National Forest, 1993.

Dickson, Tom. Barbed-Wire Bears. *Montana Outdoors*, July/August 2005.

Doig, Ivan. *This House of Sky: Landscapes of a Western Mind*. Orlando: A Harvest Book, 1978. {SB}

Dood, Arnold, and H. Pac. *Montana Statewide Grizzly Bear Mortality Studies–1986-88*. Helena, MT: Montana Fish, Wildlife, and Parks, 1989. {KA}

Dood, Arnold R., and Helga Ihsle Pac. *Five Year Update of the Programmatic Environmental Impact Statement: The Grizzly Bear in Northwestern Montana, 1986-1990*. Helena, MT: Montana Department of Fish, Wildlife, and Parks, 1993.

Dood, Arnold R., R. D. Brannon, and R. D. Mace. *Final Programmatic Environmental Impact Statement: The Grizzly Bear in Northwestern Montana*. Helena, MT: Montana Department of Fish, Wildlife, and Parks, March 1986. {KA}

Dood, Arnold R., Robert D. Brannon, and Richard D. Mace. "Management of Grizzly Bears in the Northern Continental Divide Ecosystem, Montana." *Transactions of the 51st Northern American Wildlife and Natural Resource Conference* (1986): 162-177.

Dood, Arnold R., Shirley J. Atkinson, and Vanna J. Boccadori. *Grizzly Bear Management Plan for Western Montana: Final Programmatic Environmental Impact Statement 2006-2016.* Helena, MT: Montana Department of Fish, Wildlife, and Parks, 2006.

Dormaar, John F. *Sweetgrass Hills: A Natural and Cultural History.* Lethbridge, AB: Lethbridge Historical Society, 2003.

DuBois, Kristi. *Rocky Mountain Front Raptor Survey.* Helena, MT: Montana Department of Fish, Wildlife, and Parks, 1984.

Dupuyer Centennial Committee. *By Gone Days and Modern Ways: Dupuyer Centennial.* Havre, MT: Griggs Printing and Publishing, 1977.

Dusenberry, Verne. The Rocky Boy Indians. *Montana Magazine of History,* Winter 1954.

———. Waiting for a Day That Never Comes. *Montana: The Magazine of Western History,* Spring 1958.

Dyck, Ian. "Does Rodeo Have Roots in Ancient Indian Traditions?" *Plains Anthropologist* 41, no. 157 (1996): 205-219.

Dyck, Paul. Lone Wolf Returns to That Long Ago Time. *Montana: The Magazine of Western History,* Winter 1972.

Earhart, Robert L., and Lawrence Y. Marks. "Scapegoat Wilderness and Additions, Bob Marshall and Great Bear Wildernesses, and Adjacent Study Areas, Montana." In *Wilderness Mineral Potential: Assessment of Mineral-Resource Potential in U.S. Forest Service Lands Studied, 1964-1984,* edited by S. P. Marsh, S. J. Kropschot, and R. G. Dickinson, 741-43. Washington, D.C: Government Printing Office, 1984.

East, Ben. *Bears: A Veteran Outdoorsman's Account of the Most Fascinating and Dangerous Animals in North America.* New York, NY: Outdoor Life, 1977.

Eckberg, Scott. Review of *Fort Union and the Upper Missouri Fur Trade* by Barton H. Barbour. *Montana: The Magazine of Western History,* Winter 2001.

Edwards, Vickie. *Northern Continental Divide Ecosystem Front Country Survey of Attractant Sites 2002-2003.* Missoula, MT: Brown Bear Resources, 2003.

Erickson, Grace V. The Sun River Stampede. *Montana Magazine of History,* January 1953.

Erickson, G. L. "The Ecology of Rocky Mountain Bighorn Sheep in the Sun River Area of Montana with Special Reference to Summer Food Habits and Range Movements." Master's thesis, Montana State University - Bozeman, 1972.

Evans, G. Edward. "Prehistoric Blackduck - Historic Assiniboine: A Reassessment." *Plains Anthropologist* 6, no. 14 (1961): 271-275.

Evans, Sterling, ed. *The Borderlands of the American and Canadian Wests: Essays on Regional History of the Forty-ninth Parallel.* Lincoln, NE: University of Nebraska Press, 2006.

Ewers, John C. *The Blackfeet: Raiders on the Northwest Plains.* Norman, OK: University of Oklahoma Press, 1958.

———. *Indian life on the Upper Missouri.* Norman, OK: University of Oklahoma Press, 1968.

———. Iroquois Indians in the Far West. *Montana: The Magazine of Western History*, Spring 1963.

———. Plains Indian Reactions to the Lewis and Clark Expedition. *Montana: The Magazine of Western History*, Winter 1966.

Ewing, Sherm. *The Range.* Missoula, MT: Mountain Press Publishing Co., 1990.

Fairfield Heritage Committee. *Boots & Shovels: A History of the Greenfield Irrigation District, Division of the Sun River Project, Fairfield Montana.* Fairfield, MT: Fairfield Times, 1978.

Fanning, T. J. *Looking Back on the Front: A Bridging of Historical Perspectives.* New York, NY: Stonesong Press, 2011.

Farnell, Brenda. "Dynamic Embodiment in Assiniboine (Nakota) Storytelling." *Anthropological Linguistics* 44, no. 1 (2002): 37-64.

Farr, William E. Going to Buffalo: Indian Hunting Migrations across the Rocky Mountains: Part 1, Making Meat and Taking Robes. *Montana: The Magazine of Western History*, Winter 2003.

———. Going to Buffalo: Indian Hunting Migrations across the Rocky Mountains: Part 2, Civilian Permits, Army Escorts. *Montana: The Magazine of Western History*, Spring 2004.

———. Troubled Bundles, Troubled Blackfeet: The Travail of Cultural and Religious Renewal. *Montana: The Magazine of Western History,* Autumn 1993.

Fenenga, Franklin. "Appraisal of the Archaeological and Paleontological Resources of the Sun River Basin, Montana." In *Appraisal of the Archaeological and Paleontological Resources of Sites in the Missouri River Basin.* [Washington, D.C.]: Smithsonian Institution, 1951.

Fickes, Clyde P. *Recollections: Forest Ranger Emeritus*. Missoula, MT: U.S. Forest Service, Northern Region, 1972.

Finnegan, Pat. *Rare Furbearer Observations Along the Rocky Mountain Front 1989-1992*. Great Falls, MT: Lewis and Clark National Forest, 1992.

Fitzpatrick, Dola. Two Rounds With a Grizzly. *Western Sportsman*, November/December, 1950.

Flanagan, Darris. *Indian Trails of the Northern Rockies*. Stevensville, MT: Stoneydale Press Publishing. Co., 2001.

Fleming, Walter C. *The Complete Idiot's Guide to Native American History*. Indianapolis, IN: Alpha Books, 2003.

———. Review of *The History of the Assiniboine and Sioux Tribes of the Fort Peck Indian Reservation, Montana, 1800-2000*, by David Miller, Dennis Smith, Joseph R. McGeshick, James Shanley, and Caleb Shields. *Magazine of Western History*, Autumn 2008.

Flora, Gloria. "Science and Public Policy—The Moratorium on New Oil and Gas Drilling Along the Eastern Face of the Rocky Mountain Front: Interview with Gloria Flora." By Jackie Yamanaka and Jim Gransbery. *Yellowstone Public Radio*, November 3, 2003.

Flowers, Alice Blood. "Assessing the Effectiveness of a Place-Based Conservation Education Program by Applying Utilization-Focused Evaluation." PhD diss., University of Montana - Missoula, 2007.

Forbis, Richard G. "Fletcher: A Paleo-Indian Site in Alberta." *American Antiquity* 33, no. 1 (1968): 1-10.

Forbis, Richard G., and John D. Sperry. "An Early Man Site in Montana." *American Antiquity* 18, no. 2 (1952): 127-133.

Ford, Lee M., and A. B. Guthrie, Jr., Bob Ford, Sun River Cowman. *Montana: The Magazine of Western History*, Winter 1959.

Forsgren, Dean, and Oscar Oliveira. Oil and Gas in Wilderness Areas: The Need for Compromise. *Western Wildlands*, Fall 1987.

Foster, Martha H. "'Just Following the Buffalo': Origins of a Montana Métis Community." *Great Plains Quarterly* 26, no. 3 (2006): 185-202.

Foster, Martha Harroun. *We Know Who We Are: Métis Identity in a Montana Community.* Norman, OK: University of Oklahoma Press, 2006. {MS}

Fourstar, Jerome. "Assiniboine Stories." Unpublished manuscript, April 1997.

Fourstar, Robert F. History of the Assiniboine People from the Oral Tradition. *The Montana Professor*, Winter 2003. Reprint with revisions from *Nakodabi*, October 1992.

Fraley, John. *Wild River Pioneers: Adventures in the Middle Fork of the Flathead, Great Bear Wilderness and Glacier National Park.* Whitefish, MT: Big Mountain Publishing, 2008.

France, Tom. "Politics, Forest Management, and Bears." *Bears: Their Biology and Management* 9 (1995): 523-528. Ninth International Conference on Bear Research and Management.

French, Steven P. and Marilynn G. French. "Predatory Behavior of Grizzly Bears Feeding on Elk Calves in Yellowstone National Park, 1986-88." *Bears: Their Biology and Management* 8, part 1 (1990): 335-341. Eighth International Conference on Bear Research and Management.

Frey, Charles R. The Rocky Mountain Front: A Chronology of Exploration. *Western Wildlands*, Fall 1987.

Friskics, Scott. "Dialogue, Responsibility, and Oil and Gas Leasing on Montana's Rocky Mountain Front." *Ethics and the Environment* 8, no. 2 (2003): 8-30.

———. "Wilderness and Everyday Life." Master's thesis, University of North Texas, 2011.

Gates, C. Cormack, Curtis H. Freese, Peter J. P. Gogan, and Mandy Kotzman, eds. *American Bison: Status Survey and Conservation Guidelines 2010.* Gland, Switzerland: International Union for Conservation of Nature, 2010.

Gilbert, Barrie K. *Motorized Access on Montana's Rocky Mountain Front: A Synthesis of Scientific Literature and Recommendations for Use in Revision of the Travel Plan for the Rocky Mountain Division.* Wilderness Society, 2003.

Gildart, Robert C. *Montana's Early-Day Rangers*. Helena, MT: Farcountry Press, 1985.

Gleason, Alice. The Hundred Year Flood. *Home Front: The Life and Times of Montana's Rocky Mountain Front Country*, Spring 1994.

Gleason, Alice, Genny Barhaugh, and Carol Guthrie. Starting From Scratch: *The Adventures of a Lady Dude Rancher.* Choteau, MT: Star Route Publishing, 2000.

Godtel, Donald, et al. *Cumulative Effects Analysis Process for the Rocky Mountain Front Northern Continental Divide Grizzly Bear Ecosystem*. Great Falls, MT: Lewis and Clark National Forest, 1987.

Graetz, Rick. *Montana's Bob Marshall Country: The Bob Marshall, Scapegoat, Great Bear Wildness Areas and Surrounding Wildlands.* Helena, MT: *Montana Magazine*, 1985. {SB}

Graetz, Rick, and Susie Graetz. *The Rocky Mountain Front.* Montana Geographic Journal, Issue 1. Helena, MT: Northern Rockies Publishing, n.d. {BC}

Graetz, Rick, Susie Graetz, and Gene Sentz. *Montana's Rocky Mountain Front*. Helena, MT: Northern Rockies Publishing, 2000.

Grafe, Steven L., ed., *Lanterns on the Prairie: The Blackfeet Photographs of Walter McClintock.* Norman, OK: University of Oklahoma Press, 2009.

Gramlich, C. R. *Raptor Nesting Inventory*, East Front. Unpublished report. Butte, MT: Bureau of Land Management, 1979.

Grant, Madison. *Early History of Glacier National Park, Montana.* Washington: Govt. Print. Office, 1919.

Greer, K. and V. Craig. *Bear Hunting in Montana.* Helena, MT: Montana Fish and Game Department, June 1971.

Greer, Kenneth. *Statewide Grizzly Investigations-Research Laboratory 1967-1990.* Helena, MT: Montana Department of Fish, Wildlife, and Parks, n.d. {KA}

Greer, Kenneth R. *Montana Grizzly Bear Management—and Public Harmony.* Bozeman, MT: Montana Department of Fish and Game, 1973. {KA}

Greiser, Sally T. "Errata: Middle Prehistoric Period Adaptations and Paleoenvironment in the Northwestern Plains: The Sun River Site." *American Antiquity* 51, no. 1 (1986): 220.

———. "Late Prehistoric Cultures on the Montana Plains." In Plains Indians, A.D. 500-1500: *The Archaeological Past of Historic Groups,* ed. Karl H. Schleiser, 34-55. Norman, OK: University of Oklahoma Press, 1994.

———. "Projectile Point Chronologies of Southwestern Montana." *Archaeology in Montana* 25, no. 1 (1984): 35-51.

Grieser, Sally Thompson. "Memoir 20: Predictive Models of Hunter-Gatherer Subsistence and Settlement Strategies on the Central High Plains." *Plains Anthropologist* 30, no. 110, part 2 (1985): i-134.

Greiser, Sally T., and T. Weber Greiser. *Blackfoot Culture, Religion, and Traditional Practices in the Badger-Two Medicine Area and Surrounding Mountains.* Final Report. Prepared for Lewis and Clark National Forest. Missoula, MT: Historical Research Associates, Inc., July 1993.

Greiser, Sally T., T. Weber Greiser, and Susan M. Vetter. "Middle Prehistoric Period Adaptations and Paleoenvironment in the Northwestern Plains: The Sun River Site." *American Antiquity* 50, no. 4 (1985): 849-877.

Grinnell, George B. "The Medicine Wheel." *American Anthropologist*, n.s., 24, no. 3 (1922): 299-310.

Gustafson, R. W. *Captain Lewis Explores the Rocky Mountain Front.* Conrad, MT: R. W. Gustafson, 2003.

———. *Room to Roam: More Tales of a Montana Veterinarian.* Conrad, MT: R. W. Gustafson, 1996.

———. *Under the Chinook Arch: Tales of a Montana Veterinarian.* Conrad, MT: R. W. Gustafson, 1993.

Guthrie, A. B., Jr. *Fair Land, Fair Land.* Boston: Houghton Mifflin, 1982. {MS}

———. The Rocky Mountain Front: One Man's Religion. *Montana Magazine,* September/October 1987.

Hagedorn, Herman. *Roosevelt in the Bad Lands.* Publication of the Roosevelt Memorial Association. Boston, MA: Houghton Mifflin Company, 1921. {JP}

Haines, Francis. *The Buffalo: The Story of American Bison and Their Hunters From Prehistoric Times to the Present.* Norman, OK: University of Oklahoma Press, 1995.

Halfpenny, James C. *Scats and Tracks of the Rocky Mountains: A Field Guide to the Signs of Seventy Wildlife Species.* Guilford, CT: Falcon, 2001.

Halfpenny, James C., and Michael H. Francis. *Yellowstone Bears in the Wild.* Helena, MT: Riverbend Publishing, 2007.

Hall, Robert L. "Medicine Wheels, Sun Circles, and the Magic of World Center Shrines." *Plains Anthropologist* 30, no. 109 (1985): 181-193.

Hallowell, A. Irving. "Bear Ceremonialism in the Northern Hemisphere." *American Anthropologist.* 28, no. 1 (1926): 1-175.

Hamlin, L. L. and M. Frisina. *Special Grizzly Bear Survey.* Job Progress Report W-130-R-6. Helena, MT: Montana Department of Fish, Wildlife, and Parks, 1975. {KA}

Hampton, Bruce. Shark of the Plains: Early Western Encounters with Wolves. *Montana: The Magazine of Western History,* Spring 1996.

Hanna, Rebecca R. *Summary of Oil and Gas Development Issues Along the Rocky Mountain Front of Montana.* San Francisco: The Energy Foundation, July 2010.

Hansen, Matthew. *Clearing*. Missoula, MT: Kutenai Press, 1986.

———. *The South Fork of the Teton River: A History of Its People.* [Montana?]: M. Hansen, printed by author, 1980.

Hansen, Peter Allen. "Geology of the Blackleaf Canyon Area, Heart Butte Quadrangle, Montana." Master's thesis, Washington State University, 1962.

Hardee, Jim, ed. *Selected Papers of the 2010 Fur Trade Symposium at the Three Forks.* Three Forks, MT: Three Forks Area Historical Society, 2011.

Harmon, Daniel Williams. *Sixteen Years in the Indian Country; The Journal of Daniel Williams Harmon, 1800-1816.* Toronto, ON: Macmillan Company of Canada Limited, 1957.

Harrington, Heather. "A True Western Woman: Alice Gleason." Unpublished manuscript, 1993.

Harting, Albert L., and Maurice N. LeFranc. *Grizzly Bear Compendium.* Sponsored by Interagency Grizzly Bear Committee. Washington, D.C.: National Wildlife Federation, 1987.

Harvey, Stephen J. *The Potential and Current Vegetation of the Sun River Game Range.* Helena, MT: Montana Department of Fish, Wildlife, and Parks, 1980.

Hazel, Paul. Interviews by Bob Cooney, February 22, 1979 through June 5, 1979. Oral History Collection (OH 687), Montana Historical Society, Helena, MT.

Headwaters Economics. *Montana's Rocky Mountain Front.* Bozeman, MT: Headwaters Economics, September 2012.

Heidenreich, C. Adrian. The Native Americans' Yellowstone. *Montana: The Magazine of Western History,* Autumn 1985.

Hendrix, Marc S. *Geology Underfoot in Yellowstone Country.* Missoula, MT: Mountain Press Publishing Co., 2011. {KP}

Henry, Alexander. *Travels & Adventures in Canada and the Indian Territories Between the Years 1760 and 1776*. Boston, MA: Little, Brown, & Company, 1901.

Herrero, Stephen. *Bear Attacks: Their Causes and Avoidance.* Guilford, CT: Lyons Press, 2002.

Herrero, Stephen, Andrew Higgins, James E. Cardoza, Laura I. Hajduk, and Tom S. Smith. "Fatal Attacks by American Black Bear on People: 1900-2009." *Journal of Wildlife Management* 75, no. 3 (2011): 596-603.

Hill, Christopher L. "Pleistocene Mammals of Montana and the Geologic Context." In *Mesozoic and Cenozoic Paleontology in the Western Plains and Rocky Mountains, Guidebook for the Field Trips: Society of Vertebrate Paleontology 61st Annual Meeting,* 127-144. 2001.

Hill, Pat. The Mystery of the Big Boom: After 200 Years, Still Unsolved. *Montana Pioneer,* July 2005.

Hilts, George B., Robert J. Spokas, Rory W. Steinke, and Steven G. VanFossen. *Soil Survey of Choteau-Conrad Area; Parts of Teton and Pondera Counties, Montana, Part 1.* [Washington, D.C.]: U.S. Dept. of Agriculture, Natural Resources Conservation Service, 2003.

Hinchman, Hannah. *Little Things in a Big Country: An Artist and Her Dog on the Rocky Mountain Front.* New York, NY: W. W. Norton and Company, 2004.

Hogue, Michel. Disputing the Medicine Line: The Plains Crees and the Canadian-American Border, 1876-1885. *Montana: The Magazine of Western History,* Winter 2002.

Holterman, Jack. *Place Names of Glacier/Waterton National Parks.* [West Glacier, MT]: Glacier Natural History Association, 1985.

———. *The Twenty-Fifth Infantry in Glacier Park Country.* West Glacier, MT: Glacier Natural History Association, 1991.

Hook, D., G. Olson, and L. Irby. *East Front Wildlife Monitoring Study: Mule Deer.* Annual Report, November 1981 - March 1982. Helena, MT: Montana Department of Fish, Wildlife, and Parks, 1982.

Hook, D. L. *Rocky Mountain Front Wildlife Studies.* Helena, MT: Montana Department of Fish, Wildlife, and Parks, 1984.

Horejsi, Brian L. "Ranching in Bear Country: Conflict and Conservation." In *Welfare Ranching: The Subsidized Destruction of the American West,* edited by George Wuerthner and Mollie Matteson, 221-225. Washington, D.C.: Island Press, 2002.

Hornocker, Maurice G. and Sharon Negri, eds. *Cougar: Ecology and Conservation.* Chicago, IL: University of Chicago Press, 2010. {JW}

Howard, Joseph Kinsey. *Montana: High, Wide, and Handsome.* Lincoln, NE: University of Nebraska Press, 1943. {MS}

———. *Strange Empire: A Narrative of the Northwest.* Whitefish, MT: Kessinger Publishing, 2009. {MS}

Howser, Tammy, Sandy Morris, Wanda Raschkow, and Jennifer Spencer. "Archaeological Survey—Sun River Game Preserve." Unpublished manuscript, Fall 1992.

Hoxie, Frederick E., and Frank Rzeczkowski. *The Grapevine Creek Battle.* Crow Agency, MT: Crow Tribal Council, 1997.

Hubbard, W. P., and Seale Harris. *Notorious Grizzly Bears.* Denver, CO: Sage Books, 1960.

Hugo, Ripley Schemm. *Writing for Her Life: The Novelist Mildred Walker.* Lincoln, NE: University of Nebraska Press, 2003. {MS}

Hungrywolf, Adolf. *The Blackfoot Papers.* 4 vols. Skookumchuck, B.C.: Good Medicine Cultural Foundation, 2006. {MS}

Ihsle Pac, Helga, Wayne F. Kasworm, Lynn R. Irby, and Richard J. Mackie. "Ecology of the Mule Deer, *Odocoileus hemionus,* Along the East Front of the Rocky Mountains, Montana." *Canadian Field Naturalist* 102, no. 2 (1988): 227-236.

Irby, L. R. and R. J. Mackie. *Mule Deer Monitoring, Rocky Mountain Front.* Final Report. Helena, MT: Montana Department of Fish, Wildlife, and Parks, 1983.

Isakson, Triston, and Wyatt Ostberg. "Baseline Water Quality Data From Streams Along the Rocky Mountain Front, Montana and the Implications for Native Trout." Unpublished manuscript. Fairfield, MT, [2010?].

Jackson, John C. Who Were Those Indians, and How Many Died? *We Proceeded On,* February 2006.

Jackson, W. Turrentine. "The Fisk Expeditions to the Montana Gold Fields." *Pacific Northwest Quarterly* 33, no. 3 (1942): 265-282.

Johnson, Olga W. *Bears in the Rockies.* Libby, MT: Olga W. Johnson, 1960.

Johnston, Alex. *Plants and the Blackfoot.* Lethbridge, AB: Lethbridge Historical Society, 1987.

Jones, Charles Jesse, and Henry Inman. *Buffalo Jones' Forty Years of Adventure.* Topeka, KS: Crane & Company, 1899.

Jones, William R. *Frontland.* Unpublished poem.

Jonkel, Charles. *Annual Report Border Grizzly Project.* Border Grizzly Project Annual Report No. 1. Missoula, MT: University of Montana, March 1976.

———. *The Antelope Butte-Blackleaf Area and Oil Development.* Border Grizzly Project Special Report No. 42. Missoula, MT: University of Montana, 1980.

———. *Antelope Butte-Muddy Creek Grizzly Bear Habitat.* Border Grizzly Project Special Report No. 35. Missoula, MT: University of Montana, 1979.

———. *Delineation of Grizzly Habitat in the Border Grizzly Area.* Border Grizzly Project Special Report No. 3. Missoula, MT: University of Montana, 1976.

———. *Grizzlies and Black Bear Interrelationships.* Border Grizzly Project Special Report No. 70. Missoula, MT: University of Montana, June 1984.

———. *Grizzly Bear "Critical Habitat."* Border Grizzly Project Special Report No. 4. Missoula, MT: University of Montana, November 1976.

———. Grizzly Bears and Livestock. *Western Wildlands,* Summer 1980.

———. *Interim Report on Border Grizzly Project (BGP) Studies and Plans.* Border Grizzly Project Special Report No. 10. Missoula, MT: University of Montana, 1977.

———. *Rocky Mountain East Front Grizzly Studies, 1977 Annual Report.* Border Grizzly Project Special Report No. 27. Missoula, MT: University of Montana, 1979.

———. *The Wariness of Hunted Grizzly Populations vs Non-Hunted Populations.* Border Grizzly Project Special Report No. 73. Missoula, MT: University of Montana, February 1985.

Jonkel, Charles, et al. *Grizzly Bear-Livestock Competition in Riparian Areas.* Missoula, MT: University of Montana, 1980.

Jonkel, James Jason. "Grizzly Maulings . . . As Reported by *Outdoor Life*, *National Enquirer* and *The Missoulian.*" Bachelor's thesis. University of Montana - Missoula, 1984.

Jope, Katherine L. "Implications of Grizzly Bear Habituation to Hikers." Wildlife Society Bulletin 13, no. 1 (Spring 1985): 32-37.

Joslin, Harry. Destiny: Reflections on the Front. *Montana Wildlife,* July/August 2011.

Joslin, Gayle. *Distribution and Population Characteristics of the Rocky Mountain Goat Along the East Slope of the Rocky Mountains in Northcentral Montana.* Progress Report. Helena, MT: Montana Department of Fish, Wildlife, and Parks, 1981.

———. Linking Prehistory to Posterity. *Montana Outdoors*, March/April 1997.

———. *Montana Mountain Goat Investigations Along the East Front of the Rocky Mountains, Lewis and Clark National Forest.* Progress Report. Helena, MT: Montana Department of Fish, Wildlife, and Parks, 1982.

———. *Montana Mountain Goat Investigations Along the East Front of the Rocky Mountains, Lewis and Clark National Forest.* Helena, MT: Montana Department of Fish, Wildlife, and Parks, 1983.

———. *Montana Mountain Goat Investigations, Rocky Mountain Front.* Final. Helena, MT: Montana Department of Fish, Wildlife and Parks, August 1986.

———. "Mountain Goat Population Changes in Relation to Energy Exploration Along Montana's Rocky Mountain Front." Paper presented at the Fifth Biennial Symposium of the Northern Wild Sheep and Goat Council, Missoula, MT, April 1986.

Jourdonnais, Craig S., and Donald J. Bedunah. "Prescribed Fire and Cattle Grazing on an Elk Winter Range in Montana." *Wildlife Society Bulletin* 18, no. 3 (1990): 232-240.

Kaniut, Larry. *Alaska Bear Tales.* Anchorage, AK: Alaska Northwest Publishing Co., 1983.

———. *Bear Tales For the Ages: From Alaska and Beyond.* Anchorage, AK: Paper Talk, 2001.

Kasworm, Wayne F. "Distribution and Population Characteristics of Mule Deer Along the East Front, Northcentral Montana." Master's thesis, Montana State University - Bozeman, 1981.

Kasworm, Wayne F. and Lynn R. Irby. *East Slope Rocky Mountain Front Mule Deer Study and Investigation.* Annual Report. Bozeman, MT: Montana Department of Fish, Wildlife, and Parks, 1979.

Kasworm, Wayne F., Lynn R. Irby, Helga B. Ihsle Pac. "Diets of Ungulates Using Winter Ranges in Northcentral Montana." *Journal of Range Management* 37, no. 1 (1984): 67-71.

Keenan, Jerry. *The Life of Yellowstone Kelly.* Albuquerque: University of New Mexico Press, 2006.

———. Yellowstone Kelly: From New York to Paradise. *Montana: The Magazine of Western History,* Summer 1990.

Kehoe, Thomas F. "Stone 'Medicine Wheels' in Southern Alberta and the Adjacent Portion of Montana: Were They Designed as Grave Markers?" *Journal of the Washington Academy of Sciences* 44, no. 5 (1954): 133-137.

———. "Stone Tipi Rings in North-Central Montana and the Adjacent Portion of Alberta, Canada: Their Historical, Ethnological and Archaeological Aspects." Bureau of American Ethnology Bulletin 173, *Anthropological Papers,* 62 (1960): 417-73.

———. "Tipi Rings: The 'Direct Ethnological Approach' Applied to an Archaeological Problem." *American Anthropologist* 60, no. 5 (1958): 861-873.

Kehoe, Thomas F., and Alice B. Kehoe. "Observations on the Butchering Technique at a Prehistoric Bison-Kill in Montana." *American Antiquity* 25, no. 3 (1960): 420-423.

Keller, David W. "An Environmental History of the Rocky Mountain Front." Master's thesis, University of Montana - Missoula, 1996.

———. *The Making of a Masterpiece: The Stewardship History of the Rocky Mountain Front and the Bob Marshall Wilderness Complex (1897 - 1999).* Missoula, MT: Boone and Crockett Club, 2001.

———. *Prehistoric Cultures of the Rocky Mountain Front.* Boone and Crockett Wildlife Conservation Program Progress Draft Report 94-1. Missoula, MT: University of Montana, April 1994.

Kelly, Carla, ed. *On the Upper Missouri: The Journal of Rudolph Friederich Kurz, 1851-1852.* Norman, OK: University of Oklahoma Press, 2005.

Kelly, Luther S. and Milo Milton Quaife. *Yellowstone Kelly: The Memoirs of Luther S. Kelly.* New Haven: Yale University Press, 1926.

Kenck, Richard. Interview by Melinda Livezey, June 7, 1994. Oral History Collection (OH 1653), Montana Historical Society, Helena, MT.

———. Interview by Melinda Livezey, June 22, 1994. Oral History Collection (OH 1660), Montana Historical Society, Helena, MT.

Kenck, Richard C. "Growing Up in the Vicinity of the Old North Trail." Interview with David Louter, February 14, 1987. Oral History 167-3. Archives and Special Collections, Mansfield Library, University of Montana, Missoula, MT.

———. "Twentieth Century Fur Trade in Montana." Interview with Ed Nentwig, December 12, 1981. Oral History 99-19 and 99-20, transcript. Archives and Special Collections, Mansfield Library, University of Montana, Missoula, MT.

———. "Twentieth Century Fur Trade in Montana." Interview with Ed Nentwig, April 1, 1982. Oral History 99-21, transcript. Archives and Special Collections, Mansfield Library, University of Montana, Missoula, MT.

Kendall, Katherine C., Jeffrey B. Stetz, David A. Roon, Lisette P. Waits, John G. Boulanger, and David Paetkau. "Grizzly Bear Density in Glacier National Park." *Journal of Wildlife Management* 72, no. 8 (2008): 1693-1705.

Kendall, Katherine C., Jeffrey B. Stetz, John Boulanger, Amy C. Macleod, David Paetkau, and Gary C. White. "Demography and Genetic Structure of a Recovering Grizzly Bear Population." *Journal of Wildlife Management* 73, no. 1 (2009): 3-17.

Kennedy, Dan, and James R. Stevens. *Recollections of an Assiniboine Chief.* Toronto, ON: McClelland and Stewart, 1972.

Kershaw, Linda, A. MacKinnon, and Jim Pojar. *Plants of the Rocky Mountains.* Edmonton, AB: Lone Pine Publishing, 1998.

Keyser, James D. "The Central Montana Abstract Rock Art Style." Papers from the Fourth Biennial Conference of the Canadian Rock Art Research Associates. British Columbia Provincial Museum, Heritage Record No. 8 (1977): 153-177.

———. "Variations in Stone Ring Use at Two Sites in Central Montana." *Plains Anthropologist* 24, no. 84, part 1 (1979): 133-143.

Keyser, James D., and George C. White. "The Risley Bison Kill: West-Central Montana." *Plains Anthropologist* 21, no. 74 (1976): 291-300.

———. "The Rock Art of Western Montana." *Plains Anthropologist* 21, no. 71 (1976): 1-12.

Kiesling, Robert J. "Strategies for Preserving the Biological Diversity of the Rocky Mountain Front." Master's thesis, University of Montana - Missoula, 1991.

Kinley, Henry J., and Daisy. *An Indian School Diary.* USA: unknown, 1975.

Kipp, Darrell Robes, and Ronald B. Tobias. View From the Shore: A Native American Perspective on the Lewis & Clark Bicentennial. [Bozeman, Montana]: Black Dog Films, 2005, DVD, 28 min.

Kipp, Woody. Looking Behind and Beyond: A Blackfeet Perspective of the Front. *Home Front: The Life and Times of Montana's Rocky Mountain Front Country,* Spring 1993.

Kinsner, John J. *Paleoindian Land Use in Glacier National Park.* Final Report. [West Glacier, MT]: Glacier National Park, 2010.

Kittredge, William and Annick Smith, eds. *The Last Best Place: A Montana Anthology.* Helena, MT: The Montana Historical Society Press, 1988. {JP}

Knight, Richard R., and M. R. Mudge. "Characteristics of Some Natural Licks in the Sun River Area, Montana." *Journal of Wildlife Management* 31, no. 2 (1967): 293-299.

Knight, Richard R. "The Sun River Elk Herd." *Wildlife Monographs* 23 (1970): 3-66.

Koch, Elers. "Big Game in Montana from Early Historical Records." *Journal of Wildlife Management* 5, no. 4 (1941): 357-370. {JP}

Kotynski, Tom. *Discover the Rocky Mountain Front: A Hiking Guide.* Great Falls, MT: *Great Falls Tribune,* 2006.

Kudray, Gregory M., and Stephen V. Cooper. *Montana's Rocky Mountain Front: Vegetation Map and Type Description.* Report to the United States Fish and Wildlife Service. Helena, MT: Montana Natural Heritage Program, February 2006.

Kujala, Quentin. The Elk Pasture: Sun River Wildlife Management Area. *Montana Outdoors,* November/December 1996.

Kunkel, Kyran E., Toni K. Ruth, Daniel H. Pletscher, and Maurice G. Hornocker. "Winter Prey Selection by Wolves and Cougars in and Near Glacier National Park, Montana." *Journal of Wildlife Management* 63, no. 3 (1999): 901-910.

Lahren, Larry. "Montana Archaeological Society Conservation 2001 Award to Bud Bisnett." *Archaeology in Montana* 41, no. 2 (2000): 1-3.

Lapinski, Michael. *True Stories of Bear Attacks: Who Survived and Why.* Portland, OR: West Winds Press, 2004.

Larpenteur, Charles. Forty Years a Fur Trader on the Upper Missouri: The Personal Narrative of Charles Larpenteur 1833-1872. Lincoln, NE: University of Nebraska Press, 1989.

Lavender, David Sievert. *The Way to the Western Sea: Lewis and Clark Across the Continent.* Lincoln, NE: University of Nebraska Press, 1998.

Lee, Lyndon and Charles Jonkel. Grizzlies and Wetlands. *Western Wildlands*, Fall 1981.

Leopold, Aldo. *A Sand County Almanac: and Sketches Here & There.* London: Oxford University Press, 1949. {SB}

Lesica, Peter. "Vegetation and Flora of Pine Butte Fen, Teton County, Montana." *Great Basin Naturalist* 46, no. 1 (1986): 22-32.

Lewis, H. P. "Buffalo Kills in Montana." Unpublished manuscript, 1947. [available at University of Montana].

Lewis, Meriwether. *The Lewis and Clark Expedition.* Edited by Archibald Hanna. 3 vols. Philadelphia: J.B. Lippincott Company, 1961. {JP}

Lind, Robert W. *Brother Van: Montana Pioneer Circuit Rider.* Las Vegas, NV: R.W. Lind, 1992.

Long, Ben. *Great Montana Bear Stories.* Helena, MT: Riverbend Publishing, 2002. {KA}

———. "The Grizzly of Falls Creek." *Montana Outdoors,* July/August 2002.

Long Standing Bear Chief. Piegan, Pikuni, or Perhaps Piikani? *Piikani Sun*, Book 1, Chapter 2 [2004].

———. The Spirit of Beings in the Backbone of the World. *Piikani Sun,* Book 1, Chapter 1, August 2004.

Lowie, Robert H. "The Assiniboine." *Anthropological Papers of the American Museum of Natural History* 4, part 1 (1909): 1-270.

———. *Indians of the Plains.* Lincoln, NE: University of Nebraska Press, 1982.

MacDonald, Douglas H. *Montana Before History: 11,000 Years of Hunter-Gatherers in the Rockies and Plains.* Missoula, MT: Mountain Press Publishing, 2012. {HP}

Mace, Richard, K. Aune, W. Kasworm, R. Klaver, and J. Claar. "Incidence of Human Conflicts by Research Grizzly Bears." *Wildlife Society Bulletin* 15, no. 2 (1987): 170-173. {KA}

Mace, Richard, S. Minta, T. Manley, and K. Aune. "Estimating Grizzly Bear Population Size Using Camera Sightings." *Wildlife Society Bulletin* 22, no.1 (1994): 74-83. {KA}

Mace, Richard, T. Manley, and K. Aune. "Factors Affecting the Photographic Detection Rate of Grizzly Bears in the Swan Mountains, Montana." *Bears: Their Biology and Management* 9, part 1 (1995): 245-251. Ninth International Conference on Bear Research and Management. {KA}

Mace, Richard D., Daniel W. Carney, Tonya Chilton-Radandt, Stacy A. Courville, Mark A. Haroldson, Richard B. Harris, James Jonkel, et al. "Grizzly Bear Population Vital Rates and Trend in the Northern Continental Divide Ecosystem, Montana." *Journal of Wildlife Management* 76, no. 1 (2012): 119-128.

Mackie, R. J. and L. Irby. *Mule Deer Monitoring Rocky Mountain Front,* Annual Report. Great Falls, MT: U.S. Bureau of Land Management, 1982.

Madej, Ed. A Guide to the Bob Marshall Additions. *Montana Magazine,* July/August 1982.

Madel, Mike. *Grizzly Bear and Black Bear Species Report; Region Four Rocky Mountain Front Grizzly Bear Management Program.* Biennial Progress Report January 1, 1989 to December 31, 1990. Great Falls, MT: Montana Department of Fish, Wildlife, and Parks, March 1991.

———. *Grizzly Bear Ecology and Management on the Rocky Mountain Front.* Last Chance Audubon Society's 1999 Natural History Lecture Series. Helena, MT, March 17, 1999. Videocassette (VHS), 60 min.

———. A Grizzly Biologist's Journal. *Montana Outdoors,* July/ August 2004.

———. Of Prairie, Bears, and People. *Montana Outdoors,* May/June 1989.

———. *Region Four Bear Management and Inventory Report 89-90.* Helena, MT: Montana Fish, Wildlife, and Parks, 1990. {KA}

———. *Rocky Mountain Front Grizzly Bear Management Program.* Four-Year Progress Report 1991-1994. [Great Falls, MT]: Montana Department of Fish, Wildlife, and Parks, July 1996.

Mahoney, Shane. The North American Conservation Model: Triumph for Man and Nature. *Bugle Magazine*, January/February 2005. {JP}

Mails, Thomas E. *Dog Soldiers, Bear Men, and Buffalo Women: A Study of the Societies and Cults of the Plains Indians.* Englewood Cliffs, N.J.: Prentice-Hall, 1973.

Malone, Jesse. *Two Families: Two Centuries.* Helena, MT: Sweetgrass Books, 2007.

Manning, Richard. *Last Stand: A Riveting Exposé of Environmental Pillage and a Lone Journalist's Struggle to Keep Faith.* New York, NY: Penguin Books, 1992.

Martinka, C. J. "Ecological Role and Management of Grizzly Bears in Glacier National Park, Montana." *Bears: Their Biology and Management*, n.s., 3, 40 (1976): 147-156. Third International Conference on Bear Research and Management.

McAllister, David Charles. "Plant Community Development in a Minerotrophic Peatland, Teton County, Montana." PhD diss., University of Montana - Missoula, 1990.

McCarthy, Mary F. *Archaeological Reconnaissance Survey of the Blackleaf Wildlife Management Area, Teton County, Montana.* Helena, MT: Montana Department of Fish, Wildlife, and Parks, October 1992.

———. *Archaeological Reconnaissance Survey of the Ear Mountain Wildlife Management Area, Teton County, Montana.* Helena, MT: Montana Department of Fish, Wildlife, and Parks, October 1993.

McCarty, Richard. Family Ranch in Big Sky Country. *Western Horseman,* September 2001.

McClintock, Walter. *The Old North Trail: Or, Life, Legends and Religion of the Blackfeet Indians.* Lincoln, NE: University of Nebraska Press, 1968.

McCloed, Frank and Bon I. Whealdon. "Exterminating a Montana Buffalo Herd in 1836." In *"I Will Be Meat for My Salish": The Buffalo and the Montana Writers Project Interviews on the Flathead Indian Reservation,* edited by Robert Bigart, 39-41. Pablo, MT: Salish Kootenai College Press; Helena, MT: Montana Historical Society Press, 2001. {HP}

McCulloch, David G. *Mornings on Horseback*. New York: Simon and Schuster Inc., 1981. {JP}

Mergenthaler, Jake. *Central Montana Rock: Climbs Around Helena, Canyon Ferry & the Rocky Mountain Front.* Bozeman, MT: First Ascent Press, 2006.

Merriam, L. C., Jr. *A Land Use Study of the Bob Marshall Wilderness Area of Montana.* Montana State University: Forest and Conservation Experiment Station, School of Forestry, Bulletin No. 26, October 1963.

Merriam, Lawrence Campbell, Jr. "The Bob Marshall Wilderness Area of Montana: A Study in Wilderness Use." PhD diss., Oregon State University, 1963.

Messelt, Tom. *A Layman and Wildlife, and a Layman and Wilderness.* Great Falls, MT: Montana Stationery Company, 1971 {JP}

Milbrath, Joseph T. "Land-Cover Change Within the Peatlands Along the Rocky Mountain Front, Montana: 1937-2009." Master's thesis, University of Montana - Missoula, 2013.

Miller, David R., Dennis J. Smith, Joseph R. McGeshick, James Shanley, and Caleb Shields. *The History of the Fort Peck Assiniboine and Sioux Tribes, 1800-2000.* Poplar, MT: Fort Peck Community College; Helena, MT: Montana Historical Society Press, 2008.

Miller, Nathan. *Theodore Roosevelt: A Life.* New York: William Morrow and Company, 1992. {JP}

Mills, Enos A. *The Grizzly: Our Greatest Wild Animal.* Sausalito, CA: Comstock Editions, Inc., 1919.

Monkman, Olga W., ed. *Teton County History.* 1955.

Montana Department of Fish, Wildlife, and Parks. A Century of Conservation. Special Centennial Issue. *Montana Outdoors,* November/December 2000.

———. *Ear Mountain Wildlife Management Area - Salmond Ranch and Gollehon Ranch Grazing Agreement.* Draft Environmental Assessment. Great Falls, MT: Montana Department of Fish, Wildlife and Parks, March 2009.

———. *Edwards Property Conservation Easement.* Great Falls, MT: Montana Department of Fish, Wildlife, and Parks, December 1994.

———. *Environmental Assessment: Knowlton Dam Rehabilitation Project.* Helena, MT: Montana Department of Fish, Wildlife, and Parks, August 2000.

———. *Montana's Comprehensive Fish and Wildlife Conservation Strategy.* Helena, MT: Montana Department of Fish, Wildlife, and Parks, 2005.

———. *Neal Ranch Acquisition.* Environmental Assessment. Great Falls, MT: Montana Department of Fish, Wildlife, and Parks, January 2009.

———. *The Sun River Wildlife Management Area FG-N-141 Preliminary Environmental Review Before the Montana Fish and Game Commission on an Oil and Gas Lease Application.* Helena, MT: Montana Department of Fish, Wildlife, and Parks, February 1981.

Montana Fish and Game Commission. *Purchase of Grizzly Habitat by the Montana Fish and Game Commission - Salmond's Ranch, Choteau, Montana.* Helena, MT: Montana Fish and Game Commission, 1975.

Morris, Sandi. "Wildfire as a Part of Cultural Prehistory in Montana and the Implications for Public Land Managers." *Archaeology in Montana* 33, no. 1 (1992): 79-90.

Moser, David. *Transfer of Westslope Cutthroat Trout from North Badger Creek to South Badger Creek (Two Medicine River Drainage).* Environmental Assessment. Helena, MT: Montana Department of Fish, Wildlife, and Parks, January 2009.

Mosher, Dick & Ben East. "Dark Tragedy." In *Beyond ... The Shadows of the Rockies: History of the Augusta Area,* Augusta Area Historical Society, 70-75. [Augusta, Mont.]: Anderson Publication, 2007.

Moulton, Gary E. ed. *The Definitive Journals of Lewis and Clark: Over the Rockies to St. Louis.* Vol. 8. Lincoln, NE: University of Nebraska Press, 1993. {HP}

———. *The Journals of the Lewis and Clark Expedition.* Vols. 1-3. Lincoln, NE: University of Nebraska Press, 1987.

Mudge, M. R., and Earhart, Robert L., 1983, Bedrock geologic map of part of the Northern Disturbed Belt, Lewis and Clark,Teton, Pondera, Glacier, Flathead, Cascade, and Powell Counties, Montana, U.S. Geological Survey Miscellaneous Investigations Series Map I–1375. Map scale 1:125,000. {KP}

Munson, Gene. *Class III Cultural Resource Inventory on Willow Creek Reservoir, Lewis and Clark County and Pishkun Reservoir, Teton County, Montana.* Report for the Bureau of Reclamation. Butte, MT: GCM Services, September 1986.

Murie, Adolph. "Cattle on Grizzly Bear Range." *Journal of Wildlife Management* 12, no. 1 (1948): 57-72.

Murphy, Bob. *Bears I Have Known.* Helena, MT: Riverbend Publishing, 2006.

Murphy, Kerry M. "The Ecology of the Cougar (Puma Concolor) in the Northern Yellowstone Ecosystem: Interactions with Prey, Bears, and Humans." PhD diss., University of Idaho - Moscow, 1998. {JW}

Murray, Carol, Dale Fenner II, Lea Whitford, Lola Wippert, Marion Salway, Marvin Weatherwax, Earl Old Person, et al. *Days of the Blackfeet.* Browning, MT: Blackfeet Community College, 2008, DVD, 45 min.

Murray, John A. *Grizzly bears: An Illustrated Field Guide.* Boulder, CO: Roberts Rinehart Publishers, 1995.

Mussehl, Thomas W. and F. W. Howell, eds. *Game Management in Montana.* Federal Aid Project W-3-C. Helena, MT: Montana Fish and Game Department, 1971. {KA}

Napier, Norman J. "Knowlton Gas Field, Teton County, Montana." In *Geologic Studies of the Cordilleran Thrust Belt,* vol. 2, edited by Richard Blake Powers, 575-579. Denver, CO: Rocky Mountain Association of Geologists, 1982.

Neilson, Helen Parsons. *Montana Treasure: Doctor O.A. Kenck, His Life and Times.* Gig Harbor, WA: Red Apple Publishing, 2003.

Nett, Tot. "Reminiscences About Ranching in Montana." Interview with David Louter, February 15, 1987. Oral History 167-4. Archives and Special Collections, Mansfield Library, University of Montana - Missoula, MT.

Newcomb, Thomas P. "Some Fact and Much Conjecture Concerning the Sun River Medicine Wheel, Teton County, Montana." *Archaeology in Montana* 8, no. 1 (1967): 17-23.

Newton, Richard E. and Sandra French. *Gibson Archaeological Project.* (R2009011500058). Great Falls, MT: Lewis and Clark National Forest, December 2010.

Nisbet, Jack. *The Mapmaker's Eye: David Thompson on the Columbia Plateau.* Pullman, WA: Washington State University Press, 2005. {HP}

Northwest Ecosystem Alliance. *Ranching and Grizzly Bears.* Bellingham, WA: Northwest Ecosystem Alliance, 2004. DVD, 26 min.

Noss, Reed F. "Sustainability and Wilderness." *Conservation Biology* 5, no. 1 (March 1991): 120-122.

Oard, Michael J. "A Method for Predicting Chinook Winds East of the Montana Rockies." *Weather and Forecasting* 8 (1993): 166-180.

Ochenski, George. "Sensitive Area" Stipulations Retained for Rocky Mountain Front. *Focus on Montana State Lands and the Montana Land Board,* Summer 2002.

Oetelaar, Gerald A., and D. Joy Oetelaar. "People, Places and Paths: The Cypress Hills and the Niitsitapi Landscape of Southern Alberta." In "Memoir 38: Changing Opportunities and Challenges: Human-Environmental Interaction in the Canadian Prairies Ecozone," edited by B. A. Nicholson and Dion Wiseman. Special issue, *Plains Anthropologist* 51, no. 99 (2006): 375-397.

Offerdahl, Russell James. "A Description of the Major Plant Communities on the Theodore Roosevelt Memorial Ranch." Master's thesis, University of Montana - Missoula, 1989.

Old Trail Museum. *The Mètis Between Worlds.* Choteau, MT: Old Trail Museum, n.d.

Olsen, Lance. Compensation: Giving a Break to Ranchers and Bears. *Western Wildlands*, Spring 1991.

Olson, Gary. Beefing Up the Blackleaf. *Montana Outdoors,* March/April 1992.

———. *Effects of Seismic Exploration on Summering Elk in the Two Medicine—Badger Creek Area, North central Montana.* Helena, MT: Montana Department of Fish, Wildlife, and Parks, 1981.

———. Resources in Conflict. *Montana Outdoors*, July/August 1980.

Olson, Gary and Ina Trowbridge. *Blackleaf Wildlife Management Area Management Plan.* Helena, MT: Montana Department of Fish, Wildlife, and Parks, January 1990.

Olson, Gary, Les Marcum, and Thomas Baumeister. *Theodore Roosevelt Memorial Ranch Elk Study.* [Helena, MT]: Montana Department of Fish, Wildlife, and Parks, May 1994.

Olson, Gary Roger. "Range Condition on Abandoned Croplands in North Central Montana." Master's thesis, University of Montana - Missoula, 1973.

O'Neil, Carle Francis. *The Mystery of Marias Pass*. Lakeside, MT: Bush Computing, 1998.

Pac, Helga Ihsle. "Population Ecology of Mule Deer with Emphasis on Potential Impacts of Gas and Oil Development Along the East Front of the Rocky Mountains, Northcentral Montana." Master's thesis, Montana State University - Bozeman, 1982.

Parks, Douglas R., and Raymond J. DeMaille. "Sioux, Assiniboine, and Stoney Dialects: A Classification." *Anthropological Linguistics* 34, no. 1/4 (1992): 233-255.

Parry, Ellis Roberts. *Montana Dateline.* Guilford, CT: Twodot, 2001.

Patent, Dorothy, Mary Scriver, Curly Bear Wagner, Adolf Hungry Wolf, and Victor Charlo. *Who Tells the Native American Story.* Highlights from the 2006 Montana Festival of the Book. Billings, MT: At Large Productions, Audio CD, 58 min.

Pearson, Arthur A. Topographical Relief Map (explanatory notes) [Old North Trail]. Located in Greenfields Irrigation District Office, Fairfield, Montana, n.d.

Peck, Trevor R. "Archaeologically Recovered Ammonites: Evidence for Long-Term Continuity in Nitsitapii Ritual." *Plains Anthropologist* 47, no. 181 (2002): 147-164.

Peebles, Bob. A View From the Front - Ranching: A Proud Heritage. *Home Front: The Life and Times of Montana's Rocky Mountain Front Country,* Fall 1994.

Perkins, Ira. *"Mr. Perkins, Tell Us a Story": Collected Stories of Ira Perking, A Bynum Rancher and School Teacher.* Bynum, MT: Ira Perkins, 2003.

Peterson, Jacqueline, and Jennifer S. H. Brown, eds. *The New Peoples: Being and Becoming Mêtis in North America.* Lincoln, NE: University of Nebraska Press, 1985. {MS}

Peterson, Jim. "Growing Up on Mountain Trails." Unpublished manuscript, 1995.

Picton, Harold D. "Climate and the Prediction of Reproduction of Three Ungulate Species." *Journal of Applied Ecology* 21, no. 3 (1984): 869-879.

———. "Migration Patterns of the Sun River Elk Herd, Montana." *Journal of Wildlife Management* 24, no. 3 (1960): 279-290.

———. "Use of Vegetative Types, Migration, and Hunter Harvest of the Sun River Elk Herd," Montana. Master's thesis, Montana State College, 1959.

Picton, Harold D., and Irene E. Picton. *Saga of the Sun: A History of the Sun River Elk Herd.* Helena, MT: Game Management Division, Montana Department of Fish and Game, 1975.

———. "A Wildlife Bibliography of the Sun River, Montana, 1973." Prepared for the Montana Fish and Game Department. Unpublished manuscript, 1974.

Picton, Harold D., and Terry. N. Lonner. *Montana's Wildlife Legacy: Decimation to Restoration.* Bozeman, MT: Media Works Publishing, 2008. {HP}

Pienkowski, Laura. "The Blackleaf: A Case Study of the Impacts of Oil and Gas Leasing on the Grizzly Bear." Unpublished manuscript, 1994.

Pitt, Kenneth P. "The Ceded Strip: Blackfeet Treaty Rights in the 1980's." Paper prepared for academic credit. Ruhle Library E99. S54 P58, West Glacier, MT: Glacier National Park, n.d.

Pletscher, Daniel H., Robert R. Ream, Diane K. Boyd, Michael W. Fairchild, and Kyran E. Kunkel. "Population Dynamics of a Recolonizing Wolf Population." *Journal of Wildlife Management* 61, no. 2 (1997): 459-465.

Posewitz, James A. "Observations on the Fish Population of Willow Creek Reservoir, Montana." Master's Thesis, Montana State University - Bozeman, 1961.

Posewitz, James A., John J. Fraley, Gayle L. Joslin, and Shawn J. Riley. *Limits of Acceptable Change, Bob Marshall Wilderness Complex, Fish and Wildlife Plan.* [Helena, Mont.]: Montana Department of Fish, Wildlife and Parks, December 1991.

Posewitz, Jim. "Yellowstone to the Yukon (Y2Y): Enhancing Prospects for a Conservation Initiative." *International Journal of Wilderness* 4, no. 2 (1998): 25-27.

Power, Thomas M. To Be or Not To Be? The Economics of Development Along the Rocky Mountain Front. *Western Wildlands,* Fall 1987.

Prato, Tony, and Dan Fagre, eds. *Sustaining Rocky Mountain Landscapes: Science, Policy, and Management for the Crown of the Continent Ecosystem.* Washington, D.C: Resources for the Future, 2007.

Primm, Steve, and Seth M. Wilson. "Re-Connecting Grizzly Bear Populations: Prospects for Participatory Projects." *Ursus* 15, no. 1 (2004): 104-114.

Puckett, Karl. Homeward Bound? *Montana Magazine,* July/August 2010.

Punke, Michael. *Last Stand: George Bird Grinnell, the Battle to Save the Buffalo, and the Birth of the New West.* New York: Smithsonian Books/Collins, 2007. {JP}

Rahr, Willie. *Old North Trail at Theodore Roosevelt Memorial Ranch: Inventory of Cultural and Historical Resources.* [Missoula, MT]: University of Montana, December 1993.

Rappagliosi, Philip, and Robert Bigart. *Letters from the Rocky Mountain Indian Missions.* Lincoln, NE: University of Nebraska Press, 2003.

Ratledge, Mark, ed. *From the Divide: Essays and Photographs of Wilderness.* Missoula, MT: Wilderness Institute, 1991.

Ray, Arthur J. 1974. *Indians in the Fur Trade: Their Role as Trappers, Hunters, and Middlemen in the Lands Southwest of Hudson Bay, 1660-1870.* Toronto, ON: University of Toronto Press, 1974.

Reeves, Brian. "How Old is the Old North Trail?" *Archaeology in Montana* 31, no. 2 (1990): 1-18.

———. *Ninaistako - The Nitsitapii's Sacred Mountain: Traditional Native Religious Activities and Land Use/Tourism Conflicts.* Draft. Calgary, AB: University of Calgary, January 1992.

Reeves, Brian O.K. "Culture Change in the Northern Plains, 1000 B.C. to A.D. 1000." PhD diss., University of Calgary, 1970.

———. "The Kenney Site: A Stratified Campsite in South Western Alberta." Master's thesis, University of Calgary, 1966.

Reichel, James D. *Amphibian, Reptile and Northern Bog Lemming Survey on the Rocky Mountain Front: 1996.* Helena, MT: Montana Natural Heritage Program, April 1997.

Reiger, George. A Shared Journey. *Field and Stream Magazine,* August 1995. {JP}

Reiger, John F. *American Sportsmen and the Origins of Conservation.* Norman, OK: University of Oklahoma Press, 1986. {JP}

Reuter, Lisa. American Serengeti. *Montana Magazine,* July/August 2012.

Riley, Shawn, K. Aune, R. Mace, and M. Madel. "Translocation of Nuisance Grizzly Bears in Northwestern Montana." *Bears: Their Biology and Management* 9, part 1 (1995): 567-573. Ninth International Conference on Bear Research and Management. {KA}

Riley, Shawn J., Keith Aune, Richard D. Mace, and Michael J. Madel. "Translocation of Nuisance Grizzly Bears in Northwestern Montana." *Bears: Their Biology and Management* 9, part 1 (1995): 567-573. Ninth International Conference on Bear Research and Management.

Riley, Shawn J., and D. J. Decker. "Wildlife Stakeholder Acceptance Capacity for Cougars in Montana." *Wildlife Society Bulletin* 28, no. 4 (2000): 931-939. {JW}

Rittel, John F. Interview by Kerri Blanton, April 2008. Oral History Collection (OH 2269), Montana Historical Society, Helena, MT.

Rittel, Tag. *The Blacktail Cave.* Wolf Creek, MT: Tag Rittel, 1981.

Robbins, Jim. A Town Divided By the Grizzly. *New York Times Magazine,* August 31, 1986.

———. Pine Butte: Nature Conservancy Eyes a Swampful of Marvels. *Montana Magazine*, September/October 1982.

Roberts, Dexter. Predicting the Future by Observing the Past: A New Threat to the Rocky Mountain Front. *Western Wildlands,* Fall 1987.

Robinson, Hugh S. and R. M. DeSimone. *The Garnet Range Mountain Lion Study: Characteristics of a Hunted Population in West-Central Montana.* Final Report. Helena, MT: Montana Department of Fish, Wildlife, and Parks, 2011. {JW}

Robinson, R., D. Choate, R. DeSimone, M. Hebblewhite, M. Mitchell, K. Murphy, T. Ruth, and J. Williams. "Linking Resource Selection and Morality Modeling for Population Estimation of Mountain Lions in Montana." Manuscript submitted for publication. {JW}

Rodnick, David. "An Assiniboine Horse-Raiding Expedition." *American Anthropologist*, n.s., 41, no. 4 (1939): 611-616.

———. "Political Structure and Status Among the Assiniboine Indians." *American Anthropologist*, n.s., 39, no. 3, part 1 (1937): 408-416.

———. "The Fort Belknap Assiniboine of Montana: A Dissertation in Anthropology." PhD diss., University of Pennsylvania - Philadelphia, 1938.

Rognrud, Merle. *A Preliminary Investigation of Mountain Goats in the Continental Big Game Management Unit Sun River-Flathead Area Montana*. Helena, MT: Montana Fish and Game Commission, 1946.

Rubbert, Jim. *Hiking With Grizzlies: Lessons Learned.* Helena, MT: Riverbend Publishing, 2006.

Rush, W. M. Elk Expert for More Hunting. *Montana Wild Life,* July 1930.

Russell, Andy. *Grizzly Country*. New York, NY: Nick Lyons Books, 1967.

Russell, Charles M. *Good Medicine: Memories of the Real West.* Garden City, NY: Garden City Publishing Company, Inc., 1929. {JP}

Ruth, Toni K. "Patterns of Resource Use Among Cougars and Wolves in Northwestern Montana and Southeastern British Columbia," PhD diss., University of Idaho - Moscow, 2004. {JW}

Safety in Bear Country Society, Wild Eye Productions, AV Action Yukon Ltd, and International Association for Bear Research and Management. *Staying Safe in Bear Country: A Behavioral-Based Approach to Reducing Risk.* Atlin, BC: Safety in Bear Country Society, 2001. DVD, 50 min.

Saindon, Bob. "Lewis & Clark Among the Assiniboines." *Montana Professor* 15, no. 1 (2004): 23-28.

———. "What's in a Name? Ossnobian, Nasseniboine, Assiniboi, Assinipoval, Assinibouane, Assinepoualao, Assiniboe, Assiniboil...ASSINIBOINE." *Montana Professor* 13, no. 1 (2003): 12-13.

Saindon, Robert A., ed. *Explorations into the World of Lewis and Clark: 194 Essays from the Pages of We Proceeded On.* Great Falls, MT: Lewis and Clark Trail Heritage Foundation, 2003.

———. The "Unhappy Affair" on Two Medicine River. *We Proceeded On,* August 2002.

Saterlie, C. J. *Here Comes the Wind.* New York, NY: Comet Press Books, 1956.

Schallenberger, A. *Grizzly Bear Habitat Survey, Badger Creek–South Fork Two Medicine Management Unit, Lewis and Clark National Forest.* Great Falls, MT: U.S. Forest Service, 1976.

———. "Raptor Reconnaissance Survey of Rocky Mountain Front." Unpublished report. Great Falls, MT: Lewis and Clark National Forest, 1975.

———. "Wildlife Habitat Report, Badger Creek-Two Medicine Management Unit." Unpublished report. Great Falls, MT: U.S. Forest Service, 1974.

Schallenberger, A., and C. Jonkel. *Rocky Mountain East Front Grizzly Studies, 1977.* Annual Report. Border Grizzly Project Special Report No. 18. Missoula, MT: University of Montana, 1978.

Schallenberger, A., C. Jonkel, and L. Lee. *Ear Mountain, the Teton Floodplain, and the Pine Butte Swamp Areas as Grizzly Habitat.* Border Grizzly Project Special Report No. 29. Missoula, MT: University of Montana, 1979.

Schallenberger, A., and C. J. Jonkel. *Rocky Mountain East Front Grizzly Studies, 1979.* Annual Report. Border Grizzly Project Special Report No. 39. Missoula, MT: University of Montana, March, 1980. {KA}

Schallenberger, Allen. *Reconnaissance Survey of Grizzly Bear Habitat, Rocky Mountain Division, Lewis and Clark National Forest.* Great Falls, MT: U.S. Forest Service, December 1974. {KA}

Schallenberger, Allen, and Charles Jonkel. *Critique of the USFS Rocky Mountain Front Plan.* Border Grizzly Project Special Report No. 13. Missoula, MT: University of Montana, February 1978.

Schallenberger, Allen Dee. "Food Habits, Range Use and Interspecific Relationships of Bighorn Sheep in the Sun River Area, West-Central Montana." Master's thesis, Montana State University - Bozeman, 1966.

Schlesier, Karl H., ed. *Plains Indians, A.D. 500-1500: The Archaeological Past of Historic Groups.* Norman, OK: University of Oklahoma Press, 1994.

Schneider, Bill. *Where the Grizzly Walks: The Future of the Great Bear.* Guilford, CT: Falcon, 2004.

———. *Where the Grizzly Walks.* Missoula, MT: Mountain Press Publishing Co., 1977.

———. Should We Hunt the Grizzly?: Eight Expert Opinions. *Montana Magazine,* January/February, 1982.

Schoenberg, Wilfred P. *Jesuits in Montana,* 1840-1960. Portland, OR: Oregon-Jesuit, 1960.

———. Historic St. Peter's Mission: Landmark of the Jesuits and the Ursulines Among the Blackfeet. *Montana: The Magazine of Western History,* Winter 1961.

Schwitters, Mike. *White Geese Along the Rocky Mountain Front.* Last Chance Audubon Society's 1999 Natural History Lecture Series. Helena, MT, March 3, 1999. Videocassette (VHS), 60 min.

Scott, Tristan. Glacier's First Enforcers. *Montana Magazine,* March/April 2012.

Scriver, Mary Strachan. *Bronze Inside and Out: A Biographical Memoir of Bob Scriver.* Calgary, AB: University of Calgary Press, 2007.

Secoy, Frank Raymond. *Changing Military Patterns on the Great Plains (7th Century Through Early 19th Century).* Seattle, WA: University of Washington Press, 1996.

Sentz, Gene. Don't Release the Front. Home Front: *The Life and Times of Montana's Rocky Mountain Front Country,* Winter 1994.

———. Montana's Rocky Mountain Front: Sell It or Save It. *High Country News,* June 26, 1995.

Servheen, Christopher. *Grizzly Bear Recovery Plan.* Missoula, MT: U.S. Fish and Wildlife Service, 1993.

Sexton, Mary. The Changeless Rocky Mountain Front: For How Long? *Home Front: The Life and Times of Montana's Rocky Mountain Front Country,* Spring 1993.

Shelton, James Gary. *Bear Attacks: The Deadly Truth.* Hagensborg, BC: Pogany Productions, 1998.

Shield, James Parker. Red Diaspora: The Little Shell Chippewa of Montana. *Montana Magazine,* February 1995.

Shumate, Maynard. *Pictographs in Central Montana, Part II, Panels Near Great Falls, Montana.* Anthropology and Sociology Papers, No. 21. Missoula, MT: Montana State University, 1960.

———. *The Archaeology of the Vicinity of Great Falls, Montana.* Anthropology and Sociology Papers, No. 2. Missoula, MT: Montana State University, 1950.

Siggins, Maggie. *Riel: A Life of Revolution.* Toronto, ON: HarperPerennial Canada, 2003.

Smith, Charline G., and Floyd W. Sharrock. *Identifying and Recording Archaeological Sites: A Manual for Forest Service Personnel.* Missoula, MT: University of Montana, 1974.

Smith, Dennis J. "Fort Peck Agency Assiniboines, Upper Yanktonais, Hunkpapas, Sissetons, and Wahpetons: A Cultural History to 1888." PhD diss., University of Nebraska, 2001.

Smith, Sonja Marlene. "Winter Habitat Use by Mule Deer in Idaho and Montana." Master's thesis, University of Montana, 2011.

Smith, Craig S. "Seeds, Weeds, and Prehistoric Hunters and Gathers: The Plant Macrofossil Evidence From Southwest Wyoming." *Plains Anthropologist* 33, no. 120 (1988): 141-158.

Smith, Tom S., Stephen Herrero, Terry D. Debruyn, James M. Wilder. "Efficacy of Bear Deterrent Spray in Alaska." *Journal of Wildlife Management* 72, no. 3 (2008): 640-645.

Smyth, David. "The Struggle for the Piegan Trade: The Saskatchewan vs. the Missouri." *Montana: The Magazine of Western History,* Spring 1984.

Snell, Marilyn Berlin. Cowboys Are Their Weakness: Montana Politicians Can't Ignore This Pro-Wilderness Rancher. *Sierra,* July/August 2005.

Snow, John. *These Mountains Are Our Sacred Places: The Story of the Stoney People.* Calgary, AB: Fifth House, 2005.

Spence, Mark David. *Dispossessing the Wilderness: Indian Removal and the Making of the National Parks.* New York: Oxford University Press, 1999.

———. "Crown of the Continent, Backbone of the World: The American Wilderness Ideal and Blackfeet Exclusion from Glacier National Park." *Environmental History* 1, no. 3 (1996): 29-49.

Sperry, J. Elizabeth. "Ethnogenesis of the Métis, Cree and Chippewa in Twentieth Century Montana." Master's thesis, University of Montana - Missoula, 2007.

Stalling, David. Angling for the Front. *Big Sky Journal* 12, no. 1 (2005). 134-143.

Stark, Peter, and Ted Wood. "The Old North Trail." *Smithsonian,* July 1997.

Stebinger, Eugene. "Geology and Coal Resources of North Teton County, Montana." *U.S. Geological Survey Bulletin* 621, (1916): 117-156.

———. "Oil and Gas Geology of the Birch Creek-Sun River Area, Northwestern Montana." *Contributions to Economic Geology,* Part II, (1918): 149-184.

Stetz, Jeffrey Brian. "Using Noninvasive Genetic Sampling to Assess and Monitor Grizzly Bear Population Status in the Northern Continental Divide Ecosystem." Master's thesis. University of Montana - Missoula, 2008.

Stevens, Isaac. *Reports of Exploration and Surveys to Ascertain the Most Practical and Economic Route for a Railroad From the Missouri River to the Pacific Ocean: Survey Near the 47th and 49th Parallels.* Vol.12, Book 1:120-239. Washington, D.C.: U.S. War Department, 1855. {HP}

Stivers, Thomas S. "Effects of Livestock Grazing on Grizzly Bear Habitat Along the East Front of the Rocky Mountains, Montana." Master's thesis, Montana State University - Bozeman, 1988. {KA}

Stivers, Thomas S., and Lynn. R. Irby. "Impacts of Cattle Grazing on Mesic Grizzly Bear Habitat Along the East Front of the Rocky Mountains, Montana." *Intermountain Journal of Sciences* 3, no. 1 (1997): 17-37.

Stockstad, D. S. *Grizzly Bear Investigation and Re-check.* Pittman-Robertson Job Completion Report 5, no. 2 (1954): 223-235, Job 7-A. Helena, MT: Montana Fish and Game Department. {KA}

Strachan Scriver, Mary. *Bronze Inside and Out: A Biographical Memoir of Bob Scriver.* Calgary: University of Calgary Press, 2007. {MS}

Stringham, Stephen F. "Aggressive Body Language of Bears and Wildlife Viewing: A Response to Geist (2011)." *Human–Wildlife Interactions* 5, no. 2 (2011): 177–191.

Stuart, Granville. *Pioneering in Montana: The Making of a State, 1864-1887.* Edited by Paul C. Phillips. Lincoln, NE: University of Nebraska Press, 1925). {JP}

Sumner, Jay, and John J. Craighead. *Grizzly Bear Habitat Survey in the Scapegoat Wilderness, Montana.* Missoula, MT: University of Montana, 1973.

Sun River Valley Historical Society. 1989. *A Pictorial History of the Sun River Valley.* Sun River, MT: Sun River Valley Historical Society, 1989.

Teton County History Committee. *Teton County: A History: The Story of Teton County, Montana, Its Land, Its Infancy, Its People.* Choteau, MT: *Choteau Acantha*, 1988.

Teton County Technical Action Panel. *Teton County Recreational Development.* Choteau, MT: U.S. Department of Agriculture, [1968?].

Tews, Anne, Michael Enk, Steve Leathe, William Hill, Steve Dalbey, and George Liknes. "Westslope Cutthroat Trout *(Oncorhynchus clarki lewisi)* in Northcentral Montana: Status and Restoration Strategies." Special Report. Great Falls, MT: Montana Fish, Wildlife and Parks in collaboration with the Lewis and Clark National Forest, September 2000.

Thackeray, Bill. *The Mètis Centennial Celebration Publication.* Lewistown, MT: Central Montana Publication Co., [1979?]

Thane, Eric. *The Majestic Land: Peaks, Parks, and Prevaricators of the Rockies and Highlands of the Northwest.* Indianapolis, IN: Bobbs-Merrill Company, 1950.

Their, Tim, 1988. What Bears Take for Granted. *Montana Outdoors,* November/December, 1988.

Thompson, Michael J. "Mountain Goat Distribution, Population Characteristics and Habitat Use in the Sawtooth Range, Montana." Master's thesis, Montana State University - Bozeman, 1981.

Thompson, Sally. *Long Ago in Montana.* Helena, MT: Montana Office of Public Instruction; Missoula, MT: University of Montana Regional Learning Project, 2006, DVD, 30 min.

Thompson, Sally, and Kimberly Lugthart. *Discovering Our Own Place: A Map Saga for Montana: Rocky Mountain Front/Blackfeet.* Lifelong Learning Project. Missoula, MT: University of Montana, 2004.

Thornton, Nancy. "Out of Harm's Way The History of the Four Persons Blackfeet Indian Agency 1868-1876." Unpublished manuscript, May 1, 2006. Pdf file.

Tomasko, D. 1980. *Distribution and Populations Characteristics of the Rocky Mountain Goat Along the East Slope of the Rocky Mountains in Northcentral Montana.* Pittman-Robertson Project. No. W-120-R-11. Helena, MT: Montana Department of Fish, Wildlife, and Parks, 1980.

Trefethen, James B. *An American Crusade for Wildlife.* New York: Winchester Press, 1975. {JP}

U.S. Bureau of Land Management. *Blackleaf Environmental Impact Statement.* Final. Great Falls, MT: Great Falls Resource Area Office, June 1992.

———. *Cultural Resource Report for Small Scale Class III Inventories: Ear Mountain Trailhead and Trail.* Great Falls, MT: U.S. Bureau of Land Management, June 1994.

———. *Headwaters Resource Area Resource Management Plan/ Environmental Impact Statement.* Fianl. Butte, MT: U.S. Bureau of Land Management, November 1983.

———. *Interagency Rocky Mountain Front Wildlife Monitoring/ Evaluation Program: Management Guidelines for Selected Species, Rocky Mountain Front Studies.* Billings, MT: U.S. Bureau of Land Management, September 1987.

———. *Old North Trail and Ethnographic Investigation for the Blackleaf Gas Field.* Billings, MT: U.S. Bureau of Land Management. May 2004.

———. *Rocky Mountain Front Outstanding Natural Area Activity Plan/Environmental Assessment.* Final. Lewistown, MT: U.S. Bureau of Land Management, March 1989.

U.S. Fish and Wildlife Service. *Conservation Strategy for Grizzly Bear Management in the Northern Continental Divide Ecosystem.* Preliminary Working Copy. Helena, MT: U.S. Fish and Wildlife Service, March 1996.

———. *Draft Northern Continental Divide Ecosystem Grizzly Bear Conservation Strategy.* Missoula, MT: U.S. Fish and Wildlife Service, April 2013.

———. *Environmental Assessment and Land Protection Plan: Rocky Mountain Front Conservation Area.* Great Falls, MT: U.S. Fish and Wildlife Service, April 2005.

———. "Gray Wolf Monitoring in Montana." In *The Yellowstone Wolf: A Guide and Source Book,* edited by Paul Schullery, 102-7. Wordan, WY: High Plains Publishing, 1996. {HP}

———. *Grizzly Bear (Ursus arctos horribilis): 5 Year Review.* Summary and Evaluation. Missoula, MT: U.S. Fish and Wildlife Service Grizzly Bear Recovery Office, 2011.

———. *Land Protection Plan: Rocky Mountain Front Conservation Area Expansion.* Lakewood, CO: U.S. Fish and Wildlife Service, Mountain-Prairie Region, 2011.

———. Nez Perce Tribe, National Park Service, Montana Fish, Wildlife and Parks, Blackfeet Nation, Confederated Salish and Kootenai Tribes, Idaho Fish and Game, and USDA Wildlife Services. *Rocky Mountain Wolf Recovery 2007 Interagency Annual Report.* Helena, MT: U.S. Fish and Wildlife Service, Ecological Services, 2008.

U.S. Forest Service. *Analysis of Recreation Resident Use Continuance, Arsenic Creek Neighborhood, Sun River Ranger District.* Great Falls, MT: Lewis and Clark National Forest, April 1975.

———. *Animal Damage Control Environmental Assessment.* Great Falls, MT: U.S. Forest Service, July 1992.

———. *Benchmark Fuels Reduction Project Environmental Assessment.* Great Falls, MT: Lewis and Clark National Forest, April 2009

———. *Bob Marshall, Great Bear, and Scapegoat Wilderness Areas.* Map scale 1:100,000. ISBN 978159351094-7, 2011. {KP}

———. *Decision Memo, Rocky Mountain Ranger District, Pool Creation South Fork of Dupuyer Creek.* Choteau, MT: Rocky Mountain Ranger District, September 1998.

———. *Environmental Assessment, EPS Natural Gas Facilities on Federal and State Land Along the Blackleaf Road.* Great Falls, MT: Lewis and Clark National Forest, 1989.

———. *Environmental Assessment for Oil and Gas Leasing on Nonwilderness Lands.* Great Falls, MT: Lewis and Clark National Forest, February 1981.

———. *Environmental Assessment, Management of the Little Badger Sheep and Goat Allotment # 112,* Rocky Mountain Ranger District. Great Falls, MT: Lewis and Clark National Forest, September 1993.

———. *Final Environmental Impact Statement for Exploratory Oil and Gas Wells Near Badger Creek and Hall Creek.* Great Falls, MT: Lewis and Clark National Forest, October 1990.

———. *Environmental Assessment Oil and Gas Leasing: Deep Creek and Reservoir North Rare II Further Planning Areas.* Great Falls, MT: Lewis and Clark National Forest, January 1981.

———. *Environmental Assessment, South Fork of the Sun River Prescribed Burn.* Choteau, MT: Rocky Mountain Ranger District, April 2000.

———. *Establishment and Modification of National Forest Boundaries and National Grasslands.* USDA FS 612, November 1997. {JP}

———. *Fina Oil and Chemical Company Exploration Oil/Gas Well Federal South Glacier No. 1-26 Glacier County Montana,* Great Falls, MT: U.S. Forest Service and U.S. Bureau of Land Management, February 1991.

———. Lewis and Clark National Forest Plan, Monitoring and Evaluation Report, Fiscal Years 2000-2001. Great Falls, MT: Lewis and Clark National Forest, June 2002.

———. *Lewis and Clark National Forest Oil and Gas Leasing, Final Environmental Impact Statement.* Great Falls, MT: Lewis and Clark National Forest, September 1997.

———. *Revised Environmental Assessment for the Gibson Lake Trail Rocky Mountain Ranger District.* Great Falls, MT: Lewis and Clark National Forest, January 1993.

———. *Rocky Mountain Ranger District Travel Management Plan: Record of Decision for Badger-Two Medicine.* Great Falls, MT: Lewis and Clark National Forest, March 2009.

———. *Summary Draft Environmental Impact Statement Rocky Mountain Ranger District Travel Management Plan.* Great Falls, MT: Lewis and Clark National Forest, June 2005.

———. *Summary of the Environmental Impact Statement for the Proposed Rocky Mountain Front Mineral Withdrawal.* Great Falls, MT: Lewis and Clark National Forest, September 2000.

Valley County Historical Society. *Assiniboine Chief Rosebud Remembers Lewis and Clark.* Glasgow, MT: Valley County Historical Society, 2004, DVD, 18 min.

———. *In the Land of the Assiniboine.* Glasgow, MT: Valley County Historical Society, 2009, DVD, 55 min.

Van Kirk, Sylvia. *Many Tender Ties: Women in Fur-Trade Society, 1670-1870.* Norman: University of Oklahoma Press, 1983. {MS}

VanRooy, Susan. Life on the Front: The Harlequin Duck. Home Front: *The Life and Times of Montana's Rocky Mountain Front Country,* Winter 1994.

Vaughan, Jack C. Colonel. *Alfred Jefferson Vaughan, The Frontier Ambassador.* (Dallas?), 1957. {HP}

Vaughn, Robert. *Then and Now, or, Thirty-Six Years in the Rockies: Personal reminiscences of Some of the First Pioneers of the State of Montana.* Helena, MT: Farcountry Press, 2001.

Vest, Jay Hansford C. The Medicine Wolf Returns: Traditional Blackfeet Concepts of *Canis Lupus. Western Wildlands,* Summer 1988.

Viola, Herman J. *After Columbus: The Smithsonian Chronicle of the North American Indians.* Washington, D.C.: Smithsonian Books, 1990.

Vollertsen, John. "A Critical Analysis of the Biography of Robert Marshall." Unpublished manuscript, May 2001.

———. "A Report on House Bill 131, Human Skeletal Remains and Burial Site Protection Act, Before Montana's 52nd Legislative Assembly 1991-1992." Unpublished manuscript, May 1991.

———. Blackleaf Canyon: Deception Unmasked. *Journal of the Rocky Mountain Front,* Spring 1991.

———. Blackleaf Canyon: Part 2: "Deception Unmasked." *Words on Wilderness,* June 1991.

———. "Does the Regulatory Schematic of the U.S. Government Fulfill the Cultural Interests of the Blackfeet Tribe as Described in the Badger-Two Medicine Final Environmental Impact Statement?" Unpublished manuscript, June 1991.

———. "Historical Evidence of Blackfeet Use of the Badger-Two Medicine Area." Unpublished manuscript, November 1990.

———. "Political Activism and Sacred Land Issues Involving the Blackfeet Traditional Religion." Master's professional paper, Montana State University, 1992.

———. "Using Multiple Regression Analysis to Associate Education Levels and Financial Compensation with Livestock Producers' Tolerance for Grizzly Bears in the Northern Continental Divide Ecosystem." EdD diss., Montana State University, 2005.

Vrooman, Nicholas. *Strange Empire: A Presentation on Mètis Culture.* Augusta, MT, December 17, 1993. Audiocassette. In possession of author/editor.

Vrooman, Nicholas C.P. *"The Whole Country Was ... 'One Robe'": The Little Shell Tribe's America.* Helena, MT: Little Shell Tribe of Chippewa Indians of Montana and Drumlummon Institute, 2012.

Vuke, S. M., Porter, K. W., Lonn, J. D., and Lopez, D. A., 2007 (ed. 1.0), Geologic map of Montana, Montana Bureau of Mines and Geology, Geologic Map GM 62. Map scale 1:500,000. {KP}

Wagner, Curly Bear, and Dennis Neary. *Two Worlds at Two-Medicine: The Blackfeet Meet Meriwether Lewis.* Arcadia, IN: Going-to-the-Sun Institute and Native View Pictures, 2004. DVD, 35 min.

Walchek, Ken. Montana Wildlife - 170 Years ago. *Montana Outdoors,* July/August 1976.

Waldt, Ralph. *A Naturalist Looks at the Rocky Mountain Front.* Last Chance Audubon Society's 1999 Natural History Lecture Series. Helena, MT, April 8, 1999. Videocassette (VHS), 60 min.

———. *Crown of the Continent: The Last Great Wilderness of the Rocky Mountains.* Helena, MT: Riverbend Publishing, 2004.

———. Tooth & Tine: Solving the Riddle of an Epic Battle. *Bugle,* Fall 1997.

Waller, John S. "Movement and Habitat-Use of Grizzly Bears Along U.S. Highway 2 in Northwestern Montana, 1998-2001." PhD diss., University of Montana - Missoula, 2005.

Walter, Dave. Gabriel Dumont: Mètis Prince of the Prairies. *Montana Magazine,* February 1995.

———. *More Montana Campfire Tales: Fifteen Historical Narratives.* Helena, MT: Farcountry Press, 2002.

Walter, David. The Baker Massacre. *Montana Magazine*, March/ April 1987.

Walter, Marcella. The Old North Trail. *Montana Magazine*, April 1994.

Warren, Louis S. *The Hunter's Game: Poachers and Conservationists in Twentieth-Century America.* New Haven, CT: Yale University Press, 1997.

Weide, Bruce. *Trail of the Great Bear.* Helena, MT: Falcon Press, 1992.

Weisel, George. Life on the Front: The Bob Marshall Fishery. *Home Front: The Life and Times of Montana's Rocky Mountain Front Country,* Spring 1994.

Welsch, Jeff. Protecting the Backbone of the World. *Montana Quarterly,* Fall 2011.

Wenzel, E. O. *Raptor Observations, Notes and Nest Locations: Rocky Mountain East Front, 1979-81.* Unpublished Report, Butte, MT: U.S. Bureau of Land Management, 1982.

West, Helen B. Blackfoot Country. *Montana: The Magazine of Western History,* Autumn 1960.

———. *Meriwether Lewis in Blackfeet Country.* Browning, MT: Museum of the Plains Indian, 1964.

———. Starvation Winter of the Blackfeet. *Montana: The Magazine of Western History,* Winter1958.

Whipple, N. J. *Serenity.* Brownsville, TX: Border Press, Inc., 1974.

Whipple, Nels. *Interlude: Verse of the West.* Choteau, MT: Nels Whipple, 1981.

White, Don, Jr., Katherine C. Kendall, and Harold D. Picton. "Seasonal Occurrence, Body Composition, and Migration Potential of Army Cutworm Moths in Northwest Montana." *Canadian Journal of Zoology* 76, (1998): 835-842.

White, Don W., J. Berardinelli, and K. Aune. "Reproductive Characteristics of the Male Grizzly Bear in the Continental United States." *Ursus* 10, (1998): 497-501. Tenth International Conference on Bear Research and Management. {KA}

———. "Seasonal Differences in Spermatogenesis, Testicular Mass and Serum Testosterone Concentrations in the Grizzly Bear." *Ursus* 16, no. 2 (2005): 198-207. {KA}

White, Don W., J. G. Berardinelli, K. Aune. "Age Variation in Gross and Histological Characteristics of Testis and Epididymis in Grizzly Bears." *Ursus* 16, no. 2 (2005): 190-197. {KA}

White, Linda Harper, and Fred R. Gowans. Traders to Trappers: Andrew Henry and the Rocky Mountain Fur Trade: Part 2. *Montana: The Magazine of Western History,* Summer 1993.

White, Thain. *Tipi Rings in the Flathead Lake Area, Western Montana.* Missoula, MT: Montana State University, October 1959.

Whitehorn, W. Clark. Pine Butte Swamp Preserve and the Rocky Mountain Front. *Montana: The Magazine of Western History,* Autumn 2005.

Whitman, David. The Return of the Grizzly: Parts of the West are Braced for a Second Coming. *Atlantic Monthly,* September 2000.

Williams, Jim. "Ecology of Mountain Lions in the Sun River Area of Northern Montana." Master's thesis, Montana State University - Bozeman, 1992. {JW}

Williams, Jim S., J. J. McCarthy, and H. D. Picton. "Cougar Habitat Use and Food Habits on the Montana Rocky Mountain Front." *Intermountain Journal of Science* 1, (1995): 16-28. {JW}

Wilson, Seth. "The Social and Political Viability of Biological Corridors on Private Lands: A Case Study in Lewis and Clark County, Montana." Master's thesis, University of Montana - Missoula, 1996.

Wilson, Seth M. "Landscape Features and Attractants that Predispose Grizzly Bears to Risk of Conflicts with Humans: A Spatial and Temporal Analysis on Privately Owned Agricultural Land." PhD diss., University of Montana - Missoula, 2003.

———. The Science of Coexistence: What's Behind Grizzly Bear Conflicts on Rocky Mountain Front Ranches. *Wild Guardian,* Winter 2004.

Wilson, Seth M., Michael J. Madel, David J. Mattson, Jonathan M. Graham, James A. Burchfield, Jill M. Belsky. "Natural Landscape Features, Human-Related Attractants, and Conflict Hotspots: A Spatial Analysis of Human-Grizzly Bear Conflicts." *Ursus* 16, no. 1 (2005): 117-129.

Wilson, Seth M., Michael J. Madel, David J. Mattson, Jonathan M. Graham, Troy Merrill. "Landscape Conditions Predisposing Grizzly Bears to Conflicts on Private Agricultural Lands in the Western USA." *Biological Conservation* I30 (2006): 47-69.

Wiseman, Alfred. Interview by Melinda Livezey, February 10, 1994. Oral History Collection (OH 344-4), Montana Historical Society, Helena, MT.

———. Interview by Melinda Livezey, November 29, 1993. Oral History Collection (OH 344-2), Montana Historical Society, Helena, MT.

Wiseman, Cecelia. Interview by Melinda Livezey and Al Wiseman, February 18, 1994. Oral History Collection (OH 344-5), Montana Historical Society, Helena, MT.

———. Interview by Melinda Livezey and Al Wiseman, March 1, 1994. Oral History Collection (OH 344-6), Montana Historical Society, Helena, MT.

Wissler, Clark. "The Influence of the Horse in the Development of Plains Culture." *American Anthropologist* 16, no. 1 (1914): 1-25.

———. "Material Culture of the Blackfoot Indians." *Anthropological Papers of the American Museum of Natural History* 5, part 1 (1908): 1-175.

———. "Riding Gear of the North American Indians." *Anthropological Papers of the American Museum of Natural History* 17, part 1 (1915): 1-38.

Wissler, Clark, and D. C. Duvall. "Mythology of the Blackfoot Indians." *Anthropological Papers of the American Museum of Natural History* 2, part 1 (1908): 1-163.

Wojtowicz, Richard. "Coyotes, Grizzlies and Native Americans: Then and Now Grizzlies." In *A Confluence of Cultures: Native Americans and the Expedition of Lewis and Clark,* 190-93, Missoula, MT: University of Montana Printing and Graphics Services, 2003.

Wood, Michael D. "An Exploration of the Pikuni World View: Pikuni Water Rights in the Ceded Strip." Master's thesis, University of Montana - Missoula, 1994.

Worcester, D. E. "Spanish Horses Among the Plains Tribes." *Pacific Historical Review* 14, no. 4 (1945): 409-417.

Wright, John. *Where the Mountains Meet the Plains: Oil and Gas Leasing and the Conservation Legacy of the Rocky Mountain Front.* Helena, MT: Montana Wilderness Association, September1995.

Wright, John B. "Society Conservation's Radical Center in Geography." *Geographical Review* 91, no. 1/2 (2001): 9-18.

Wylie, Allan. "Hydrologic Investigation of Durr and McDonald Swamps, Teton County, Montana." Master's thesis, University of Montana - Missoula, 1991.

Yetter, Bob. *Badger-Two Medicine: The Last Stronghold: Sacred Land of the Grizzly, Wolf and Blackfeet Indian.* Missoula, MT: Badger Chapter of Glacier-Two Medicine Alliance, 1992.

———. Mètis on the Front: A Refuge From Repression. *Home Front: The Life and Times of Montana's Rocky Mountain Front Country,* Spring 1993.

Yung, Laurie. "The Politics of Cross-Boundary Conservation: Meaning, Property, and Livelihood on the Rocky Mountain Front in Montana." PhD diss., University of Montana - Missoula, 2003.

Yung, Laurie, and Paul Wick. *Community Land Use Survey: Obtaining Public Opinion About Teton County's Future.* Draft Summary of Survey Results. Collaborative Project of Teton County, Growth Policy Citizen's Advisory Committee, and University of Montana. Choteau, MT: Teton County, March 2002.

Yung, Laurie, Wayne A. Friedman, and Jill M. Belsky. "The Politics of Place: Understanding Meaning, Common Ground, and Political Difference on the Rocky Mountain Front." *Forest Science* 49, no. 6 (2003): 855-866.

Zion, Robert. Interview by Melinda Livezey, June 27, 1994. Oral History Collection (OH 344-10), Montana Historical Society, Helena, MT.

Zion, Scotty. *Been Any Bigger I'd Have Said So!* Great Falls, MT: Scotty Zion, 2002.

Zumbo, Jim. War Over Grizzlies. *Outdoor Life,* November 1991.

INDEX

ABOUT THE AUTHOR

Photo by Crystal Images, Big Sky, Montana

Dr. Vollertsen is one of only three individuals known to accomplish both master's and doctoral research on Montana's Rocky Mountain Front.

He is a recipient of Montana Wilderness Association's coveted Sedlack Award for his work on the Rocky Mountain Front.

Semi-retired and staying busy, he is an adjunct instructor for Montana State University-Bozeman and teaches an online graduate course in American Indian Studies. He resides in Helena, Montana.